BAD KARMA

Deborah Blum

BAD KARMA

A True Story of Obsession and Murder

Atheneum   NEW YORK   1986

The lines quoted on page vi are from the song "Somebody to Love." Lyrics and music by Darby Slick. ©
1967 Irving Music, Inc. (BMI). All rights reserved.
International copyright. Used by permission.

Library of Congress Cataloging-in-Publication Data

Blum, Deborah.
   Bad karma.

   1. Murder—California—Berkeley—Case studies.
2. Tarasoff, Tanya. 3. Poddar, Prosenjit. I. Title.
HV6534.B44B48 1986   364.1'523'0979467   85-48129
ISBN 0-689-11617-9

Copyright © 1986 by Deborah Blum
All rights reserved
Published simultaneously in Canada by Collier Macmillan Canada, Inc.
Composition by Heritage Printers, Inc., Charlotte, North Carolina
Manufactured by Fairfield Graphics, Fairfield, Pennsylvania
Designed by Harry Ford
First Edition

For BEA *and* PINK

Illustrations

(following page 152)

Tanya, Lidia, Alex, and Vitally Tarasoff, 1952

Prosenjit's village: Balurghat, West Bengal, 1982
(photograph: Deborah Blum)

People's Park demonstration: Berkeley, May 1969
(photograph: AP/Wide World Photos)

Tanya and Lidia at family party
(photograph: Lidia Tarasoff)

Tanya, age seventeen
(photograph: Lidia Tarasoff)

Prosenjit Poddar, student at IIT: Kharagpur, West Bengal, 1966

Dr. Larry Moore, 1974
(photograph: The Clinical Psychiatry News)

Dr. Harvey Powelson, 1969
(photograph: The Daily Californian)

Prosenjit Poddar, police mug shot: October 28, 1969

Tanya, high school graduation photograph

Author's Note

In 1969, when Tanya Tarasoff was murdered, I was a sophomore at the University of California at Berkeley. I didn't know her, I didn't know the guy who killed her, but I remember feeling that what happened to Tanya might just as easily have happened to me.

It was not until seven years later that the incident resurfaced in my life. An article on the front page of the *Los Angeles Times* reported that the California Supreme Court had ruled, in a landmark case, that doctors or psychotherapists have a legal duty to warn intended victims of patients believed dangerous to them. Such a duty, the court said, was not a breach of the therapist-patient privilege of confidentiality. I was surprised to learn that this precedent stemmed from the slaying of Tanya Tarasoff.

As if compelled, I began to piece together the story from court transcripts, police reports, newspaper accounts, letters, and interviews with the many people directly involved. It was only over the course of the next eight years that I came to realize how closely I could identify with the emotions of not only the victim, but also of her murderer. In order to better communicate the nature of their relationship, I found it preferable to portray events in a dramatized rather than a documentary style. In so doing, it often became necessary to reconstruct dialogue and, occasionally, to create scenes where there were gaps in available information. However, all such passages were drawn from the recollections of one or more of the actual participants, or someone else reliably informed, so as to capture either the essence and the spirit of the moment or the personality and style of the people involved. In no instance was this "dramatic license" taken in such a way as to distort actual events.

In an effort to safeguard the privacy of certain individuals, I have changed names and, in some cases, disguised identifying characteristics or created composite characters. This applies to "Cindy Vogel," "Janice Kaplan," "Gunnar Stanfil," "Jal Mehta," "Natalie Gorlov," "Jeff Flanders," and the DasGupta brothers, "Dilip" and "Amit." With regard to people such as Dr. Larry Moore and the friends and families of Prosenjit Poddar and Tanya Tarasoff who cooperated with me in the preparation of this book, I remain forever thankful. Particular gratitude, however, is reserved for Lidia Tarasoff, who allowed herself to revive often painful memories of her daughter and without whose assistance this book would not have been possible.

DEBORAH BLUM, *January 1986*

BAD KARMA

Don't you want somebody to love?
Don't you need somebody to love?
Wouldn't you love somebody to love?
You better find someone to love.

JEFFERSON AIRPLANE, 1967

Prologue

Berkeley, California, 1968.

The folk dance was held in an auditorium which had been cleared for the occasion. It was a cavernous mustard-colored room. The ceiling was carved with arabesque swirls like some ancient mosque, and rose in a dome shape, high, high above them. From the great height, an elaborate chandelier was suspended on a spindly wire pole. Many of its globes were burned out, and it threw off a dim yellow glare. The dance floor was hardwood, so worn and frayed that none of its varnish remained. In the center a circle of about thirty young men and women held hands and shuffled back and forth. They were concentrating on learning the steps of a Greek dance. Music blared out of an old record player that spat and crackled every time the needle ran over a scratch. A Balkan with rolled-up sleeves stood in the center of the circle, calling out instructions. He held one arm akimbo, darting forward and back to demonstrate the dance steps.

Tanya and Cindy stepped forward, close to the moving circle. Joining the dance was like jumping onto a merry-go-round. When Tanya saw an opening she yelled, "Now," grabbed Cindy's hand, and took a running leap. They broke in between two bodies. On one side Tanya held Cindy's hand, on the other, the clammy palm of some young man. The circle kept sweeping to the right, dipping and twisting to the beat. Laughing and out of breath, Tanya tried to fall in with the rhythm, but following the intricate steps was next to impossible. She was conscious of Cindy fumbling behind her, faking the steps, kicking her big legs out in the wrong direction. "Thanks," yelled Tanya, when she felt a stabbing pain in her calf.

"I can't do this," groaned Cindy.

"Yes you can—just watch me," and as she said this, Tanya brought the full weight of her body down on the toe of the young man dancing next to her. She snuck a look at him. His face was dark and screwed up in intense concentration. He was obviously struggling to learn the dance himself. She turned away to smother a giggle and whispered to Cindy, "Oh, God, I just mashed this poor guy's toe. Really hard."

"Good. He probably deserves it," Cindy said, laughing.

Tanya glanced back at the boy and saw that he was watching his feet and moving them with machinelike precision. She became even more conscious of his sweating palm and pulled her own away to wipe it on her skirt. When she slipped her hand back into his, he clutched at her, as if to steady himself.

But Tanya was exhilarated by the music. It was a haunting melody played in a minor key, and the dance enacted an ancient ritual. The Balkan told them that back in Athens, centuries ago, it had been a courting dance for maidens of marriageable age. The steps the girls did were coy and teasing; those that the boys followed had an assertive thrust. The music had that edge of expectancy that goes along with first love, and as it built in intensity toward its climax, male and female dancers were paired off in a symbolic betrothal. To Tanya, it was thrilling. She was a natural dancer and was entirely caught up in the music. Even though Cindy ridiculed her for coming to the International House, she was in her element here; she was happy.

As the dance went on, Tanya's eyes traveled the room to see if anyone was watching her. The third time around she caught the eye of the guy with the clammy hand whose toe she had mashed. He was now standing awkwardly on the opposite side of the circle, and she could have sworn he was watching her. He looked like he was from some place like India or Pakistan. He had a slight, wiry body and a solemn expression. The idea that a man, any man, was watching her dance excited Tanya. Coyly she cocked one elbow and pressed her hand against the small of her back. She kicked her toes out in front of her in high, perky jabs, and she felt transported back to that dusty Greek village on festival day.

When they circled around again, she caught the young man's timid eye for a second time. Even though he was a foreigner, and looked like a drip, she was flattered and felt the flush spread from her cheeks to her fingertips.

Cindy had noticed him too and said, "Hey, Tanya. Check that guy out. He's really giving you the eye."

"Who is?" she said, with feigned innocence.

"That cretin right over there," hissed Cindy, inclining her head in a certain direction. "The one that looks like a Hare Krishna reject."

"Oh, him," said Tanya. "Mr. Mellow Yellow," and she laughed. "Just pretend we're engrossed in conversation so he doesn't come over here."

"If he does, tell him to fuck off."

"You're so mean," teased Tanya, and she let her eyes wander back to where the Indian boy was standing.

"If you let another one of these creeps come on to you, I'm leaving."

Tanya ignored the jibe and threw herself completely into the dance. With her head thrown back and her lips slightly parted, she gave herself to the magic of the moment. There was no way she could know that there, in that musty auditorium, with music chirping out of an old record player, she had begun a dance of death.

ON an October evening in 1968, Tanya Tarasoff sat tensely on the edge of her bed. It was a rainy Saturday night, around seven o'clock, just the hour when the rest of the world was going out. She could picture them, hordes of happy faces, streaming down Telegraph Avenue, eating pizza at Giovanni's and heading into San Francisco to hear the Jefferson Airplane at the Fillmore. And there she was, stuck in her bedroom waiting for her brother to come get her. He had promised a ride over to her girlfriend Cindy's apartment. What was keeping that numbskull, she wondered. If she was late, Cindy might leave without her, and then where would she be? Stuck again with nothing to do on another Saturday night.

Tanya was nineteen years old and just a month earlier had begun her freshman year at Merritt Junior College in nearby Oakland, only twenty minutes away by the Nimitz Freeway. To her constant dismay, she was still living at home with her parents. Most of her girlfriends had their own apartments, but her father was old-fashioned and refused even to consider letting her move out. He accused her of chasing after anything in pants, but in reality, she was shy and naive. Awkward around boys, Tanya always assumed they wouldn't like her. Why should they when she felt certain she had nothing interesting to say? Dogged by terrible insecurities, looking for signs that maybe she wasn't so bad, she only sniffed around at life like a timid animal.

Although she was a striking girl with wide Slavic cheekbones, dark hair, and green eyes that tilted upward, Tanya couldn't accept her good looks. When friends complimented her on her exotic features, she automatically dismissed their remarks with a self-effacing shrug. And it was true that her face, while lovely, was marred by a disconcerting passivity, a tentative quality that caused her to be nearly invisible. She made such a slight impression on people that those who were introduced to her rarely remembered her on a second meeting. If they did remember, they were left thinking that this was a shy girl who could be beautiful if only she let down her guard and relaxed. But she cared too much about what others thought to relax. Hiding behind her sweet smile, she observed them all with fine-tuned antennae, recording their every gesture, weighing their every word, in an attempt to read their minds. Yet there were times, after a glass of wine, or while she was dancing, that she would forget to care. Then a spark would shine in her eyes and she would glow with a radiance that made her the envy of every girl in the room.

Even more than most teenage girls, Tanya was painfully aware of her shortcomings. She often complained that her slim body didn't have any shape. She had been one of the last girls in her high school class to develop, and she still fretted that her breasts were too small. Some nights, when she went out, she stuffed Kleenex in her bra to fill out a tight sweater. Tonight she glanced in the mirror and adjusted the tilt of her bra to make sure the padding looked natural.

There was a shuffling noise in the hall, and she whirled around. Her seventeen-year-old brother, Alex, stuck his head in the door. He was in his stocking feet and held a pair of Hush Puppies in one hand. "Move it, dumbbell," he hissed.

In a flash, Tanya whisked up her raincoat and boots and padded after Alex down the dingy, narrow hall. When he reached the dining room, Alex came to an exaggerated halt and held up his hand like a stop sign. Tanya tiptoed around him and peeked in. Her mother was sitting at the table, staring at a plate of jelly cookies, absentmindedly pushing one in her mouth. Her lumpish body looked like a piece of overstuffed furniture covered with a dust cloth. Tanya's five-year-old sister, Helen, sat on the floor filling in a coloring book.

Tanya caught her mother's eye. There was a passivity in her mother's face too, as if the life force had been sucked out of her. An unspoken signal passed between them, a language of their own making. Her mother resignedly motioned her on, and Tanya tip-toed past her, followed by Alex. Tanya peered into the dimly lit front room before she entered. The television set flickered. It was *I Love Lucy*, which always came on after the evening news. Her father was slumped before the TV on the Naugahyde sofa. His breathing came thick and labored. As Tanya tiptoed by, she could see that his face hung slack with drink and a thread of spittle dribbled down his chin. At his side sat a half-empty bottle of vodka. For a second he gave a start and jerked his head up, as if a thought had flitted through his sodden mind, but then his chin bounced down again on his chest.

"Oh, Jesus," breathed Alex. Tanya took a running leap and skidded to the front door. Alex scrambled after her. They were both holding in the laughter, and when they got outside, they convulsed in hysterics. It was one of the few moments when brother and sister felt close.

Alex's souped-up Dodge Charger sat in the driveway. He swung in behind the wheel, released the brake, and let the car roll silently back into the street. Tanya tossed her boots in ahead of her and slid in by his side.

"Too fuckin' much," said Alex. He had a raw-boned handsome face and long dark hair.

Images of her father's face, contorted in rage, filled Tanya's mind. He had told her if he ever caught her sneaking out, he'd beat her into a pulp. Like a possessive lover, he couldn't stand the idea of her venturing out on her own. She had to beg to get his permission, and mostly he said no. Even when she made plans with a girlfriend to see a movie, he sank into a sullen mood. Dating was out of the question. He was so exasperating that she had given up trying to reason with him, and it was only on the evenings when he passed out from drinking that she could escape. And even then she had to pray he'd still be in a coma when she got home.

The Tarasoffs lived on a quiet block on Tacoma Street, in the Berkeley flatlands, three miles below the University of California. It was a tacky neighborhood of bungalows wedged closely together. Most of the families who lived on the block were, like the Tarasoffs, working-class people who had little or no connection with the campus and were thankful that they were situated far enough from it to discourage students from moving into their midst. Most vociferous in this point of view was Tanya's father, Vitally Tarasoff. It infuriated him that while he was working eight hours a day as a car mechanic, hippies down on Telegraph Avenue were despoiling public property. Whenever he'd had too much to drink, he ranted that it was his tax money that was helping to put those spoiled brats through college.

Vitally was known to his neighbors as a man with a short fuse. Although he was considered a good provider, it was gossiped that his temper easily raged out of control after too many beers. By the time Tanya was eighteen years old, the Comm Center at the Berkeley Police Department had received over a dozen complaints against Vitally Tarasoff for such offenses as disorderly public conduct, felony assaults, and driving under the influence. Not only that, the "alpha tapes," the department's official records, logged numerous dates when officers had been called to the house by neighbors to break up family squabbles. For those living on the 1800 block of Tacoma Street, a patrol car slowly cruising by the Tarasoff home was not a surprising sight.

As they drove along, Tanya rolled down the window and fresh air hit her face. The Berkeley streets still glistened from the rain that had fallen all day, and the sidewalks gave off that metallic smell she loved. She positioned herself in the car seat so she could pull on her boots.

Dylan's "Rainy Day Women" came on the radio, and Alex turned up the volume. He had a certain glint in his eyes that the girls at Berkeley High found irresistible. Tanya, on the other hand, had decided long ago that he was impossible. As he turned into the parking lot of the liquor store on the corner of Shattuck and Vine, his big hands shimmied and danced over the steering wheel, causing the car to careen in a wild U-turn. He screeched to a stop in front of the neon entrance. "Corners like a Porsche," he said proudly.

Tanya gave him a dirty look. "You're so immature."

He kept the motor running and, reaching into his pocket, pulled out a wad of bills. "Six-pack Bud," he said, handing her a few dollars. She got out of the car and headed into the store. Tanya didn't have a driver's license; Alex wasn't old enough to buy liquor. Although Tanya wasn't old enough to buy it either, she had no trouble passing for twenty-one. It was an arrangement that benefited them both. But it burned Alex up that he had to rely on Tanya for anything, and he often threatened her that her days were numbered.

When she got back into the car he said, "What're you and Pig Face doing tonight?"

"None of your business," said Tanya, resenting the way he put down Cindy. Especially since she considered the guys he hung around with to be a bunch of immature bums. They ditched class and bragged about how far they'd gone with their girlfriends. She referred to Alex's crowd as "little bitty hoods."

"I don't know why you go around with that pig," said Alex. "She looks cheap."

"You're starting to sound like Dad."

"Shut the fuck up."

"Just drop me off here," said Tanya. They had stopped for the light at the corner of College and Durant. "I'll walk the rest of the way." She got out and slammed the door.

As she was walking away he called out, "Hey, Tanya." She turned. He leaned out of the window and said, "Give me the signal when you get back."

"You'll be home?"

"Yeah, sure." He winked.

It was their secret pact. Brother and sister had devised a system of rapping on the kitchen window to alert each other if Vitally Tarasoff was still passed out and it was safe to enter the house.

"See you." She walked toward Cindy's apartment, and heard the engine rev and the screech of tires as Alex laid a patch of rubber behind him.

Tanya cinched up her trench coat and adjusted the angle of her wool beret. She walked along, conscious of the click of her heels on the sidewalk. With her hair tucked up under the beret, she felt like the heroine in one of her beloved Helen MacInnes thrillers. Tanya always imagined herself in one role or another, mostly as the unsuspecting beauty caught in a web of danger. She was a hopeless romantic who believed that someday, when she grew up, her "soul mate" would come along and whisk her away. Love was a tumultuous struggle that endured through great suffering, something like the love between Heathcliff and Catherine in *Wuthering Heights*, her all-time favorite movie. She was forever seeing her soul mate on the street, in a restaurant or passing in a car, and she'd make up stories to go along with his face. Of course, she never had the nerve to put any of her fantasies into action.

When she arrived at Cindy's place, just three blocks south of Telegraph, she could hear the driving beat of "Foxy Lady" coming from the second-story window, and it made her spine tingle. Foxy was just what she wanted to be. She ran up the wooden steps. When she leaned on the buzzer, no one came to the door, so she opened it and went in. A rush of incense shot up her nose and made her eyes cloud.

"Oh, hi," said Cindy. She was standing in front of a full-length mirror, trying to zip up a pair of jeans that were two sizes too small. From the back they looked like tourniquets around her thighs, cutting off the circulation to the top half of her body. Above the waist, she wore only her bra.

"Sorry I'm late," said Tanya, dismayed to see that her friend wasn't close to being ready.

"Shit. What do I do?" asked Cindy, surveying her image in the mirror.

Cynthia Ann Vogel had long brown hair, bangs that capped her forehead, and a sweet, clownish face. At twenty-one years old, she considered herself quite worldly and was convinced that she had "deep insights" to impart. On first seeing Tanya she had decided the girl was a wounded bird and had resolved to take her under her wing.

Tanya watched as Cindy sucked in her midriff and jutted out her ample bosom. Cindy had a big, loose-limbed body that was so double-jointed she could wrap herself up like a pretzel. Her personality was just as loose. She was always up for trying anything; nothing shocked her. That's what drew Tanya to her.

The girls had met a few months earlier in a biology class at Merritt Junior College, where they were both students. Merritt was a trade school for high school graduates who hadn't done well enough to get into Berkeley. The campus was down on Grove Street in Oakland, smack in the middle of a black ghetto, and consisted of a series of low-slung trailers beached on an asphalt parking lot. Crabgrass grew willy-nilly through the splayed blacktop. Abandoned cars were rusting out in front of the classrooms, and courses in metal shop and weaving were most popular. It was not the kind of atmosphere that inspired serious scholarship, which suited Cindy just fine. She was muddling through her second year, carrying the minimum number of units and halfheartedly studying to be a nurse. She hadn't told her parents yet, but she was close to flunking out.

Tanya was another matter altogether. In high school she had been an overachiever, extremely conscientious about her homework and concerned about making a good impression on her teachers. She had had the grade point average to get into Berkeley, but her father had played on her insecurities and convinced her that she was "too dumb" to succeed at the university. Now, two months into the first semester of her freshman year, she could kick herself for listening to him and was desperate to transfer to Berkeley.

"How about a long blouse?" ventured Tanya.

Cindy gave her a look in the mirror, then began rummaging through the mound of sweaters stuffed inside her dresser drawer. "I was good all week," she moaned. "Then Janice brought home some chocolate-chip cookies. That bitch. Talk about overdosing on sugar." Janice was her roommate, Janice Kaplan, also a sophomore at Merritt.

"Where is she?" asked Tanya, hoping that Janice wasn't home.

"Where do you think?"

"Someone new?"

"Some bozo. He took her to the Fillmore last night and she never came home."

"I wish someone would take me to the Fillmore," said Tanya, wandering over to a refrigerator smudged with greasy fingerprints. "The Jefferson Airplane are playing."

"The Fillmore? How about having someone to take an overnight with?"

Tanya sighed and yanked open the refrigerator door. A cheesy odor wafted out. She peered inside, but the bulb was burned out and all she could see was an unsavory dark hole.

"Forget it, there's nothing good in there," said Cindy. "Janice is on some crazy protein diet where all she eats are scrambled eggs and hamburger patties. What really pisses me off is, she never washes out the pan."

Tanya let the door slam shut. From where she was standing she could see a frying pan soaking in the sink, with a crust of hardened egg at the bottom. The rest of the apartment was a wreck, too. The only furniture in evidence was two beanbag chairs and a mattress. During the day, the mattress served as the living-room couch, and at night, as Cindy's bed. It was covered with a flimsy Indian spread and smelled vaguely of incense. Tacked on the wall, over the mattress, was a life-size poster of Bob Dylan, his singular profile exaggerated in silhouette and his hair fanning out in the colors of the rainbow, like a psychedelic crown. By his face, Cindy had scribbled the words to one of his songs, "She makes love just like a woman, but she breaks like a little girl."

"Hey," said Tanya, looking up at Dylan, "have you heard anything from the Toothpick?"

Cindy was sticking her head into a loose-fitting tie-dyed shirt. When she emerged from the folds of fabric she said, "No, goddammit. I'll die if he doesn't call."

The Toothpick was the teaching assistant in Cindy's music class, and Cindy had been mooning over him ever since the semester started. A few weeks earlier she had found out that he played the flute in a modern jazz ensemble, and she had goaded Tanya into accompanying her to one of his concerts. The concert was given on a Sunday morning in a futuristic church in the hills near Tilden Park. The girls had traveled up there by bus and trudged through the rain looking for the address. They were early, and had to wait in the cold pews for nearly an hour. When the Toothpick finally stepped out onstage, Cindy gripped Tanya's knee and whispered, "Oh, God, I can't stand it." Even Tanya felt a twinge of excitement. His lean body was accentuated by skin-tight black jeans that he wore tucked into his boots. His hair hung down his back in a long pigtail that swung back and forth when he played. When the music was over, Cindy said, "Wait here," and ran toward the stage to intercept him. A moment later, she came back and said, "I'm so bummed. He didn't even recognize me."

"Did he ask for your number?"

"Not exactly. I gave it to him anyway." And she explained how she had written her number on a deposit slip from her checkbook and said jokingly, "Either call me or make a deposit."

"Of course he might have called while I was out," Cindy was saying as she checked herself out in the mirror, and then Tanya heard her mutter something about the Goodyear blimp.

"Give him a chance. It's only been a few days," said Tanya, wondering why it was so hard to connect with guys. Life was a never-ending search for romance. On some mornings she'd wake up sure it was going to happen. She'd dress in anticipation of the event. She had outfits that were sexy, innocent, or classic, depending on how she was feeling. She'd play songs on the record player to put her into the right mood. One of her favorites was a sultry tune by the Shirelles called "Will You Still Love Me Tomorrow?" While she put on makeup, she'd sing along with the music. On her sexy days, she applied an extra coat of mascara to make her eyes look more mysterious. Every time she passed in front of the mirror, she'd suck in her cheeks and let her eyelids droop. With the music pounding and her cheeks flushed from dancing, she'd work herself into a joyous frenzy. Then she'd charge out of the house, ready for romance. But so far, the only guys who came on to her were the wimps at Merritt College.

Cindy was combing out her hair for the tenth time, turning her head in front of the mirror. "What a waste. The minute I get out into the fog, it'll frizz up. Come on. Let's check out the Med."

Once they were on the street, Tanya felt renewed hope. There were bound to be some interesting men at the Med. When they came to the corner of Telegraph, the avenue was alive with students, street people, and all manner of riffraff surging toward campus. To Tanya, this vibrating life was a constant source of wonder. Every trip to campus held the prospect of adventure—adventure which Tanya yearned to be a part of. So did everyone else, it seemed. There was a vibration in the air that made one feel something extraordinary was happening.

By the fall of '68, the world as Tanya knew it had been turned topsy-turvy, and she thrilled to every astonishing new aspect of it. Boys let their hair grow past shoulder length and girls went bra-less. The mandatory dress code was a pair of faded jeans and a blue workshirt. Sit-ins, love-ins, and bed-ins were part of daily news. Draft cards, deferments, 1-A, 4-F, Selective Service boards, and conscientious objectors were constant topics of conversation. Tear-gas levels were posted alongside the morning weather report in the *Daily Cal*, patchouli oil had taken the place of perfume, and psychedelic poster art adorned nearly every dorm-room wall. Pledging a sorority or a fraternity was as good as committing social suicide. Alpha Epsilon Phi, the number-one Jewish sorority, had gone bankrupt, and that bastion of young WASP womanhood the Kappa Kappa Gamma House, at the corner of Channing and Piedmont, had been converted into the Maharishi's Transcendental Meditation Center. In fact, anything that smacked of India was in vogue, including Ravi Shankar's sitar music, gurus, ashrams, the *Kama Sutra*, saffron robes, mantras, and kundalini yoga. Collegiate sports had so fallen out of favor that the California Bears, the university's famed football team, was ridiculed, and attendance at games had plummeted. For Friday-night entertainment—and Tanya yearned most of all for this—university students hitched across the Bay Bridge to hear music at the Fillmore. There, as Cindy had described it, they would sit cross-legged on the floor of a pitch-black auditorium, passing joints and Cokes spiked with LSD, while an overhead projector flashed psychedelic images on the screen that swirled in a mad sea of color. Every weekend, groups like the Jefferson Airplane, Big Brother and the Holding Company, and the Creedance Clearwater Revival turned their amps all the way up and blasted their benumbed audiences.

And benumbed they were. Although she hadn't yet had the courage to try it, Tanya was aware that dope was everywhere. Getting high was treated as a ritual experience. There was an unspoken competition over who could hold the shortest roach or roll the tightest joint. Most of Tanya's acquaintances kept a supply of Zig-Zag papers on hand, and owned strobe lights and water pipes. These same people loved to brag about the super lid of Acapulco Gold or Panama Red they had bought down on Telegraph Avenue, and from time to time, someone would even claim the discovery of a legal substance, like dried banana peels or catnip, that had the same effect as marijuana. Getting stoned was so commonplace that ex-sorority girls were baking hash brownies and dropping LSD into the party punch. If Tanya wanted, she could buy any type of acid—Purple Micro Dot, Orange Sunshine, Window Pane, or White Lightning—in tabs on the street. Many of her favorite songs charted the wondrous journey of an acid trip, like the Beatles' "Strawberry Fields Forever" and Jimi Hendrix's "Purple Haze."

Tanya knew that drugs and sex went hand in hand. She had heard that smoking dope enhanced sex because it lowered inhibitions and created the illusion of intimacy. Indeed, one-night stands between strangers were the norm. To Tanya, this world of sexual freedom and psychedelics seemed just out of reach. No matter how hard she tried—cruising Telegraph in her faded jeans and buying Beatles albums as soon as they came out—she was still an outsider. She had never even smoked pot, much less gone to a concert at the Fillmore, or experienced anything close to a one-night stand. To her acute embarrassment, her classmates considered her straight as an arrow. In her mind it was all her overprotective father's fault. Now that she had started college, she was determined to do anything necessary to change her image, except perhaps dropping acid, which she admitted to Cindy seemed "much too heavy to handle."

"There's the Med," said Cindy, pointing to some plate-glass windows fogged with steam. "Hang a right," and she turned in under a striped awning that sagged over the street.

The Mediterranean Café was the most infamous espresso joint on Telegraph Avenue. It had originally been modeled after a Parisian café, and during the days of the Free Speech Movement had flourished as a haven for beatnicks and rabble-rousers. In recent years it had degenerated into a rather seamy establishment, yet even in its unkempt condition, the Med still had an aura of intellectual arrogance.

They squeezed inside the door. The place was crammed with phony marble tables, and the stink of unwashed bodies and patchouli oil permeated the room. The noise was so dense, Tanya couldn't hear her own voice. She tapped Cindy on the shoulder and yelled, "Upstairs?" She pointed to a spiral staircase that led to another floor.

"No way." To Cindy's mind, going upstairs was like being banished to Siberia. "Let's wait."

They stood by the door, scanning the room for possibilities. Tanya spotted a table of three hippies and nudged Cindy.

Cindy glanced at them. "Not bad. Definitely fuckable." To Cindy and Tanya, "fuckable" stood for the most meaningful measurement of human achievement. Men fell on one side or the other of this invisible fault line. Not that either of the girls had had much opportunity to test it out. Cindy had presumably chalked up several one-night stands that had ended, the next morning, in awkward goodbyes. The only time Tanya had nearly gone all the way was in high school, with a boy named Wally, whom she'd had a crush on for two years. Finally, two months before graduation, they had ended up together at a party, in a dark room full of couples rolling around on the floor under blankets. The sex, such as it was, had been over so fast she wasn't completely sure what had happened. When Wally never so much as called to ask her out, she suffered greatly, and tortured herself with the thought that she wasn't worthy of any man's love.

A table opened up on the far side of the room, but to the girls' great disappointment it wasn't near the three hippies.

"Damn," said Tanya. "What do we do?"

Cindy shrugged and edged her way through the crowded room, going out of her way to pass the boys' table. Tanya followed, and as she neared their table, her heart began to flutter. One of the boys was just her type, dark, with a gaunt face. She sucked in her cheeks and pretended to look straight ahead. As she passed him by, she brushed against an Army jacket that was slung over the back of a chair, tipping it over. She whirled around to pick it up and found herself looking into a pair of dazed brown eyes. He looked loaded. "I'm sorry," she mumbled, flushing bright red.

"No problem," he said, putting the chair upright.

For a moment she was certain that a spark had passed between them, and she scampered after Cindy to their waiting table.

"Oh God!" she moaned.

"What did he say?" demanded Cindy.

"I think we made eye contact."

"Far out."

Tanya glanced over her shoulder to see if he was watching her. She wondered if he had felt the same overpowering vibes. Unfortunately, he was now facing in the wrong direction, and she couldn't see his face. How was she to know if she had made an impression? "Here, I'm going to switch seats," she said, scrambling to get onto another chair so she could have a better view of his table. The three guys had their heads thrown back and were laughing. "They're so darling," she said. "They remind me of the Three Musketeers."

They ordered café au lait. Tanya sipped hers, trying to make it last as long as possible, while she kept glancing over to see if the Musketeer was looking her way. He wasn't.

"Hey, did I tell you the latest about Janice?" asked Cindy.

"No, what?"

"Well, a few days ago she went in for a pregnancy test. She thinks it was that guy Stuart she was with after the Doors concert."

"Oh sure. After one time?" said Tanya disgustedly. Janice had been broadcasting to the world that her period was five days late. An image of her, lighting up her cigarette and bragging about her latest fuck, flitted through Tanya's mind, and she said, "She exaggerates everything."

"What else is new? The test came up negative, *of course.* But guess what. The gyno told her to get on the Pill."

"You're kidding," said Tanya, sinking back in her chair. To both girls, being on the Pill was a mark of real prestige.

"When she came home last night she showed them to me. They're in a baby-blue compact, and when you open it up, there's a wheel inside with twenty-eight tiny pills. You just dial one up for each day of the month."

"Has she started yet?"

"Yeah. Yesterday."

"Boy," sighed Tanya. Something like that would just never happen to her. Sometimes she thought that Tanya Tarasoff, whoever she was, didn't exist. She was doomed to be stuck at home with a telephone that didn't ring.

"Let's split," said Cindy, rummaging around in her purse.

Tanya stole another glance at the Musketeers, but to her shock, their table was empty. A lump rose in her throat, and she swore inwardly. As she followed Cindy out, she was filled with self-pity. The thought of going back to her bedroom filled her with despair. Nothing was ever going to change.

ON a morning in October, Prosenjit Poddar got up at five-thirty to catch the university car pool out to the East Bay docks. The International House cafeteria was still dark, so he skipped breakfast and dogtrotted, tool chest and tiffin carrier in hand, to the corner of Piedmont and Bancroft. A knot of young men dressed in overalls stood in the fog—the same group of graduate students he saw every Tuesday and Thursday when he waited for the minibus. As he approached, they glanced his way, and he nodded politely. He didn't join them, but stopped short and set his tool chest on the sidewalk. Long ago, he had learned to hold himself aloof. He was a thin, angular young Hindu, twenty-three years old, with a face that could be appealing were it not so remote. In India, his friends had called him a *gabhir jaler mach*, "deep water fish," because so little of him met the eye.

What failed to meet the eye this particular morning was the song in his heart. He didn't quite understand it himself—this strange and unbidden melody of lightness and joy—except that he knew it came from the girl. The girl. That vision of raven-haired, green-eyed lissomeness, with her hands on her hips, thrusting forth her dainty feet almost in challenge. She must have known he was staring; she must have felt he was under her spell.

Dropping to his knees beside his tool chest, he opened the lid and surveyed the contents. The compartments were arranged with meticulous care, and the metal tools gleamed. He fingered a row of drill bits, taking comfort in the faint smell of machine oil the tools gave off. Sometimes, just sifting through his chest in this way, he came up with an idea for a new invention. Electronic and mechanical designs were his passion, as well as his refuge from loneliness. Now, with the vision of the girl in his mind, it occurred to him that there was no telling what wonder he might conceive. From where he crouched, he could barely overhear the others. The even drone of their conversation hummed in the background. Every so often a wisecrack would elicit a snort of laughter, and he was able to identify who the laugh was coming from without looking up. As usual, he felt excluded from their jokes, but now he didn't mind one bit. He clenched his fist around some chunky nuts and bolts and shook them around in his hand like dice. When the bus pulled up, he snapped the chest shut and bounced to his feet. He waited until the others climbed in before he boarded, then he took the seat across from the driver so he could look out the front.

The ride to the docks took forty minutes. To Prosenjit, with his spirit soaring, it was forty minutes of unimaginable pleasure. Locals referred to this East Bay drive as the armpit of California, but today this was the world he loved. He stared straight ahead, mesmerized by the gray seascape, barely able to make out the waterfront, still blanketed by fog. From the distance, muffled foghorns signaled the arrival of freighters from the Orient. He thought of the ships, heavy with cargo, waiting offshore for tugs to pull them in, and felt as if he were at the very center of world commerce.

The van wove its way toward Richmond, up Highway 17. Before he came to America, Prosenjit had never even ridden in an automobile, and now he was hurtling down the freeway at sixty miles an hour. With the bus vibrating beneath him, he was transported by the thrill of having left the rickshaws and bullock carts of India far behind.

He had been born in the Ganges Delta, in a village two hundred miles north of Calcutta, on the border of Bangladesh. Rice paddies, the color of pea soup, stretched as far as the eye could see. The land was so flat, nothing broke the horizon but an occasional mango tree. Balurghat, the village where Prosenjit had grown up, had remained unchanged for a thousand years. It consisted of a few hundred thatched huts, sprawled along the banks of the Atreyi River, a tributary of the Ganges. Its only link with the rest of the world was one dirt highway, ten miles off, scored with potholes. But in Balurghat, no one went anywhere. Sometimes the rickshaw wallahs waited all day without a commission, their conveyances stacked in the sunbaked marketplace, with flies swarming around the wallahs' heads.

The house that Prosenjit was raised in was without running water, toilet, or electricity. Every morning, he or one of his five brothers lugged in buckets of water to fill a stone cistern in the kitchen for that day's supply. His mother cooked the family's meals over a fire fueled by cow-dung patties, and he and his brothers ate their dinner by the light of a kerosene lamp.

But Prosenjit was pleased to recall how he had deliberately severed these and other memories of Balurghat. He was in the States now. Never mind the fact that Americans were cold and inhospitable. To a boy who loved electronic and mechanical design as much as he did, the opportunities seemed boundless. He had immediately become immersed in the world of technology and within a few months of his arrival had assembled a sophisticated sound system and a reel-to-reel tape recorder. His letters home were full of detailed descriptions of the gadgets he had designed, like a portable burglar alarm, a remote-control cigarette lighter, and a telephone-answering device. He knew that to his five younger brothers his achievements seemed incredible, and it swelled his heart to think that he had become a hero in their eyes.

As the bus took an off-ramp and pulled into the Richmond Field Station, Prosenjit rose and picked up his tool chest and tiffin carrier. The Field Station was a training ground for graduate students who specialized in ship design. During World War II, it had been a bustling naval base where transports and destroyers were built. When the war ended, the shipbuilding stopped and the base was left deserted. For years it lay empty, until the university acquired the land and converted it into a research facility. It still had the feel of a ghost town. A layer of crusty sea salt had settled over the row of wood-frame barracks, and an enormous airplane hangar loomed over the docks.

Prosenjit hurried along the gravel path into the hangar. In the early-morning gloom, the cavernous room was bone-chilling cold.

After switching on the lights, he picked up a rag and began to wipe the mist off the gauges.

His pulse quickened when he heard the crunch of tires over gravel and the sound of a car door slamming. From the window he could see the beefy figure of Gunnar Stanfil, chief mechanic, walking up the path. Stanfil had fuzzy Brillo-pad hair and a walrus mustache, and sported a rose tattoo on his arm. As usual, he was dressed in a red plaid Pendleton and wore a visor pulled down over his eyes. Prosenjit lowered his eyes and said in a deferential tone, "Good morning, Mr. Stanfil."

Stanfil gave him a curt nod and grumbled, "Give me a holler when you're ready," as he disappeared down the hall, into his office.

Gunnar Stanfil had run the Field Station for the last five years. He had little formal education and liked to brag that all his knowledge came from on-the-job training in the Navy. At age forty-five, he was turning to flab from too much beer. He thought of his job with the university as a stopgap and kept repeating that he was fed-up with sitting on his can and babysitting wimps who were "all brain, no brawn." On Orientation Day, he had announced to a fresh crop of graduate students, "I got my Ph.D. in the university of hard knocks. The only thing I flunked was reading." As far as Stanfil was concerned, a background in calculus and physics was all well and good, but nothing took the place of firsthand experience at sea. He was especially caustic with students who fumbled with tools and lathe. He'd bark monosyllabic orders meant more to intimidate than instruct. In private, he once told his second engineer that all the grads were "pussies." When he first spotted Prosenjit, standing with hands in pockets of neat khaki trousers, asking polite questions, he grunted in contempt and made up his mind he was going to give the Little Hindu, as he called him, a hard time.

It especially griped Stanfil that the Hindu prided himself on being adept with his hands. A few weeks earlier, Stanfil had stayed late, as he often did, to tidy up after his charges, and had heard a noise coming from the machine shop. "What the devil," he muttered, and strode into the room. He was shocked to see Prosenjit hunched over a cast-off propellor and casing. His arms were elbow-deep in grease and on his face was a look of utter concentration.

Prosenjit gave Stanfil a wide smile. "Sir," he said, "I am restoring the propellor and dynamometer."

"Oh, really?"

"Whenever I find a broken-down machine, I must rehabilitate it."

"Well, you aren't going to rehabilitate that frozen hunk of shit."

Prosenjit only smiled and kept on working. Stanfil turned and stalked out. Over his shoulder he grumbled, "Shut off the lights when you're done."

Since then, Stanfil had been aware that the Hindu had stayed after work nearly every Tuesday and Thursday. He had searched his brain for a reason to run him out, but the machine shop was always left spick and span, and the tools were all in place. There was nothing for Stanfil to do but tolerate it, and he did so with little grace.

For his part, Prosenjit barely noticed that he had been singled out for abuse. Although he held Gunnar Stanfil in high esteem, and would have liked nothing better than to have earned his respect, he simply accepted the chief mechanic's ill humor without complaint and went about his work. This just rankled Stanfil all the more. Sometimes, when Prosenjit was immersed at the drafting table, his agile fingers moving over a sketch pad, Stanfil found himself watching him, wondering what fluke of nature had endowed this slip of a boy with so much natural dignity.

There was no way Stanfil could know what Prosenjit had undergone to earn that dignity. There was no way that he could even imagine, in his wildest dreams, what secret this boy harbored in his breast.

For Prosenjit Poddar had been born an *Untouchable*. By mere accident of birth, Prosenjit and every one of his ancestors, stretching back through the ages, were stigmatized as defiled human beings. They were on the lowest rung of a caste system that had had its beginnings in India's prehistoric past and had clung on for thousands of years. According to Hindu belief, society was broken down into four main divisions: the priests (Brahmans), the warriors (Kshatriyas), the merchants (Vaisyas), and the servitors (Sudras). Beneath these castes, indeed so low that they fell outside the caste system, were the Untouchables (Achyuts). As Untouchables, Prosenjit and his people were destined for their lifetime to perform the most despised and debasing jobs imaginable: sweeping and scavenging; carrying off the dead and cremating their remains; tanning the skins of dead animals and eating their flesh; cleaning latrines and disposing of human excrement.

Prosenjit could never forget the stories that his grandmother, Bhagabati, told of her youth. In those days before Gandhi, Untouchables were treated with less humanity than animals. They were forced to live outside the village in order not to contaminate its inhabitants. Contamination was believed possible by breathing the same air, drinking from common water, or even stepping into the shadow cast by an Untouchable. Bhagabati and the other Untouchables were allowed to enter the village only to perform unclean jobs, and on such occasions they were obliged to carry brooms to sweep away the footprints they left in the dirt. As a child of eight, Bhagabati went to work for an upper-caste family to whom her family claimed service as a hereditary right. Each morning before it was light, she slipped into town and crept up a wooden staircase to their latrine to collect the contents of an earthenware jar. She emptied the excrement into a bucket and carried it outside the village to the refuse heap. As she performed this duty, Bhagabati adhered to two strict taboos: never to enter a room in which food was prepared and, above all, never to be seen by the family she served. To ensure this, she banged on a small tin drum as she walked through the corridors of their house. The most her mistress ever saw of Bhagabati was the tail end of her sari as she scurried out of a room.

But times had greatly improved for Prosenjit's family. The breakthrough came when Prosenjit's father, Pulinchandra, became one of the first Untouchables in the Faridpur District of East Bengal to learn how to read. Even though the caste Hindus of his village had tried to bar him from school, the village teacher, an enlightened Brahman, admitted him into the first standard. He made a place for the boy in the dirt outside the schoolhouse, where Pulinchandra took all of his lessons by listening through the window. After several months, the furor died down, and Pulinchandra was permitted to move up to the verandah and squat on the pavement. He went through six years of primary education in this manner.

Thanks to this rudimentary schooling, Pulinchandra was able to find work as a court inspector in the magistrate's office in the Dinajpur District of West Bengal, in the town of Malda, just a few miles from Balurghat. As a court inspector he earned what was for him the unprecedented sum of nine hundred rupees a year, equivalent to one hundred and fifty dollars.

Pulinchandra saw to it that his firstborn, Prosenjit, went even further. He boarded him, at the age of nine, with relatives so he could attend high school, and with gratifying results; Prosenjit demonstrated an uncanny aptitude for mathematics and chemistry. He erected a makeshift chemistry lab in his second cousin's home and was forever mixing formulas over a Bunsen burner. It was at this time that he became consumed with designing and building mechanical devices, such as a miniature steam engine and a telephone. This in a village that did not have running water or electricity.

When he was sixteen, Prosenjit sat for the Joint Entrance Examination for the Indian Institute of Technology, the best engineering college in India. Competition was fierce; eighty thousand students vied for twelve hundred places. He scored in the upper tenth of one percentile and was admitted to the branch at Kharagpur, in West Bengal. Although it had become a government policy to reserve places at the university for members of the Scheduled Caste (the name given to Untouchables when Gandhian law abolished discrimination against them in 1949), Prosenjit had earned his seat by merit, and was the only Untouchable admitted to the IIT. He took up the study of naval architecture and after five years "passed out a topper in his batch"—he graduated second in his class. The caption under his yearbook photo stated, "A topper with dreams of going abroad." And indeed, the desire to pursue higher studies at an American university was the driving force in his life.

Admission to graduate school at the University of California at Berkeley was nothing short of a miracle. Of the tens of millions of students in India, only a tiny few earned the privilege of attending a foreign university. Historically, this domain had been reserved for the scions of upper-caste families who could afford to send their sons abroad. It was almost unheard-of for a member of the Scheduled Caste to go abroad. When word of Prosenjit's intent first leaked out, his classmates jeered and accused him of *gache kanthal gofe tel*, building sand castles in the air. He said nothing until he received notice from the West Bengal government that he had qualified for a scholarship. With the official papers in hand, he went to his father and knelt at his feet. Pulinchandra received the astonishing news in silence. For one week he ruminated over a course of action, and then, in a gesture that shocked even the most well-to-do of Balurghat, he took out a loan of six thousand rupees to pay for his son's passage to the United States.

In the fall of 1967, Prosenjit Poddar stepped into an airplane at Calcutta's Dum Dum Airport and became one of only a handful of Untouchables, in the whole of India, ever to leave for an American university. When he arrived at the International House, lugging his two trunks, the latches bound together with hemp, he was determined to shed his identity as an Untouchable and conquer the whole world. But he was quite taken aback when Americans seemed unwilling even to meet his eye and went out of their way to avoid noticing him. There was never a direct insult; he just didn't exist. Not realizing that, as a rule, American students turned a cold shoulder to foreigners, he came to suspect that somehow they had discovered the secret of his past; somehow they instinctively knew he was an Untouchable. Even with his great triumph, even with his great opportunity to make a new life for himself, he could not shake off the stigma of his birth.

He had always been reserved, but now he was an utter recluse. The weekdays weren't so bad because he had classes to attend, but the weekends offered only emptiness. On Friday nights he would loiter in the cafeteria after coffee and then unwillingly mount the tile stairs to his cell on the sixth floor, where he stayed for the duration of the weekend. In that first year he never so much as spoke to an American outside his courses. He felt that he had been "bambooed," and seriously considered going home; but then his father's face, full of pride for his accomplishments, and the loan of the six thousand rupees, quickly put an end to those thoughts.

He knew too that the future education of his younger brothers depended on the pittance he earned from his job at the towing tank. So he trained himself to put up a brave front, and whenever loneliness descended upon him, he'd pick up a manual on ship propulsion systems and burrow in deeper. Consequently, he had done brilliantly in that first critical year of his master's program. But his self-containment was so thorough he seemed plunged within himself like the nucleus of a cell, feeding on its own substance. That is, until today, when he felt his world opening up.

Now, on this chill October morning, he was going to run a seakeeping test on his model ship, the *Sita*, named after the heroine of the Hindu epic the *Ramayana*. It had taken him five months to design and construct the model. If the experiment succeeded, he believed, his studies in the United States would be validated. After setting the gauges, he resolutely approached Gunnar Stanfil's office and rapped on the door. The chief mechanic was behind his desk, reading the sports section and cradling a steaming cup of coffee.

"Mr. Stanfil? I am ready for you."

"Let's get going, then," said Stanfil, pushing back and following Prosenjit into the hangar. From the corner of his eye, Stanfil could see the model ship waiting on a pedestal. There was no denying it; the lines of that ship had been exquisitely crafted.

Prosenjit lowered the *Sita* into the water. The towing tank was a shallow pool four hundred feet long, stretching the length of the hangar. At one end was a wave-making device that could churn up the water like a North Sea squall. On the other end was a carriage on rails that pulled ship models the length of the tank. Along the walls were gauges that measured the model's water resistance and energy consumption. By tabulating the results, one could predict precisely how a ship would fare on the high seas.

Stanfil yanked the switch on the wave-making machine, and the drone and pounding of heavy machinery shook the room, making conversation impossible. Prosenjit hoisted himself over the carriage and adjusted the *Sita*, then he let her go. On the ship's return trips, Prosenjit ran back and forth, excitedly calling out the marks on the gauges. It was a painstaking experiment that took over two hours. When it was finished, there was no doubt in his or Stanfil's mind: The *Sita* was a resounding success.

A few hours later Stanfil was surprised to find the Little Hindu standing behind him. The boy was grinning slyly, rubbing the palm of his hand on the side of his trousers.

"Mr. Stanfil, could you spare a moment?"

"For what?"

"You remember, previously I was keen on fixing the propellor housing. Well, it gave a good deal of trouble. Please can you come?" He walked swiftly into the machine shop, pointed to the far end of the room, and said, "I had another bash at it. Please observe."

Stanfil squinted and walked toward a shining shape. He ran his hands over the blades and gave them a spin. "Sure as shit," he muttered under his breath. Somehow, the Little Hindu had transformed a useless, frozen apparatus into a spinning whir. The boy was the best goddam mechanical engineer to cross his path since the Navy. Suddenly, with a gush of warmth, he found himself slapping Prosenjit on the back. "How about some lunch?" This was an unheard-of invitation.

Prosenjit, out of habit, smiled bashfully, his eyes fixed on the ground. "My regrets, Mr. Stanfil, but I must decline. It is necessary for me to log the results of the test."

"Bullshit," said Stanfil.

"Please, sir," Prosenjit began to stammer, but Stanfil wouldn't take no for an answer. Prosenjit was swept out of the room.

This marked the beginning of an odd friendship. Every Tuesday and Thursday they brought their bag lunches down to the docks and watched as ships' cargoes were off-loaded. Stanfil's lunch invariably was a foot-long submarine sandwich and a thermos of black coffee, while Prosenjit contented himself with soggy fish patties and rice dished out of his tiffin carrier. It was apparent that Stanfil had taken a fancy to the Hindu not just because he was a crack engineer, but because he was an avid listener. He told himself that he liked to "shoot the shit" with Poddar because he had a different scope on the world, but what he really relished was the opportunity to talk about his own great days in the Navy. He regaled the youth with stories that bordered on the incredible. Prosenjit hung on every word, often begging to hear more about hair-raising engine burnouts and narrowly averted maritime disasters.

For Prosenjit, it was the first time that he had felt close to an American—something he had never believed would happen. Their biweekly bull sessions bolstered his self-confidence and triggered an astonishing reaction; the acceptance by this one American made him feel welcomed by the culture as a whole.

It was not until a few weeks later that he came to a simple but profound realization. *In America there were no Untouchables.* The rules and regulations that had separated him from other human beings had never existed here, and they need not persist in his own mind. The door to human contact had been opened, if only a crack, and he was free to walk through it. For Prosenjit, this signified the beginning of a new life. And indeed, it was this newfound confidence that encouraged him to think that if he returned to the folk dance, he might once again encounter that green-eyed girl, and that just maybe she would not reject him.

ON the evening of November 15, Tanya Tarasoff was dancing to rock 'n' roll in front of her full-length mirror. It was a Friday night and she was getting ready to go out. She was wearing only a bra and bikini underpants. The underpants were pink with a red heart embossed over one pelvic bone, and she thought of them as her good-luck charm. On the floor by her bed lay a heap of discarded clothes that was growing all the time. As she pranced back and forth between closet and bed, she watched herself in the mirror to see how she looked.

"Shut that noise off," her father bellowed from the kitchen.

"Gotta get you into my life," she sang to an imaginary man as she skipped to the record player to turn down the volume. Her father had agreed to let her go to tonight's folk dance on the Berkeley campus. It would be a disaster if she pissed him off now.

"Gotta get you into my life," she sang, as she sat down to take the rollers out of her hair. Her dressing table was her favorite place in the house, because it reminded her of a princess's throne. It was antique white with gold-leaf rubbings on it—a real find her father had picked up at the Sunday flea market, where he shopped for bargains. On it she kept a cluster of perfume bottles chiseled in glass. They had romantic-sounding names like Prince Matchabelli and Madame Rochas, and they made her dream about what it would be like when she fell in love.

She opened one of the drawers of her dressing table, rooted around, and took out a pouch full of cosmetics. She dropped the bag into her purse. Her father had forbidden her to wear blusher or mascara, so she would sneak it out of the house to put on later.

She jumped up from the stool and examined herself for the last time, admiring her flared skirt and boots that laced up the front.

She put her hands on her hips and puckered her lips at the mirror. She liked to imagine she had a pout like her idol, Brigit Bardot. She bared her teeth and shook her hair out like a sex kitten.

"Dad, I'm ready," she called. She could hear him ranting in the kitchen, telling her mother that Alex had to be punished for cutting class. "Wait till I get my hands on that punk, I'm going to take him apart." Then there was the sound of her mother's voice, too muffled to make out, and her father's ferocious, "What? What did you say?" No doubt her mother had tried to intercede on Alex's behalf, always a mistake.

She ducked her head into the hall and called, "Dad, it's time." There was no answer from the kitchen, only the continuous din of voices. She stomped her foot and called, "Dad . . . Dad," in a louder voice.

"In a minute you're not going anywhere," he yelled back.

Then she heard the back door slam. She held her breath until she heard the groan of the garage door opening, then she dashed down the hall into the kitchen. Her mother, Lidia, was standing at the sink, her hands submerged in dishwater. Tanya's little sister, Helen, was sitting at the table, putting together a jigsaw puzzle.

When she saw Tanya, Lidia said, "You must wear something more. The air, it is so cold." She spoke with a heavy Russian accent.

"Please, Mama." It embarrassed Tanya that after so many years in America, her mother still had trouble speaking the language.

Drying her hands on her apron, Mrs. Tarasoff walked up to Tanya and started to fuss with her hair, brushing the loose curls away from her face. Her hands were coarsened by housework. "Be careful not to upset your father."

"He already *is* upset."

Her mother sighed. The sigh, so unconscious and heartfelt, was the utterance of one who was resigned to going through life as a victim. She often complained that her husband didn't want a wife, but a maid. Because of his drinking, she had been forced to take on many of the responsibilities he shirked. Now, from standing on her feet endlessly, she suffered from varicose veins that wound up her legs and swelled her ankles in the cold, obliging her to wear spongy opaque support hose, even around the house.

"Mama, I'm going to take driving lessons and get my license. And he's not going to stop me."

"You need to go somewhere, Alex will drive you."

"Mama, you know I can't depend on Alex!"

"Most of the time, Alex is okay."

"How can you say that?" It irritated Tanya that her brother was so unreliable. Whereas she had responded to the situation at home by becoming the dutiful daughter, adjusting to the needs of everyone else, Alex had rebelled against it. Even as a child he had been a troublemaker, and now, in high school, he was incorrigible. To make matters worse, Alex had recently made Tanya the unwilling guardian of his secret. Just last week, he had dropped out of school and taken a job at the Union 76 gas station on Solano Avenue, right around the corner from their house. If their mother ever found out that Alex was pumping gas, she'd be heartsick. In the meantime, Alex thought it hilarious that neither of their parents had seen him, especially because Vitally passed the station every day on his way to work. Tanya was tempted to blow his secret, even though he threatened to beat her face in if she "finked." All that prevented her from doing so was a weariness with the whole hopeless scene.

Lidia was shaking her head and saying, "Your father always picks on him."

"Yeah, but what about me? What do you think he does to me?"

"Don't make your father mad," Lidia warned. "You know you can't talk to him."

"He's not going to even know when I take my driver's test," she said. "I'm going to do it secretly."

Mrs. Tarasoff only pursed her lips.

There was a blast from the horn in the driveway.

"Coming, coming!" Tanya sang out, as she ran from the door.

Her father owned an old blue Pontiac which he was still paying for on time. He always made a big deal about warming the engine up, especially because it drove the others up the wall to wait. As Tanya slid into the front seat, she said, "Don't forget, first we have to pick up Cindy."

"You've got another think coming if you think you can run

around with that slut," said Vitally Tarasoff. Even though he had only glimpsed Cindy for a moment, he had already labeled her boy-crazy and a bad influence.

"What's wrong with Cindy?"

"Don't give me that. She's cheap."

"She is not."

Vitally fell into a sullen silence, and Tanya was careful not to say anything more to provoke him. She caught a whiff of his sour breath. He had been drinking. He was still dressed in the gray over-alls that he wore to work, and his big hands were smudged with grease. A shock of black hair had fallen across his forehead like a wild sprout. Under the light of a streetlamp, he looked almost boyish. It always amazed Tanya that he could look so young when he got blitzed every other night on beer and vodka. He really did have a remarkable constitution. Tanya fancied that once he must have been a dashingly handsome man. Looking at him now, she wondered what had happened to sour him so. His life had been full of adventure, and everyone, especially Tanya, loved to hear his stories. No matter what, he had a great knack for making people and places come alive. Whenever he told a story, he'd rise from his chair, pace the floor, and gesture with his thick hands. Tanya would listen enthralled, even though she'd heard it fifty times before.

Vitally Tarasoff had grown up in Harbin, the old Russian metropolis of Manchuria. As a boy he had worked on the Trans-Siberian Railroad hammering spikes. But by the time he was in his early twenties, the work had been phased out and the Russians were an unwelcome presence in China. It was a hand-to-mouth existence, and he grew used to living off rations. It was around this time that he met Tanya's mother, Lidia Gabrilov, a shy girl with a proud eagle's nose and sturdy legs. The courtship had been typical of Vitally's reckless nature. On their first outing he persuaded her to go for a ride on the back of his motorcycle, through the twisted cobblestone streets of Harbin. Not heeding her pleas to slow down, he leaned into a hairpin turn and skidded, head-on, into a vegetable cart. He pulled himself out of the wreckage uninjured. Lidia, on the other hand, had a mangled knee. Suffused with guilt, Vitally brought flowers and candy to her bedside, and it was there while she was recuperating that he proposed.

Shortly after they were married, World War II ended and the Russians were expelled from Manchuria. It was on the train to Shanghai that he announced to Lidia that he had made up his mind to emigrate to America. When they arrived in Shanghai, they were told that securing visas would be difficult, maybe impossible, but that only made him more determined. They traveled by steamship to São Paulo, Brazil, where Vitally got a job as a car mechanic and Lidia worked in the flea market. Two years passed. On January 22, 1949, their first daughter, Tanya, was born, and fifteen months later, their son, Alex. In 1963 the long-awaited visas were issued, and the Tarasoffs moved to Berkeley, California.

During the first few years, Vitally struggled as an auto mechanic with the hope of buying his own garage. By working two shifts and pooling his money with another Russian, he managed to lease an auto repair shop on San Pablo Avenue. But it wasn't long before he realized that he had bitten off more than he could chew. Although an expert with his hands, Vitally had no business sense at all and couldn't get along with any partner. Their frequent altercations ended, finally, with Vitally grabbing up a jack handle and chasing the frightened man around the garage. Before the year was out, Vitally's auto repair shop went bankrupt. It was the greatest disappointment of his life.

Now, he was utterly defeated. At the age of forty-eight, he worked grudgingly as a mechanic at a Rambler dealership in San Francisco and lived only for the weekends, when he cut loose at the Mercury Club, a Russian tavern on Sutter Street, and had to be conducted home. Tanya felt a twinge of pity as she glanced at the powerful hands all chewed up and toughened. He still had fine, baby-soft skin on his face, and when he got excited, his cheeks flushed pink. He had the eyes of a man whose dreams had been lost.

"So where does this friend of yours live?" asked Vitally, as he braked for the light at Dwight and Telegraph.

She was too irked to answer. He knew perfectly well where Cindy lived, because he had taken her there twice before. Not only that, she could have sworn she'd seen him cruising by the apartment, spying on her.

"Well?" he asked again.

"Dad, you've been there before."

"When?"

She couldn't help herself. "How about all the times you've driven by?"

"What are you talking about?"

"I've seen you. It's like you're spying on me."

"You're out of your mind."

"I wish you'd mind your own business."

"I can do anything I damn well please."

"That's what you think."

"It's my right to know what's going on. I'm your guardian until you're out of my house."

"Some guardian." And then, losing all control, "You can't even take care of yourself."

He slammed on the brakes, and the car swerved on the wet road. "You lousy little bitch." He reached out and grabbed her wrist, squeezing it until the flesh turned white.

"Don't. Don't." She struggled to break loose.

"Don't you ever talk to me like that," he rasped. "You're going home."

"No, please! We're here already. Cindy lives right there," and she pointed at the doorway.

"I'm taking you home."

"Please. Dad, oh please! I'll be good from now on." She started to sob. "Please, I can't just not show up."

He pounded his fists on the steering wheel.

Tanya hissed at him, "Here she comes," as Cindy appeared under a streetlight. Tanya opened the door and leaned forward so she could climb into the backseat.

Cindy ducked her head in and said in a chipper voice, "How are you tonight, Mr. Tarasoff?"

He lifted his head and muttered, "As good as can be expected."

Tanya felt Cindy tweak her arm. She turned around and with a wan smile said, "Nice dress."

"I'm into a heavy purple phase," said Cindy, adjusting her neckline. "It's my new favorite color."

The girls exchanged looks, then Tanya faced forward in her seat. Vitally shifted into low and the car began to mount the hills. They rode in painful silence. The Pontiac climbed up to the corner of College and Piedmont, and the International House came into view. Vitally pulled up alongside the curb.

The I House, as it was called, was a gloomy dormitory that reminded Tanya of the Spanish Inquisition. Dark Moorish arches framed the front entry. The I House was a long-standing campus joke. It had been built in 1930 with the idea that the best minds from around the world would intermix with American scholars. Instead, Americans turned out to be discriminatory and impatient with foreign accents, and suspicious of other cultural traditions. They shunned the I House as if it were full of lepers. Although the dormitory, with its six hundred occupants, sat smack in the middle of Fraternity Row, it was definitely off limits. The only attraction that lured a few Americans inside was the regular Friday-night folk dances.

To Tanya's annoyance, her father waited in front with the motor idling. When they were safely inside, she permitted herself a sigh and said, "Can you believe my father?"

"No," said Cindy, marching through the lobby. "What's with him?" They pushed through the swinging doors of the ladies' room. Tanya slung her coat on a metal counter and leaned over the row of sinks to get a good look at herself in the mirror. Fishing through her purse, she found her makeup pouch and dug out a small bottle of Ivory Dawn foundation. Putting a glob on her fingertips, she began to spread it over her wide cheeks.

"I wish I had skin like yours," said Cindy, as she hoisted her rear end up on a sink. Her wide hips spilled over the sides of the sink bowl. Throwing Tanya a look, she said, "This dance better not suck."

"Who knows, you might meet the love of your life."

"Oh, right." Cindy snorted. Turning on the faucet, she flicked a few drops of water in her direction.

"Hey," shrieked Tanya, jumping out of the way. "You never

know. I'm hoping that maybe that cute guy from the Med will be here. The Musketeer. You know, the one with the bedroom eyes?"

"Be serious. What would a guy like that be doing in a dump like this?"

"This place isn't so bad."

"I promise you," said Cindy, "you're not going to find him here."

"Well, where?"

"A demonstration."

"You mean a noon rally?"

"Yeah, a noon rally or a riot down on Telegraph. I guarantee that's the best way to meet someone."

"We definitely have to go," said Tanya.

"Hey," said Cindy. "What's with your dad, anyway?"

"What do you mean?"

"He seems so uptight about everything. So paranoid."

Tanya shrugged, trying to make light of it. "He's not that bad."

"I don't see how you put up with him," said Cindy, thinking that this was one of the odd things about Tanya. Ever since they had known each other, she had been struck by how defensive Tanya became whenever her father's name was brought up. Cindy knew from bruises she had seen that Tanya's old man beat her up. But Tanya never complained, and only once had she revealed something about her father, saying, of all things, that back in China he had been a diplomat with the Russian embassy. Somehow the notion that Vitally Tarasoff, with his grease-smeared overalls, was once a diplomat was too hard to fathom, and Cindy suspected that it was a lie.

"Yeah," Tanya was saying, "he's been really down lately."

Cindy looked her in the eye. "Why don't you move out?"

"Are you kidding? He'd never let me."

"Yeah, well, that's what my parents said, too. They never want you to move out. You just do it."

"It's not the same thing. Besides, I don't have the money."

"It doesn't cost that much. My parents aren't supporting me. You can get a part-time job or something."

"He'd kill me." Tanya stopped applying mascara, and stood for a moment, rubbing the brush back and forth over the cake.

"What kind of a hold does he have on you, anyway?" asked Cindy narrowly.

Tanya allowed her eyes to meet Cindy's, then turned away.

Cindy reached out and touched her shoulder. "One of these days you've got to deal with it."

Tanya didn't say anything else.

For a moment Cindy thought she saw tears welling in the corner of her friend's eyes. "Don't sweat it. Nothing says you have to do it now."

Tanya swallowed hard.

"Aren't you finished yet?"

"Yeah, almost."

"Come on. Nobody good's going to be out there, anyway."

Tanya gave her a look in the mirror and snapped the mascara compact shut.

"If some turkey asks me to dance," said Cindy, "I'm going to sic him on you." She began humming "If you can't be with the one you love . . ."

Tanya finished it, ". . . love the one you're with," and they waltzed through the swinging doors, toward the dance.

AT eight-thirty that evening, after carefully shaving and slicking his hair back with oil, Prosenjit descended in the elevator and crossed the I House lobby. All day long he had thought of nothing but the green-eyed girl. He could hear strains of music and whoops of laughter coming from the auditorium, and in his mind he imagined her, her head thrown back and lips slightly parted, and the tingle of excitement shot up his spine.

He crept to the doorway and peeked in. In the center of the room was a circle of about thirty young men and women, whirling around and around to an Israeli *hora*. His shyness made him so tense and nervous that beads of sweat were beginning to form on his upper lip. For a few minutes he remained paralyzed, his heart racing, his eyes scanning the moving bodies for the girl.

Then he saw her, dancing on the opposite side of the circle. She had a slim, graceful body, and her eyes were the color of the sea. She looked so childlike, not more than sixteen years old. He couldn't stop staring at her. She tossed her head in a coy gesture and cocked her arm, reminding him of his favorite film star, Suchitra Sen, who played the role of the heedless child-woman in so many Bengali films. He was fascinated by her dainty feet. He thought about how at the last dance she had accidentally stepped on his toe, and how in that moment of confusion she had put her hands up over her mouth to smother a reckless laugh. He had noticed then that she had the hands of a woman. Her long, tapered fingers had moved in quick gestures, drawing his eyes to her and holding him like a snake charmer.

He inched forward, close to the spinning circle, wondering how he could possibly break in and make a place for himself next to her. She did not seem the least bit aware of his presence, and as the circle kept sweeping to the right, dipping and twisting to the beat, he hovered close by, until he was able to dive in and take her hand.

The touch of her hand was divine. He tried to fall in with her rhythm, but the thrill of having her delicate fingers entwined in his own made following the intricate steps impossible. For about half an hour, he shuffled back and forth, pretending to keep up. Then the dance instructor changed the record, putting on a fast-paced Greek *sirto*, and he completely lost his footing. He fixed his eyes on the ground, his face screwed up in painful concentration, trying to follow the flashing movement. When finally he mustered the courage, he looked up. Her hair had swung over one cheek, and he could just barely see, through the dark strands, that her moist lips were parted. She seemed to sense his eyes on her, and she turned her face away to smother a giggle, whispering something to the girl on her other side.

The other girl laughed, and he felt a flush creep across his face.

A few minutes later, he felt her drop his hand and withdraw from the circle. Alarmed, he watched her skip across the dance floor. He felt the impulse to go after her until he realized that she was merely taking off her sweater, which she casually tossed on a chair. The sight of her bare shoulders and shapely arms gave him a start. When she rejoined the dance, it was on the opposite side of the circle.

There was something about her that was spellbinding. He longed to know her name, where she came from, and something of her family background. As he watched her dance he came to the conclusion that she must be an American. Only an American girl would dance in public with such wild abandon. The thought depressed him. Thus far, all of the American students he had met had snubbed his attempts at friendship, reacted with impatience at his halting English, and been repelled by the darkness of his complexion. Why, he wondered, should this girl be any different?

But when they circled around again, he caught her eye, and this time he could have sworn that he saw the corners of her lips curl up in a smile before she turned away from his stare. He was almost certain it wasn't his imagination. She seemed to be flirting with him. His heart fluttered and he was short of breath. In that instant he made up his mind that he would return to the folk dance every week until he made her acquaintance.

A few days later, Prosenjit Poddar was at work in the towing tank, running an experiment with the help of two other graduate students. Prosenjit ran to and fro, calling out instructions to his bored and weary colleagues. Ever since the last dance, an energy had pulsed through his veins that made it hard to sleep and even harder to remain idle. Just as he switched on the wave-making machine, a door opened at the far end of the hangar and a voice boomed out, "Okay, boys. Let's knock off early today. We've got a surprise for you." It was Gunnar Stanfil. He had a grin on his face and was stroking his walrus mustache. There were grunts of relief from the others as they moved toward the door. Reluctantly, Prosenjit turned off the wave-maker, wiped his hands on the side of his trousers, and followed Stanfil down the hall. When they reached his office, Prosenjit saw that the rest of the engineering staff were already there, joking among themselves.

The chief mechanic's desk had been cleared of the usual ship models he kept on display, and in their place sat a huge bowl of crimson-colored punch. Stanfil shoved out a large platter that was covered with damp cheesecloth. With a flourish, he whisked away the cloth, revealing a mound of turkey sandwiches. "Help yourselves," he urged. When no one made a move he said, "Don't mind if I do," and snatched one off the tray, stuffing it in his mouth.

It was the annual party thrown by Gunnar Stanfil a few days before Thanksgiving vacation. He always brought the sandwiches, and his assistant, Ed Spies, laced the punch with rum. Most of those working in the tank were foreign students and thought they were experiencing an authentic taste of American life.

Prosenjit made several trips to the punch bowl without realizing it had been spiked. Pretty soon, Spies nudged Stanfil and said, "Get a load of Poddar. He's really snockered." Stanfil looked over at Prosenjit, who stood with a giddy smile on his face, in the center of a small circle of colleagues, gesturing vociferously.

"The minute you get a Hindu happy," said Stanfil, "he runs around telling lame Indian jokes." Then he called out, "Hey, Poddar. What about that sea-keeping test? We need results."

"Fock it," said Prosenjit, mispronouncing the expression he had heard so many times around the tank, and Stanfil watched with pleasure as his charge launched into yet another joke that seemed to elicit several guffaws. Prosenjit seemed to be soaring.

Like most unmarried Indian boys of his age, Prosenjit was an innocent when it came to women. Not only did he come from a culture that enforced strict separation between the sexes, but he had grown up in an all-boy household. There had been only two times in his youth when he had had private conversations with girls. These had been preceded by secret sidelong glances and the passing of notes. He was thankful that his parents had never found him out. At the age of sixteen he had gone off to board at an all-male college. By the time he reached Berkeley at the age of twenty-two, he had never so much as shared an intimate moment with a girl, let alone a romance.

Up until now, this segregation from the opposite sex had been perfectly agreeable to him. He had deemed it unseemly to make the acquaintance of any women at all. He knew that when the time came to make a match, his parents would either retain the services of a *pandit*—an astrologer—or consult the matrimonial advertisements in the Sunday newspaper. They would review the candidates, investigate the girls' backgrounds, and present proposal photographs for him to inspect. Of course, he would have some voice in the decision-making process, but his parents would make the final selection. In India, ninety percent of all marriages were still arranged, and Prosenjit, a village boy, didn't dream of challenging the custom. Like other traditional Hindus, he looked upon "love matches" as less desirable than unions engineered by the parents, who were so much more experienced when it came to matrimonial matters. He firmly believed that the emotion called "love" was something one grew into, gradually, long after the marriage vows had been spoken.

But the encounter at the folk dance had upset all that. He felt nothing but the urge to get to know this green-eyed girl. The light in her eyes and the smile on her lips had turned him inside out, and now it was all sheer expectancy. Suddenly, on a wave, he called out, "Mr. Stanfil, sir, how did you meet your wife?"

"Wife? What wife?" asked Stanfil, with raised eyebrows. "What makes you think I have a wife?"

Prosenjit was caught off balance. In India, all respectable men were married. It was the done thing. A professional man needed a wife the way a ship needs a rudder. She was his most valued possession. He suddenly felt sorry for his friend and protector, Gunnar Stanfil, and was abashed that he had asked the question. But Stanfil was not about to let the subject drop. Apparently he found the idea of his being married uproariously funny. Slapping his thigh and choking with laughter, he called Ed Spies over to let him in on the joke. Then, having knocked back more than a few himself, he began to hold forth on his favorite subject, his sexual exploits. He had, it seemed, won the favors of a girl from every race on earth. He was replete with comparative data and announced he had a ratings list on performance, measurement, and special attributes. Strutting about, reliving his past glories, he completely forgot the Little Hindu's existence.

Prosenjit sat with eyes lowered, fidgeting with an empty Styrofoam cup. In India, sex was not treated so cheaply. Marriage was a sacrament, and any physical relationship before marriage was out of the question. Girls were idealized, like goddesses, and were sequestered in their parents' home to avoid temptation. Whenever they went out in public, they were admonished never even to look a young man in the eye. Occasionally, boys and girls were permitted to attend plays and concerts together, but only in groups and accompanied by a chaperon. Holding hands or kissing was out of the question. The rare peck on the cheek was considered the greatest personal favor a girl could bestow on a boy. This prohibition against even the most innocent physical contact before marriage was so strong that scenes of couples kissing were censored from Indian films. Prosenjit had never once questioned the Victorian morals of his culture. He never dreamed of kissing a girl, nor had he ever considered the possibility of buying the favors of a "lady of the night." He had always assumed that when he went for marriage, his bride would be chaste, and so would he.

"And what about you, Little Hindu?" asked Stanfil, suddenly noticing him. "How many times have you crossed the Equator?"

Prosenjit wrinkled his brow. "I beg your pardon?"

"How many times have you been with a broad?"

"In Kharagpur there were no ladies at all," Prosenjit said, still not understanding the implication of Stanfil's question.

"Kharagpur? What the hell is Kharagpur?"

"That's where I took my B. Tech degree."

"Guess I've got to start you from scratch, then," said Stanfil, slurping down the last of his drink. "Like the time in the Navy the recruits were so green I had to open up a College of Cocksology." He turned to the others. "What he needs is some basic training." They all agreed.

Prosenjit squirmed. "Mr. Stanfil, I'm afraid my mother would object to that course of study." The disapproving face of his mother, Provabati Biswas Poddar, loomed large in his mind.

"Your mother! Hell, she should be grateful to me for taking you under my wing."

"Before I left India, she made me take a sacred vow. No beef. No alcohol. No involvement with an American girl," said Prosenjit, remembering how, when he was packing his trunks for the journey, his mother had stood before him and said, "If you mix with an American girl you will become dead for me." Then she had begun to cry softly into the fold of her sari. It was only after he had knelt in front of the holy altar, promising to abide by her wishes and kissing her bare feet, that she had allowed herself to be consoled.

"You've already broken one of those vows," Stanfil said, jabbing his finger at Prosenjit's Styrofoam cup. "That's spiked . . . and last week I gave you a hunk of my hamburger. That's two down. So what's the big deal about the third? Especially when you're getting coached by the top banana?"

"She would consider involvement with an American girl a very serious matter."

"Why you worried about getting involved? Your problem is you're *not* involved."

"But . . ." he stammered.

"No buts about it," said Stanfil. "Do you want a lesson or don't you?"

Prosenjit thought to himself that perhaps Mr. Stanfil had a point. Why shouldn't he learn how to approach the girl? His mother need never know a thing about it. "Yes, perhaps I would like a relationship," he ventured.

Stanfil slapped him on the arm. "Relationship, my ass. A relationship is the one thing these campus chicks don't want. They jump in the sack before they even know your name. All they want is a quick in and out."

It suddenly dawned on Prosenjit that Stanfil had been referring to the sexual act itself, and he turned crimson. "Please, Mr. Stanfil," he started to say, but Stanfil sailed blithely on. "Don't worry about a thing, Little Hindu. We'll get you laid."

Prosenjit shook his head strenuously, "Not to bother, not to bother," and bowing with palms pressed together in a *namaste*, he backed out of the room.

SITTING in his study alcove in the naval architecture building, his thoughts were splintered. No matter how he tried, he couldn't focus on the tanker plans he was drafting. He had been fighting the impulse all morning long, but now, in a fit of temper, he gave in to it. Crumpling the sheet of tracing paper on his desk, he rose, grabbed up his windbreaker, and headed out the door.

The naval architecture department was located on the north side of campus, far from the tumult of Telegraph Avenue. During his sixteen months at Berkeley, Prosenjit had rarely left the safety of this quadrangle. He had been content to burrow in like a mole, shut off from the turmoil that rent the rest of campus.

But now he was crossing that invisible line into the demilitarized zone. With hands jammed in his pockets, he charged along the cement path that snaked through campus. It irked him that, over a matter so delicate, he had to turn to Jal Mehta, his old school chum from India. But he had no choice. As he made his way, the sloping hills leveled out into broad lawns, where hippies lolled in spotches of sun. When he reached Dwinelle Hall, he spotted a chunky girl with a sympathetic face, and trotted up to her to ask for directions. She pointed him toward a complex of buildings on the far side of a cement plaza, and he made a beeline for it.

As he neared the plaza, he was surprised to see that there were a few hundred students milling about, listening to the drone of a man's voice blaring out of a loudspeaker. Many were eating ice-cream cones or hot dogs, and the ground was littered with paper wrappers. Behind them, the imposing edifice of Sproul Hall rose in the noon sky, its elephantine Doric columns glowing white in the sunlight. A row of about fifty officers from the California Highway Patrol stood in a solid array along the steps. Their faces were hard and impassive, and they wore flak jackets and shin shields. Many of them cupped the butts of riot clubs in their hands. Somewhat shaken, he pushed his way through the crowd.

The campus cafeteria called the Terrace was so jammed that Prosenjit could hardly get in the door. He had heard from Jal that this was the most popular eating place on campus. Hunched over plates of enchiladas and containers of yogurt, revolutionaries plotted their next assault on Sproul Hall. Their discussions were volatile, fever-pitched. The scene cast such a spell that even sorority types hung around, soaking up the ambience and trying to pick up men. As Prosenjit edged his way through the room, everyone seemed to be clamoring for a place in line. The smell of beef tamales hung in the air. He pushed forward until he reached sliding glass doors that opened onto an enclosed patio. His eyes scanned the faces that sat around tables shaded under colored umbrellas. Then he spotted Jal, and all the irritation he had ever felt against the man welled up inside. Jal's pose was so predictable, a lion in repose, stretched out to catch the California rays, with legs propped up and head thrown back in an attitude of enjoyment. Even the clothes, the faded jeans and workshirt, were galling. They were so American. Prosenjit felt the urge to turn away and leave before Jal noticed him. Why should he put himself through such an ordeal? But the other impulse was stronger. Bracing himself, he pushed forward.

Jal Mehta did not look like he came from India. Italy perhaps, France maybe, but certainly from somewhere on the Riviera. An aquiline nose came down from his forehead in a straight line, and a mop of springy black hair crowned his head. With his fair complexion and aristocratic features, he might be mistaken for European nobility. He positively oozed Old World charm. His gestures were big and sweeping. His voice, if sometimes theatrical, was always commanding. He glided through even the most difficult situations with the utmost aplomb. In short, he was everything Prosenjit was not—sophisticated, outgoing, opinionated, and pompous.

They had met at the age of sixteen, during their first year at the Indian Institute of Technology. Even as a freshman, Jal had been regarded as a controversial figure on campus. For one thing, he had the habit of championing unpopular causes and driving home his points with a self-righteous fervor. For another, he was a Parsi, a member of the wealthiest and most eccentric minority community in India. Jal's family came from the city of Pune, near Bombay. His mother had been widowed, and enjoyed a thriving practice as a physician. Their house was a paradise of cool marble floors and spacious rooms that looked onto the exclusive River and Yacht Club. Like so many Parsis, Jal's European education had begun on the day he was born. He had been raised by a clutch of maidservants, and at the age of eight had been sent to board at a prestigious private school in a hill station near his home. His English was Oxonian and he could speak with knowledge about European art, literature, and music. He was completely at ease in the salon atmosphere his mother cultivated, and his very being bespoke the advantages of his youth and a proclivity for the life-style of the West.

It was this Westernized facade, assumed to be superior to the Indian, that especially rankled Prosenjit, who had been raised to take pride in the simple values of village life. Sometimes he suspected that Jal treated him in a condescending manner just to put him in his place. Whenever they were together, he was vaguely conscious that Jal was having fun at his expense, pulling his leg and manipulating him into playing the role of a *chamcha*, a flunky.

Soundlessly, Prosenjit approached the lounging Jal. He could see that his friend had his eyes closed. Clearing his throat, he said, "Don't let me disturb. Please, carry on," but before he could pull out a chair for himself, Jal had bounded to his feet and gripped him in a bearhug. "Prosenjit Poddar! I can't believe it. My eyes must be deceiving me."

Prosenjit stiffened and extricated himself from the embrace.

"So," said Jal. "You've taken the plunge and left your cave. To what do I owe this honor?"

He cleared his throat again and said, "I have met a girl." He was about to go on, but Jal cut him off.

"Good man. You're beginning to get the hang of it. Practice makes perfect, isn't that what they say? Now, let's go meet some others." Pointing to a nearby table, he dropped his voice and said,

"Those young ladies are in my physics section, and the blonde is doing quite well. Let me introduce you." Grabbing Prosenjit's elbow, he steered him toward the table.

To his annoyance, Prosenjit let himself be guided. It was still a sore point with him that somehow Jal had managed to land himself the position of teaching assistant when everyone else in the department, including himself, had been competing for the honor. Now Jal, who needed it not at all, had his tuition covered and scads of spending money. Worse, Prosenjit had to listen to him boast about the perks, which to Jal meant freshman girls who developed crushes on their teaching assistants.

At the sight of Jal, a flutter of laughter rose from the table. Prosenjit hung back and watched while Jal bantered with the girls. A minute later he turned, a grin on his face, and elbowed Prosenjit in the ribs. "Hey. What happened to you? You disappeared."

Prosenjit shrugged, his face set in a stiff, disapproving mask.

"Well, that's no way to approach the American scene, old chap. You've got to be assertive or you'll never get off the mark. Anyway, sit down and fill me in."

Prosenjit perched stiffly on the edge of a wire chair. He had half a mind to leave the subject untouched. But something goaded him on.

Jal sank back into his seat. "What a life," he sighed, stretching his arms in a wide arc and clasping his hands behind his head. With his eyes closed and his handsome face inclined toward the sun, he looked like a dauphin. Prosenjit felt a surge of resentment, and then heard himself blurt out, "I have seen a girl. She is very nice. She comes to the folk dance."

"The folk dance?" said Jal. "You mean that ring-around-the-rosy that the I House sponsors?"

"Yes, yes, at I House. I have been with her at I House."

"That's nice. So you too are becoming a Casanova. Tell me about her," he said, his eyes still shut.

"No. I hardly know her," said Prosenjit. "What I mean is, I think she has smiled at me."

"Let me guess. Is it Miss Chatterjee or Veena Das?"—two dowdy Indian girls who roomed at the I House.

"She is American," he said hotly. It angered him that Jal would naturally assume his love interest to be an Indian lady, and a not very attractive one at that.

Jal's eyes popped open. "American? You're joking? Oh, man. Prosenjit Poddar and an American chick. That's too much!"

"She is a nice girl," said Prosenjit.

"How did you ever get to know her?" asked Jal, now sitting on the edge of his seat.

"I told you, I have only seen her. Dancing. We have not talked."

"Well, you'd better get yourself up to speed. These American birds will hop all over you." He smirked. "I hope you're up to it. They're not like Indian ladies, you know—they expect a whole lot more."

"I'm prepared."

"I sure hope so." Jal chuckled.

Prosenjit perceived that, as usual, Jal was having fun at his expense. This patronizing attitude was well known to him, for they had shared a long history, stretching back through five years of college at the Indian Institute of Technology in Kharagpur. During their freshman year they were thrown together because they lived in Azad Hall, and were both studying naval architecture. Almost at once, Prosenjit became aware of Jal's importance because he was a "Guy." The Guys, as they called themselves, were an exclusive clique of suave, Westernized chaps who considered themselves "cosmopolitan," listened to Elvis Presley and Beatles records, and peppered their conversation with American slang. They were extremely particular about whom they admitted into their circle and treated everyone else with indifference. Jal was one of their ringleaders, while Prosenjit was just the opposite, so shy and backward he completely escaped everybody's notice. His friends were a couple of village boys who spoke in only the vernacular, went to the dining hall in white pajamas, and ate with their fingers. The Guys derisively referred to this rustic crowd as the "Paps."

It was not until the ragging—hazing—period that Jal became aware of Prosenjit's existence. Easygoing chaps like Jal took their punishment in stride, but for others, like Prosenjit, ragging was a demeaning ordeal. Not only was he a Pap, which made him a natural target, but he was Scheduled Caste, an Untouchable, and it was an unspoken rule that SCs would be singled out for abuse.

One Sunday in the mess hall, Prosenjit arrived early to avoid the rush of boys queueing up for the special lunch, Sunday being the only day that chicken was served. Prosenjit was standing toward the front of the line, balancing a tray, when one of the upperclassmen strode up to him, jabbed a finger in his face, and said in a loud voice, "Hey, Poddar, get to the back of the line."

Prosenjit felt the color drain out of his face. He stared straight ahead and did not move. Around him, the dining hall became silent.

"Hey, you. We don't eat with Scheduled Caste. I told you to get to the end of the line," the boy repeated.

Just at that moment, Jal walked into the dining room, trailed by his gang of Guys. When he heard the reference to caste, he stopped dead in his tracks.

Then the upperclassman knocked the tray out of Prosenjit's hands.

"What's this?" cried Jal, marching up to the upperclassman. "You have no business treating him like that!"

The upperclassman snapped back, "Listen to the freshman, acting fresh."

"Listen to the Guy," said Jal, turning to the others. "One year senior to me and he's still carping about caste. You'd have thought he'd have grown out of that barbaric behavior by now. You'd think he might have heard of Mahatma Gandhi." The offending boy was shocked into silence. Jal handed Prosenjit a new tray and strutted off.

Word spread quickly through Azad Hall that Jal had publicly bested an upperclassman. It was just like him to take up the cause of the underdog, particularly in a theatrical way. As a Parsi, he rejected the Hindu system of classifying human beings according to caste and took every opportunity to denounce it.

Later that afternoon, Jal walked into the common room of Azad Hall and spotted Prosenjit at the caroms table. Sauntering up, he casually remarked, "What the hell, Poddar, if you come into the dining hall in your pajamas, you're bound to kick up a massive ruckus." He waited with a smug grin on his face, expecting Prosenjit to fawn over him in gratitude.

"One doesn't really notice such things," said Prosenjit sullenly. He was sure that Jal had taken up his cause more for his own aggrandizement than a real sense of commitment. "He was attacking me, not my garments."

"Rubbish," said Jal, surprised by the hostility. Pointing to Prosenjit's crisp white *dhoti*, he said, "These foolish duds mark you as a village boy."

Prosenjit stiffened. "This much I can tell you. I am my own man. I hardly bother about what others have to say. And I don't need you to tell me how to dress."

Jal wondered what he had done to make the Pap flare up. He certainly was a touchy fellow, and an ungrateful one at that. Pulling himself up, he said, "It's just like you Bengalis to be stubborn. You insist on wearing pajamas, and after five years in this place, you'll still be squatting on a *charpoy*, eating rice and dal. There's more to life than that." And he walked off, leaving Prosenjit to his caroms.

They did not speak until months later, when the school year was nearly over. It was finals week, and, as usual, Prosenjit spent every waking hour in the library. Jal, too, was cramming, but his late-night forays were fraught with desperation. He had been so busy that term, running for secretary of the Gymkhana Club and acting in the drama society's production of *A Taste of Honey*, that he had neglected his course work. Late one evening, Prosenjit spotted him in the library, concentrated over a huge pile of notes and books. He walked over and asked, "How's it going?"

"I'm bambooed," moaned Jal. "Ship Hydro's way over my head. I'll be here all night, trying to pick up any damn thing I can," and he indicated the books and papers strewn about.

"It's not so difficult," said Prosenjit, looking down at his hands and smiling. "Please, as my friend, take this," and he pulled a notebook from a looseleaf binder of lecture notes. "It is a term's condensation of facts on Ship Hydrodynamics."

Jal gratefully clutched the notebook. Even in his frazzled state, he was vaguely aware that the insolent Pap considered himself intellectually superior, and was lording it over him. But at that point, nothing mattered. Leafing through the pages, he saw at once that the notes were invaluable. He was not surprised, because whenever the class sat for an exam, Prosenjit invariably came in first or second. The next day, Jal managed to make sense out of the Ship Hydrodynamics exam. When it turned out he had passed, he inwardly attributed his success to Prosenjit's help, and from that moment on, he made it a policy to borrow his new friend's notes during every finals week, even though it cost him something to do it. It always annoyed him that the village boy had a keener grasp of ship design than he did, and worse, that they both knew it.

Irked now because he had to come to Jal for advice, Prosenjit leaned forward, his elbows on the table, and looked straight into his companion's strong-featured face. As usual, the half-smile looked like a smirk. In a stiff voice he said, "You must instruct me how to behave. She comes regularly to the folk dance."

"Uh-oh. Competition." Jal chuckled. "You'd better get on it fast."

"How do you mean?"

"You know these hot-blooded Latins. When an American bird goes dancing at the I House, there's no telling what they'll do."

"Surely they would not approach her without an introduction?" exclaimed Prosenjit.

"Don't worry, we'll figure something out," said Jal, rising from his chair and stretching himself. "Let's go get some eats."

Prosenjit trailed after him into the food line. His forehead was creased in worry. He had read in *I'm Okay, You're Okay,* his main primer on American culture, that it was essential for an enterprising young man to be assertive. Indeed, "assertive" was the catch word that kept surfacing throughout the book. The question was, how should he put himself forward?

They walked through the turnstiles, past metal vats of steaming creamed corn and dull-colored roast beef. The smell of the beef made him feel queasy. As usual, none of the food looked appealing, and he thought longingly about the delicious *hilsa* fish curry his mother used to prepare. He hadn't enjoyed a single meal since he had arrived in Berkeley. He came to a refrigerated case and surveyed the items behind the glass counter with distaste. Ready-made sandwiches and limp salads rested on a bed of crushed ice. Sighing to himself, he said, "I hardly bother about food anymore," and reached for a fruit salad sunk in cottage cheese.

"Bloody hell," Jal erupted. "The grub at Kharagpur was horrible, and now you're carping about this." Prosenjit looked over and saw that his friend's tray was loaded with steaming dishes. A moment later, when they were paying the cashier, Jal pointed at Prosenjit's selection. "What's this? Sick man's food? I don't know what I'm going to do with you. You'd better be careful not to let your American chick—what's her name?"

"I do not know."

"What?" Jal jerked his head back in disbelief. "You do not know her name?

"I have not inquired."

"For God's sake, man, where are you posted?"

Prosenjit's cheeks were flaming hot.

Jal snorted. "In any case, you'd better not let the lady—whatever her name turns out to be—see you eating such sickly grub."

Prosenjit followed Jal out to the terrace. Years before, when he had begun to entertain the dream of going abroad, he had gone to Jal for advice. He was worried that he would find the life-style in the States too materialistic and fast-paced. Jal had pounced on the chance to convert him to the ways of the West. Prosenjit submitted himself to this conversion, but not without a degree of resentment for Jal's bald assumption that the American way was naturally superior to the Indian. Jal had assumed the role of guru figure almost with glee, and had enjoyed pontificating on everything from the lyrics of the Beatles' songs to table etiquette. He had even coached Prosenjit in English. Although Prosenjit had studied the language in high school, the kind of English he had been taught was the stilted Victorian variety, meant more for decoration than conversation. His instructor's poor command of the English language was made worse by the fact that only three teeth remained in his mouth. While Prosenjit had been taught grammar by rote, forced to memorize and recite Victorian poets like Browning and Tennyson, he still had trouble putting together a sentence. Jal drilled him in pronunciation, often deriding him for repeatedly substituting "*b*" for "*v*" as in "nabal architecture." He also taught the use of silverware. Prosenjit, like most Indians, ate with his hands, specifically the right—the left being reserved for "unclean" functions. Jal insisted that he practice with knife and fork, and jeered whenever he caught Prosenjit sneaking a morsel into his mouth with his fingers.

In spite of the instruction, Prosenjit was not at all prepared for what he was to find at Berkeley. His first year in the States turned out to be an ordeal. He found the food intolerable, the American idiom impossible to grasp, and the behavior between male and female vulgar and mystifying. When it came to understanding sexual mores, he was hopelessly out of touch. He had come over expecting that a '50s attitude, the kind depicted in Rock Hudson–Doris Day movies, would prevail. What he didn't realize was that American social conventions had been turned on their ear, and that Berkeley was in the midst of a sexual revolution. It wasn't possible for him to fathom that girls sometimes took the initiative and called boys on the telephone, allowed themselves to be seduced on the first date, and, in many cases, did the seducing themselves. For Prosenjit, it was far easier to ignore the differences than to adapt to them, and so he plunged ahead with blinders on.

Jal arrived a year after Prosenjit, in the fall of 1968. When he landed at San Francisco's International Airport, Prosenjit was there to greet him and help him adjust to the "strangeness" of the new world. But Jal astonished his friend by his quick grasp. Within a few days, he was making day trips into San Francisco, hopping cable cars, strolling along Fisherman's Wharf, and scarfing up spaghetti in Ghirardelli Square. At the I House, Prosenjit watched in awe as his friend moved through the common room, flirting with the ladies and hamming it up for the amusement of all. Only three weeks after his arrival, Jal was clearly the kingpin of the establishment. He dated American girls, belonged to the campus drama society, and was dominant in I House politics. Prosenjit couldn't help but be impressed.

When they found a place out on the patio, Jal settled back in his chair and propped his legs up on the table. Balancing his plate on his lap, he began to fork up a juicy cheese enchilada.

Prosenjit played with his food, pushing cubes of canned fruit around in the bowl. He coughed and cleared his throat. "What I am here to ask," he said in a shaky voice, "is, will you do me the honor of fixing up a formal introduction?"

"With the American girl?"

"Yes."

"But I've never even seen the lady!"

"That is no matter," stammered Prosenjit. "Someone has to act as a go-between and pass her a note for me. Or else how can I invite her for a date?"

"Where do you think you are? Back in Balurghat?" sniggered Jal. "This is the States. You've got to play it cool, or you're finished."

"I don't understand."

"In the States you don't need an intermediary to pass notes, go to her house, chat up the parents, and all that rubbish. You just call the lady straight away."

"With no formal introduction?" asked Prosenjit, shocked.

"Man, you're living in the Dark Ages. Just give her a jingle."

"I don't know how," he confessed miserably.

"Well, you'd jolly well better learn," said Jal, taking no small satisfaction from the desperation on Prosenjit's face. "And best of all, there's no need for those cumbersome Calcutta group dates, when you're saddled with six of her girlfriends all acting as chaperons. You'll be all on your own."

Prosenjit just stared off into space, his fingers wrapped tightly around his fork. Jal continued, "Now listen. The next folk dance, just walk up and ask her for her telephone number." When he saw how tense Prosenjit had become, he grew serious. "Hey, man, you're here now. Like it or not, you've got to embrace the American way."

"But what if she thinks I have insulted her?" asked Prosenjit.

"No way. Just get her telephone number so you can invite her to the cinema."

"The cinema?" Prosenjit was incredulous.

"Yes, yes, a film. Girls love films. They love to sit in dark theaters and eat popcorn and chocolate bonbons. It'll be smooth sailing once you've dialed the number."

Prosenjit swallowed hard. "I'll . . . do my best."

"Right on," said Jal, jumping to his feet. "Get to it straight away."

THE music came to an end, but the record player still sent waves of static cutting through the room. Finally, someone lifted the needle off the record and the noise ceased. Tanya breathed a sigh of relief and, dropping the hands she held on either side, stepped back from the circle of dancers. The last dance had been so fast-paced, carrying her around and around, that she was breathless. She made her way toward the corner of the auditorium where she had left her purse on a folding chair. She was drenched in perspiration, and the leafy material of her blouse was plastered against her skin. Even her hair was soaked, and clung to her neck in damp tendrils. She fished a brush out of her purse and began to pull it through her hair in long, hard strokes. She let her neck go slightly limp and tilted her head backward as she brushed. It felt so soothing that she kept up the even, rhythmic strokes for a few moments. Suddenly she was conscious that someone was behind her, watching her. The feeling was so strong that she whirled around. A boy with walnut-colored skin was standing a few feet away, his eyes fixed on her. She stared back at him. He looked scared out of his wits. He smiled nervously. "Begging your pardon, miss, but do you remember me?"

"No . . . ?" she said, not able to place him.

"That night at the dance two weeks ago—when you stepped on my foot?"

The memory flickered in her head. "Oh, that. It was nothing."

"You are American?" When she nodded yes, he asked, "By what name are you called?"

"Tanya."

"That is a very pretty name," he said, a smile etched on his face like a plaster cast.

"Who are you?"

He pronounced his name, but to Tanya it was a jumble of sounds. "Say it again?"

"Prosenjit Poddar," he repeated, more slowly.

"Pro-shen-jeet," she mimicked. "That's a hard one." She looked around, glad that neither Cindy nor anyone she knew was watching her. To be polite, she asked, "Where are you from?"

"My home is India."

"Oh, the Taj Mahal and the *Kama Sutra*."

"I beg your pardon?" he asked, puzzled.

"Those are the two things I know about India. Oh yeah, and Hare Krishna freaks."

"Only they are not so numerous where I come from," he said, frowning slightly.

"Well, they're all over the place here. I hope you're not one," she said, glancing around for a way to escape.

"No." He looked down at his shoes and cracked his finger joints. When he didn't say anything else, she felt a little sorry for him and found herself asking, "How long have you been here?"

"I landed up last year, but my English is not very good."

"No, it's fine. You're doing good." She noticed that he wasn't bad-looking in spite of his slightly dark complexion. He had a sweet face and tender, deerlike eyes.

The music started up. It was a Greek *sirto*, her favorite dance. She gave a little bounce and tossed her purse on the chair. "Good talking to you," she said and started to walk away, thinking that he would vanish as soundlessly as he had materialized. She got to the edge of the circle, looking for an opening to grab someone's hand. To her surprise, there was the Indian, standing by her side, watching with imploring eyes. Her conscience tugged and she said, "Want to dance?"

"I'm not too keen on dancing," he stammered.

"Oh, come on. You can do it," and she grabbed his hand and pulled him into the ring. Not only did he not know the steps, but he was quite leaden on his feet and shuffled back and forth, several beats behind the others. She was relieved when the dance was over.

He stood expectantly at her side like a dog waiting for a command. She wished she could tell him to go away, but it seemed too rude. She began to fidget with her hair, pulling a strand from behind her ear and twisting it around her finger. Finally she said, "What kind of dancing do you do in India?"

"In India, we do not dance." When he spoke he kept his eyes on the floor.

"Oh, I don't believe it. What about all those dancing girls I've seen with bells on their ankles and their stomachs showing?"

"*Nautch* girls," he said disapprovingly. "But respectable boys and girls are not permitted to dance."

"That's a bummer."

She was about to walk away when he lifted his eyes and said, "You are different from other American girls."

"Really? Why do you say that?"

"Generally speaking, American ladies seem very aggressive."

"Well, I might be too."

"I do not think so. I have been watching you and I think you are different."

She blushed. She was not used to having a man pay her such a heartfelt compliment. It was flattering, too, the way that he took what she said so seriously. She felt a rush of warmth toward him. The poor guy; it was easy to imagine how other girls had dumped all over him. His obvious lack of confidence made her feel more self-assured, and she teased, "Don't jump to conclusions. You don't even know me."

He twisted his hands and looked at her beseechingly. Then he asked in a strained voice, "There are many good films in America?"

"For sure."

"You like the cinema?"

"Yeah, when a good movie's playing. I get really bummed when I waste my money on a bad one. Have you seen *The Graduate*?"

"*The Graduate*?" He creased his forehead.

"Yeah, it's playing down on Shattuck."

"Have you seen it?" he asked hopefully.

"Yeah, twice."

His face fell and he managed to stammer, "There is much to be said for the American cinema."

She waited for him to say more, but he just stood there. "Well," she said, making a show of looking at her watch. "I've got to go. It was really nice talking to you. What did you say your name was?"

"Prosenjit Poddar."

"Well, take it easy, Pro-shen-jeet. Maybe I'll see you again."

As she turned and walked away he blurted out, "Wait. Wait for a moment," and he hurried after her. He wanted desperately to ask for her phone number, but dared not risk the question. "You will be my friend?"

"Of course I'll be your friend," and she held out her hand to shake on it. He seized it eagerly and wrung it up and down. His palm was clammy. "See you around," she called, and skipped out the door, relieved to escape into the fresh air.

THE following week, Tanya was sitting on a red swivel stool in the Top Dog on Durant Avenue, waiting for Cindy to show up. The counter was small, only four seats wide, and from where she sat she could watch the hot dogs sizzling on the grill. A student cook was absently nosing the dogs over with long silver tongs. He wore his ponytail tucked under his chef's cap. A TV set was blasting out a football game, but Tanya wasn't watching. She was concentrating on finding split ends. Holding a clump of hair in one hand, she searched the strands, and whenever she found a frayed one she snapped off the end with a rapid flick of her fingers. She gave a start when Cindy's voice erupted from behind her.

"God, have you been waiting long? I'm sorry I'm so late. You should have ordered."

"No, it's okay." Tanya swiveled around to face her. Cindy was red-faced and panting. She had obviously been running, and she clutched her huge canvas purse to her chest, trying to catch her breath.

"What a hassle," Cindy heaved. "I couldn't get a ride for the longest time, and then some flake finally picked me up." She didn't own a car and was accustomed to hitchhiking every place she went. When she traveled long distances, like into the city, she'd draw up a sign in heavy block letters that read "San Francisco or Bust" and hang it around her neck. "So what's new?" she asked, sliding onto one of the stools.

"Nada."

"No A.C.T?" A.C.T. was their code word for "action," which translated loosely into anything from making eye contact to going to bed with a cute guy. Cindy knew perfectly well that there had been no A.C.T., because they checked in with each other on the phone at least twice a day.

"Are you kidding?" Tanya made a wry face. "Null and void."

"Well, guess what," said Cindy, lowering her voice in a conspiratorial way. "I think I'm in love."

"What happened?"

"I met a guy."

"Are you serious?" An arrow of envy went through her. If Cindy got herself a boyfriend, what would happen to her? Who would she hang out with on the weekends? "That's great," she said, trying to hide her dismay.

"You won't believe it, but he sells candles out in front of Sather Gate. His name's David. Maybe you've even seen him?" She looked at Tanya questioningly. "He's got great arms. Real muscular and big. And he pushes around this wagonful of candles. They're homemade."

Tanya shook her head, "No, I've never noticed him before."

"Unbelievable bod. Next time you're there, check him out."

"So what happened?" asked Tanya, half dreading the story she was about to hear.

"It was my lucky day. I was walking through Sather Gate and I stopped to buy a cookie. You know, those raisin-and-oatmeal ones that are real chewy? Well, all of a sudden I notice this cute guy standing near the juice wagon. I really flashed on him. He didn't see me, so I go over to him and discover that he's selling candles off a rack. I pretend to be interested in the candles, you know, tell him that they're pretty colors, all orange and red like harvest."

"That was smart."

"Yeah, so we keep talking and he asks me if I want to come by and see his candle factory."

"Candle factory? That's a good one."

"Well, he's got to make them somewhere, doesn't he? He said it's in the loft of some old garage on Shattuck. A real fire hazard."

"Did you make a date?"

"No. I mean, Jesus, I just met him. Give the guy a break. My plan is to go back late one afternoon when he's packing up to leave."

"That would be good."

"Yeah. What do you think I should wear? I can't decide if my jeans and my black turtleneck or my new blouse would be better. You know, the batik one with blue and purple in it? I hope he doesn't think I'm fat."

"You're not fat," said Tanya, wondering how Cindy always managed to buy her jeans too small.

"Well, I'm going on a diet tomorrow. I could lose five pounds, easy, by next week."

"He'll like you the way you are."

"I could die for him," squealed Cindy.

Tanya looked at her face, glowing with happiness. "Why doesn't something like this ever happen to me?" she moaned, unable to control herself.

"Don't worry, it will," intoned Cindy, full of excitement. "Let's order, I'm starved," and she called out, "A kielbasa and a vanilla Coke, please." Tanya ordered a New York, and they sat munching on their hot dogs in silence. She wondered what it would be like to share intimacies with a boyfriend, to have a special name of endearment for him, and to call him by it when they were alone. Now Cindy was about to have a fabulous love affair and experience it all.

"The big question is," said Cindy, wiping her hands on a paper napkin, "what do I do about my diaphragm? I never know if I should take it with me or not."

"I don't know," said Tanya. "It's really embarrassing to carry it around in your purse when you're not sure you're going to need it." She thought about her own diaphragm, rolled up inside a nightgown and hidden at the bottom of her dresser drawer. The only time she had used it was the day she had brought it home, when she practiced inserting it with the gel.

"And how do you deal with when to put it in? Before or during?" said Cindy. "I mean, if you're not sure you're going to fuck, it's kind of presumptuous to already have it in."

"It doesn't seem like a good idea to look like you're expecting it," agreed Tanya. "You should make them think you're hard to get. Like they're seducing *you*."

"I know. It's a problem," said Cindy, mulling it over in her mind. "So how do I handle it? After we start fooling around, do I say 'Excuse me' and go running off to the bathroom with all my stuff?"

"I think that's how I'd handle it," said Tanya, wondering if Cindy would really get the opportunity to use it. She hated herself for hoping that she wouldn't.

When they had finished their dogs, Cindy wanted to go to Swensen's for an ice-cream cone. As they were walking in, she confessed to Tanya that earlier that day she had already stopped for a cone. "I hope the same girls aren't here," she whispered, and breathed a sigh of relief when she saw fresh faces working behind the counter. "Thank God. The late shift," she said as she marched up to the counter and ordered a double mocha chip. With cones in hand, they walked out to the street and turned down Telegraph.

"So what's your next move?" asked Tanya, as they walked along.

"Oh, I don't know. Sometime toward the end of next week, I'll go by Sather Gate. When I can fit into my jeans again," said Cindy, running her tongue over the ice cream. "I'm hoping we end up together over the weekend."

"Mmm . . . that'll be great," said Tanya, forcing herself to sound enthusiastic.

"Don't be so depressed." Cindy laughed. "If I don't score with the Candleman, I'll go with you to the folk dance."

"Hey, don't do me any favors," said Tanya, a sinking feeling in her stomach as she thought about what life would be without Cindy.

TANYA was barely conscious of the bus ride home, her mind was so full of Cindy's new romance. As she rushed up the front walk, she noticed her father's blue Pontiac in the driveway and it crossed her mind that it was odd that he was home so early. She let herself into the house. All was quiet, and she assumed that he was outside working in the garage. She went straight for the kitchen, grabbed a handful of chocolate-chip cookies, and headed for her bedroom.

When she opened the door, she was shocked to see her father crouched on the floor. He appeared to be sifting through the contents of her wastepaper basket. By his side lay some wadded-up balls of paper. Other crumpled papers had been opened and flattened out, and the sudden gust from the door sent them fluttering around the room. He looked up, a startled expression on his face. He was balanced on the balls of his feet, and he teetered. When he steadied himself, he gave Tanya a sheepish grin. A long moment passed between them.

"I'm fixing the plug," he mumbled and pointed at the socket in the wall.

"Oh," said Tanya. She looked at him squatting on her rug, a bottle of beer at his side. She knew he had been rummaging through her trash looking for proof that she was involved with a boy. She wanted to tell him to get the hell out, but instead she asked, "What's wrong with the plug?" enunciating each word carefully.

"Whatever it was, I fixed it," he said, and he started to gather up the loose papers and stuff them into the basket. He kept his face averted, and she watched his big hands crunching up the papers.

"Just leave it, Dad."

He straightened up to his full height. He was so tall and muscular that he filled the room. The top of her head barely reached his shoulders. He thrust a crinkled leaflet under her nose. "What's this?" he demanded.

She took it from him. It was an advertisement for the Procul Harum concert at Winterland. "Nothing," she said. "A concert I never went to," and she balled the paper up in her hand. Her heart was pounding.

"Okay," he said. "You be sure to ask my permission." He made no move to go.

"Is there something else?"

"I also found this," and he reached into his pocket and drew out a crumpled sheet of notepaper. "Is Kevin a girl's name or a boy's?"

Tanya felt her cheeks grow hot. "He's a boy in my biology class."

"What are you doing with his telephone number?"

"He's helping me study for a test."

His eyes narrowed. "All right, but I'm watching you," and he turned his back on her and walked out the door, closing it firmly behind him.

A soundless scream rose up in her. How dare he poke around in her private things? She picked up her favorite china cup, from her grandmother's tea set, and hurled it down on the floor. The shag rug cushioned the blow, and it rolled, unbroken, under the dresser. She stomped around in a silent rage, and then she noticed his bottle of beer, still standing in the corner. She picked it up, ran to the bathroom, poured it down the sink, and flung the bottle out the window. She stood for a moment looking at her face in the mirror. It looked pulled out of shape and tortured. Then she yanked open the shower door and turned the water on full blast. As she tore her clothes off, she imagined herself jumping like a cat on her father's face and clawing at his eyes. She stepped under the jet of warm water and let it run, like cleansing rain, over her.

She sat down on the tiles at the bottom of the shower so she could shave her legs. She lathered with soap, then jerked the razor up her leg, from ankle to knee, cutting a pattern of pink flesh against the white. She thought about her father's guilty look when she had walked into the room. He was searching for any flimsy shred of evidence he could find—like a boy's name scrawled across a piece of paper—to prove that she was sleeping around. He was forever watching her with his beady eyes, hounding her with accusations. She was certain that he listened in on her phone calls, too, but when she accused him of spying on her, he always denied it. Now she had caught him red-handed, but there seemed to be nothing she could do about it.

Strange as it seemed, Tanya was only vaguely aware that much of her father's unacceptable behavior stemmed from the fact that he was an alcoholic. Even though his drinking was a source of continual conflict between her parents, neither one was willing to acknowledge his addiction. As in so many alcoholic families, they had built an elaborate system of denial. Her father pretended that he didn't have a problem, lied about the amount of liquor he consumed, and blamed others for his failures. Her mother put up with his behavior in martyred silence, swallowing his insults, assuming many of the responsibilities that he shirked, and denying that there was anything wrong with their marriage. No one in the family so much as breathed the word "alcoholic" to him or even among themselves.

Whenever Tanya thought about her father, she was full of conflicting emotions. There were times, like the nights when she'd see him passed out on the living-room sofa, when she'd feel only contempt. He was pitiful, especially when she had to help drag him into his bed. But there were other times when he had a spark of life that was infectious. After a few drinks, his eyes would light up and he'd pace the living-room floor, plotting and scheming about the day, sometime off in the future, when he would open up an emergency road service that would make more money than the AAA Automobile Club. Even though Tanya knew better, she would get caught up in his grandiose fantasies and urge him on, believing that if he just sobered up, he could do anything he set his mind to.

When he expressed his love for her it was in a hot gush that flowed all over her. He liked to tell her that they were soulmates. She felt that it was he, not her mother, who understood her pain, and she always turned to him when she got her feelings hurt. She remembered the time, two years earlier, when the family had piled into the car and driven eighty miles north to Healdsburg on the Russian River, where they rented a one-room cottage on the beach. Healdsburg was one of the tiny resort towns, along with Rio Nido and Guerneville, that was popular among working-class Russian and Italian families from the San Francisco area. There were lots of other teenagers there, rowdy and fun-loving, but Tanya felt like an outsider. During the day, she kept to herself, yearning to be accepted by the group, but too timid to take any initiative. When night fell, she found herself left behind with the adults, while the other teenagers jumped into station wagons and took off to go dancing in Rio Nido. There was nothing for her to do but crawl into her cot on the porch, safe under the gauze of a mosquito net, and try to fall asleep. She lay there, listening to the hum of insects and the sound of her father's voice, louder than all the rest, telling stories and playing *pei do dna*, a Russian game in which a shot of vodka makes its way around the table until the bottle is empty. More often than not, in the middle of the night, she would be awakened by angry shouts, and minutes later she'd hear her father come in, swearing under his breath and groping his way toward his cot. She'd call out, "Dad? What's wrong, Dad?" and when he didn't answer, she knew that his feelings had been hurt. She desperately wanted to comfort him. Somehow it seemed to her that they were fused together. It was her responsibility to soothe his pain.

But while she felt protective toward him, she also feared him. His mood swings were unpredictable and his temper was apt to rage out of control over the most innocent remark. Tanya had learned to be on her toes, careful not to rock the boat. It drove her crazy that he had to be on center stage and that he pawed at her for attention if he wasn't. There had been countless times when she'd seen him sitting off to the side pouting, his face growing dark with anger. Then he'd explode, yelling that she was the reason that he drank. He could be a physically abusive man, and when carried away by rage he forgot his own strength. Their most violent arguments centered around his suspicion that she was "sleeping around." He'd goad her with rude remarks and stinging criticism, and if she dared talk back, he'd smack her hard across the face.

Whenever he had cause to believe she might be spending her time with a boy, he became obsessed with finding out who it was. What was especially embarrassing was the lengths he would go to to expose her.

The most humiliating incident had occurred a few months earlier, in her last semester of high school. There had been a party given by the drama club after the last performance of the school play, *The Madwoman of Chaillot*, and Tanya had stayed late to help clean up. She was in the cloakroom washing out the coffee percolator when one of the girls came running in, flushed and excited. "There's a guy outside creeping around in the bushes," she announced. "He's shining a flashlight through the windows." Tanya went into the auditorium. She saw a cluster of girls murmuring among themselves. Her heart was pounding as she walked up to them and asked, "What's happening?" It was explained how a man had been caught peering through one of the windows, and that Mrs. Helgesson, the drama coach, had gone outside to investigate.

When Mrs. Helgesson returned, she spotted Tanya, and motioned her over with a little wave of her hand. "I thought I should tell you this in private. It's your father outside. The girls say he's been prowling through the shrubbery, peering through the windows. I was going to call the police, but seeing who it is . . . ?" This last was phrased as a question.

"No. Please don't." Tanya felt the color rise to her face.

"What do you want me to do, dear?"

"I'd better go out there." She ran through the exit, into the night. As she stumbled through the bushes, she heard her father's rasping breath, and she yelled into the darkness, "Goddam you! How can you do this to me?" Hearing her voice, he heaved himself into her path and grabbed her arm. "Why can't you leave me alone?" she sobbed.

"You're my little girl," he said. And he dragged her off to his car.

The incident had been followed by days of remorse, maudlin apologies, and promises of reform. He was so chastened that he actually quit drinking for a while. But this period of abstinence was filled by unbearable tension while he tried to "white-knuckle" it, skulking around in frozen silence and blaming his wife and children for his unhappiness. The worst part was that the others were powerless to make things better. All they could do was wait in terror for the sound of a beer can opening or the clink of ice in the glass. It was almost a relief when the drinking began again.

Over and over again he had promised her that he would try to control himself, but thus far he had not succeeded. It seemed to Tanya that the older she got, the more possessive he became. Her mother was bothered by it too, and finally confronted him, saying, "Why do you want to put Tanya in a closet and keep her for yourself? Why do you want her beautiful? For whom? You tell her, go buy nice clothes, have nice hair. For whom?" His only response was to grunt and walk away.

The drinking, the spying, the accusations, and the violence were the pattern of Tanya's life. The fact that her father abused her didn't stop her from loving him. But the cat-and-mouse game they played was her only experience of what love and intimacy were all about, and even though these encounters were painful, Tanya had become conditioned to them. She had learned how to cope with the discomfort, even how to enjoy the excitement. Because excitement there was, a thrilling sense of being off balance and always in danger. She'd never admit it to herself, but the danger was something she craved. She hadn't chosen this condition, she had been born into it, and it had become as much a part of her nature as the skin she was in.

Tanya turned off the water and climbed out of the shower, snapping the glass door shut with a bang. As she slipped into her terry-cloth robe she told herself that somewhere out there there was somebody who would love her. There was an enormous vacancy at the center of her life that only the right man could fill. She was bound to meet him, if she kept on searching.

ON Friday night, Tanya made her way through the I House lobby. A few sagging Christmas decorations were draped along the walls, reminding her that the holidays were approaching. When she neared the auditorium she could hear the instructor's voice, calling the dancers onto the floor. She stood at the doorway, scanning the desultory crowd that had joined hands and was waiting for the music to begin. She hesitated for a moment, and then ducked out of the room.

She wandered into the cafeteria. The smell of cooking grease was so strong it had soaked into the rough plaster walls. Clusters of students were hunched around tables, talking in foreign languages. She headed through the turnstile. Her nose was level to the row of desserts displayed on a stainless-steel shelf. The sodden hunks of pie and cake looked as if they'd been sitting there for days. She reached for a slice of pumpkin pie. As she was paying, she scanned the room for a table. There was one by the windows that would let her look out over Fraternity Row and have a view of the room at the same time.

What a drag that Cindy wasn't with her. She stabbed at her pie with the fork, put a bite in her mouth without tasting it. Cindy had gone that afternoon to intercept the Candleman in front of Sather Gate. There had been a flurry of last-minute discussions about what she should wear to snare him. She had telephoned moments before she set forth for a zap of encouragement. Of course, she had promised to call the second she got back with a full report. But every time the phone had rung, it had been for Alex. That could only mean one thing; Cindy had scored. Tanya had never really expected the mission to succeed, but obviously it had. Somehow the girl had managed to end up with him on a *Friday* night.

She looked down at her watch and realized that Cindy and the Candleman had been together for at least four hours. She was surprised to feel the tears welling up in her eyes. She poked at the pie filling. When a tear ran down her cheek, she made no attempt to stop it. She didn't care if anyone noticed her crying; in fact, she almost hoped that someone would. She sat that way for about fifteen minutes, blinking out the tears, smushing up the pie filling, but no one came over to the table. Finally, she got up from her seat and drifted out the door.

She wandered aimlessly through the lobby. She could hear music coming from the auditorium, but she didn't have the heart to go in. As she was leaning on a vending machine, reading the candy-bar labels through the glass, an idea suddenly came to her and she turned and strode up to the reception desk. A blond boy with a German accent was working the switchboard, answering calls. He had an operator set clamped over his ears, and every time a call came through, a red light flashed and he plugged a long spear of wire into the waiting hole. She leaned against the counter, and when he looked up she said, "Hi."

He smiled back at her.

"Ah . . . do you know an Indian guy who lives here named Prosenjit something-or-other?"

"Yes . . . Prosenjit Poddar."

"Can you tell me what room he's in?"

"Sure," he said, thumbing through a worn directory. "He's in six-oh-seven."

She thanked him and rode the elevator up to the sixth floor. The door opened on a narrow corridor floored with brown linoleum. She walked down the hall until she found his door. She could hear hammering noises coming from inside. She hesitated, thinking to herself that she was about to give this guy the thrill of his life. Then she rapped on the door. A voice called out, "Just walk in." She tried the handle, but it was locked. She jiggled it back and forth. He yelled, "Bloody hell! Jal, my hands are tied up. Just one sec!" She could hear the sound of running water, then shuffling feet. A moment later the door swung open.

He was absolutely stunned to see her standing there.

"How're you doing, Pro-shen-jeet?" she said, as though there were nothing unusual about dropping in on him. Her body was pressed close to his in the doorway.

"Ooh. . . . I thought you were . . ."

"Someone else?" she teased, and she stepped past him into the room with a flourish of her skirt. "Who were you expecting?"

"My chum, Jal," he stammered.

"Aren't you going to invite me to sit down?" she asked, sniffing the air. The pungent odor of curry and boiled cauliflower hung in the room, and she gave a little cough.

"Please, please be comfortable here," he said, backing away from her. He seemed so suffused with astonishment it was actually painful.

"I mean, we're friends, aren't we? I thought you wouldn't mind." The fact that he was so offbalance bolstered her own confidence.

He continued to gape at her—a vision of loveliness that had floated in from another sphere. The whole thing seemed like a dream. He had just been thinking about her. In fact, he had been preoccupied with her all week long, and had been counting down the hours until the dance. In order to make the time pass, he had resorted to an old hobby and was building a model ship. The assembly lay on his desk, a miniature tanker built to scale. It had kept his hands occupied, leaving his mind free to dwell on her. All week long, while he cut and glued, he had pictured her green eyes and soft dark hair. He had imagined sitting next to her in a darkened theater, inhaling her sweet scent. He had played out conversations in which they exchanged words of endearment, and had repeated her name so many times that "Tanya" began to sound like his mantra. Just moments before he had checked his watch for the hundredth time and decided that Jal or no Jal, it was time to go down to the dance. Trembling in anticipation, he had prolonged the moment by adding a few finishing touches to the ship. Now to have her standing in front of him left him utterly incapacitated. He had never entertained any girl alone, and the intimacy of having this one in his room was overwhelming. His first thought was that he should immediately pop the question of going to the cinema, but when he cleared his throat, not a single word would come out.

His eyes darted around the room, disturbed that his work table was covered with litter and several tools were strewn about on the floor. He noticed too that a pair of trousers was slung over a chair. "I am honored that you pay me this visit," he blurted out, "only it is so much chaotic!"

"What're you up to?" asked Tanya. "I heard hammering." She tossed her purse on the floor and settled herself on his bed, kicking off her shoes and curling her stocking feet up under her.

"I'm building a ship model," he said, as he snatched up tools and hooked them on the pegboard over his desk.

She surveyed the room, which was no bigger than a cell, with one window that looked out over Piedmont Avenue, and an old-fashioned washbasin. It was obvious he was a fanatic for organization. Tools gleamed on tiny hooks, and electronic parts were neatly arranged in compartments. Technical books with off-putting titles like *Random Vibrations of Structural Systems* lined the shelves. There were no personal items except for a jar of hair oil and a small plaster statue of an elephant, painted blue and pink, that sat atop his dresser.

"Generally my room is not like this," he said as he swept the scraps on his work table into a trash basket.

"You call this messy? You've got to be kidding." She laughed. Pointing at the model, she said, "What do you do with that cute little boat, sail it in your bathtub?"

"No, no." He frowned, not realizing that she was joking. "It is for the sea-keeping experiment at the towing tank. Here, let me show you." He lifted the model off his desk and carried it to her, proud to display his workmanship. It was exquisite in every detail, made truly to scale, with even such minute details as the rivets on the boiler plates.

"Wow, how fantastic!" she gasped, genuinely impressed. "I've never seen anything so perfect." She reached out and ran her finger over the hull.

"It's an oil tanker," he said, as he put the ship into her outstretched hands. While she examined it, he rocked back and forth on his heels. "The real one's the sister ship of the *Vivekenanda*. She's over two hundred and twenty meters long and has a deadweight of eighty-eight thousand tons," and he plunged on to explain the hydrodynamic forces that determined the ship's design.

She listened with a blank expression on her face. All of his talk about torque and thrust deduction ran together into gibberish. She wanted to change the subject but didn't want to hurt his feelings. Finally, when he paused, she said, "Boy, designing ships sure sounds exciting," and she gave him a weak smile.

"No," he said. "The work is not glamorous. Many who come into the profession receive quite a shock. In my case, I work very hard. There are some who are natural naval architects, but I am not one." He was exhilarated to be speaking so frankly to her and was amazed at how his own words were pouring out.

Suddenly he heard a thump outside in the hall and stopped in midsentence. A wave of fear swept over him. It must be Jal. "Excuse me, just one sec," he said, and he tiptoed to the door and put his ear against it. All was quiet. Maybe a false alarm.

"What is it?" she asked.

"A mistake, only," he mumbled, bolting the door.

"You seem so jittery all of a sudden."

"No, it is nothing," he said. It would be a disaster if Jal came barging in now, oozing charm and good looks. There was no telling how Tanya would react. He racked his brain how to get her out before he showed up.

"So what do you do for fun?" she was asking.

"There are so many things," he said, waving his arms around. "I like to dream up machines."

"You mean you made all of these things?" she said, hoisting herself up on an elbow to get a better look. She pointed to one. "Like that?"

"That? Yes, that is a portable burglar alarm one attaches to a suitcase."

"You're really clever," she said, jumping up to examine some of the gadgets on his shelf. She especially liked the fly gun that squashed an insect when you pressed the trigger. "Here, let me try it out," she said playfully, and she aimed at him. When she fired, the plastic swatter sprang out and bounced off his chest, and she laughed. "You should try to market these. I bet you could make a fortune."

He would have been thrilled by such praise, were he not listening for those footsteps in the hall.

"No, really," she was saying. "You should get these patented before someone steals your ideas." She examined the burglar alarm. "Hey, have you ever caught anyone going through your suitcase?"

"What?" he asked distractedly. "You would like a coffee?" he said, pleased with himself for thinking of it. "They prepare super coffee in the lounge."

"No, I was already downstairs, and it's boring," she said, settling back down on the bed. "Anyway, I like it here." She spotted the canister of Darjeeling he had brought from home and said, "I wouldn't mind some tea."

Reluctantly, he forced himself to plug in his electric kettle and set out some cups. When he turned around he was embarrassed to see she was stretched out lengthwise on his bed, cupping her chin in her hand and supporting herself on one elbow. He was too respectful to look closely, but he feared that the pink of her thigh was showing from under her skirt.

"Who's that cute guy?" she asked, pointing at the plaster elephant that sat on his dresser.

"Ganesha," said Prosenjit. "The son of Shiva and Parvati"

"Who are they?"

Just then a knock sounded at the door—an insistent rap that played out a rhythm on the wood. "Hey, Poddar, open up, you lazy Bong," came Jal's voice. "Bong" was a derisive way of referring to Bengalis, who had a reputation for being indolent troublemakers. Even though Prosenjit had repeatedly requested that Jal not refer to him as a Bong, he persisted. Once they had nearly come to blows over it.

"Bloody hell," Prosenjit muttered, walking to the door.

"Who is that?" asked Tanya, rising up.

"It is nobody," said Prosenjit, sliding open the bolt and bracing himself. He heard her ask, "What does Bong mean?" but he was too distraught to answer.

"Hey, man, are you asleep?" came Jal's voice again. Then a different male voice added, "He's probably attending to matters of the left hand," and there was a howl of laughter.

Prosenjit opened the door a crack and peeked out.

Jal's big-featured face was square in front of his, buoyant and self-confident. "I've got the DasGupta brothers along," he said. "And we're going for some side eats."

Prosenjit slid his body through the crack and stepped into the hall, quickly closing the door behind him. He worried that Tanya would find him rude, but it couldn't be helped. He stood with his back against the door, hand clenched over the knob. The two DasGupta boys lounged against the opposite wall and met his stiff nod with lazy grins. As usual, they were dressed in their tennis whites, and their long legs dangled out into the hall, impeding traffic. Both played varsity tennis and were known as one of the best doubles teams in the Pac-8. Prosenjit had disliked them ever since they had snubbed him at the Gymkhana Club in Kharagpur.

"Well?" said Jal.

"Well what?" asked Prosenjit.

"Where is it? You work up a massive sweat over a toy ship, insisting I come see it, and now that I'm here I want to have a look at the damn thing."

"Yes," hedged Prosenjit. "It is not ready. There must be some finishing touches first. But generally speaking, I am pleased."

"What the hell, let's see it! You're not building the *Queen Mary*," said Jal.

"Now is not good," said Prosenjit, turning red.

"We haven't got all night, man," said Jal, and he waved his hand at the DasGuptas. "And these chaps have come clear across campus for a look-see."

"Tomorrow it will be done," said Prosenjit miserably.

"Rubbish. Tomorrow is not good enough." Turning to the DasGuptas, he said, "This calls for brute force," and laughing, he pushed Prosenjit aside and stepped through the door.

Prosenjit heard, from within the room, his friend's smooth-tongued "Why, hello!" and the trill of Tanya's laughter. Then Jal, in his theatrical voice, "May I introduce myself?" Prosenjit hurried into the room in time to see Jal step forward and, with exaggerated courtesy, take Tanya's hand as though it were a delicate flower.

Jal turned on him with a big grin. "No wonder you've been ignoring your work." He laughed. "But we're understanding chaps, aren't we?" He waved in the DasGuptas, who slouched in the doorway. Grabbing a chair from Prosenjit's desk, he said, "May I?" and straddled it as though he were mounting a polo pony. "Where is the lady from?" he asked, but before Prosenjit could answer, he whirled back to Tanya. "Surely you do not live here, in the I House?"

"Oh, no!" She giggled.

"I didn't think so. I would have noticed you before. What is your name, please?"

"Tanya Tarasoff."

He lowered his voice to a confidential tone. "Well, Miss Tarasoff, the ladies here are not nearly so lovely."

Blushing, she said to Prosenjit, "Does he talk like this to everyone?" Her voice rose in a gay lilt.

Prosenjit stood stiffly at the door, too flabbergasted to answer. The truth was that Jal did go out of his way to charm just about everyone. Back in India he was known as an "oil slicker" because of his ingratiating manner.

"One finds that beauty isn't everything," continued Jal. "The ladies who board here have other, more important attributes."

"You should know," said one of the DasGuptas.

"What does that mean?" asked Tanya, puzzled.

Jal shrugged, as though he didn't have the faintest idea, and the DasGuptas convulsed in laughter.

Tanya looked from one to the other and said, "I don't get it. Tell me."

Prosenjit felt the bile rising in his throat. This was precisely what he had feared most. He was so knotted up inside he couldn't utter a sound.

"Oh, they are referring to a small incident," said Jal, with feigned modesty. "One concerned female has a soft spot in her heart for me, and worries because I am so far away from home. I have assured her that I am quite able to stand on my own two legs, but she insists on attending to my laundry."

"You're kidding," said Tanya. "You mean she actually washes your clothes?"

Jal smiled. "And my towels and bedding too."

"She must really like you!" exclaimed Tanya.

"No, no, it's not that way at all," Jal went on. "You see, when you live in a community such as ours, we become like an extended family. I also do things for her."

More laughter came from the DasGuptas. Prosenjit glared at them, but they did not notice. In a jerky movement he stepped up to where Jal was sitting and blurted out, "Don't you want to see the ship model?"

"We can wait until it's finished," said Jal casually.

Prosenjit stood awkwardly in front of his chair and cracked his finger joints. He gulped back the misery, afraid that it showed on his face.

"So tell me," said Jal, looking at Tanya. "How have you had the good fortune to meet my friend Mr. Poddar?"

"He came up to me at the dance," she said.

"Oh?" Jal smiled, exchanging knowing glances with the Das-Guptas. "Don't tell me he's taken up dancing now?"

"Oh, yes, and he's getting pretty good," she said, not realizing that Prosenjit was being made the brunt of a joke.

"He's such a modest fellow, he's been keeping it from us," said Jal.

"Say," said one of the DasGuptas, nudging Jal, "I've got a super idea. Why don't they join us for that pizza at Giovanni's?"

Tanya sang out, "Oh, that sounds like fun," and turned to Prosenjit.

He met her entreating look with a stiff frown and said, "What about the dance?"

"The dance is for gunks," said a DasGupta, dismissing it with a wave of his hand and moving toward the door. Jal jumped up and gave an exaggerated stretch. "Let's push off, then," he said. He was all set to add that perhaps if they hurried they could catch a film too, when he noticed the misery on Prosenjit's face and checked himself. In that instant, he realized that the joke had gone too far.

As far as Jal was concerned, Prosenjit took life too seriously. The Bong attacked everything he did—schoolwork, hobbies, and inventions—with a single-mindedness that bordered on obsession. Nowhere was this intensity more pronounced than in his friendships. He allowed himself to get close to only a very few people and was fond of repeating the axiom "I mix with many people but have only one or two friends, in all my life." To Jal, this was a sentiment that belonged in the nineteenth century, and he took pleasure in pulling Prosenjit's leg about it. But while he ridiculed him for being a stick-in-the-mud, it was this steadfastness that impressed Jal the most. No man he had ever met had as much integrity as Prosenjit Poddar. No matter how many disagreements they had, Jal knew that in a pinch he could always count on Prosenjit.

Pulling himself up, Jal said, in a voice of finality, "I hate to be the one to put a damper on the evening, but perhaps now is not the time for a party. We have so much to discuss, physics and engineering problems, and I fear it would bore the lady."

Prosenjit was startled and looked at him in enormous relief, but Jal only regarded him with a blank face.

"Yes," said Jal, bowing before Tanya, "I hope you will give us a raincheck. Miss Tarasoff, a pleasure," and he extended his hand.

She accepted his handshake with an uncertain smile.

"Well, then, let's make a move," said one of the brothers, and the three of them sauntered out the door. Prosenjit ran after them excitedly and called, as they walked down the hall, "See you! Come back tomorrow—the model will be ready for viewing!"

Jal turned around, cupped his hands around his mouth, and hissed, "Don't forget. Feed her bonbons."

Prosenjit watched them as they disappeared into the elevator, and then walked back into his room. He felt drained, but immeasurably relieved.

"Boy," said Tanya, "I sure like your friend Jal."

"Yes," he said. "He's a good guy." And then he added proudly, "He's my best friend."

"I wonder . . ." She hesitated for a moment. "Did I do something to offend him?"

"No, no!"

"I thought maybe I did," she said as she stood up and smoothed her skirt. She reached for her purse and fished a brush out of it. Then, throwing back her head, she began to brush, in long, hard strokes.

Prosenjit watched, mesmerized. He had never seen a woman do anything so provocative. Even his mother had always made a point of brushing her hair in the privacy of her own bedroom. As he watched the brush travel through her hair, revealing the rounded curve of her neck with the soft, dark down on its nape, he felt a current of excitement shoot through his body.

"Okay, I'm ready," she said, dropping the brush back in her purse.

As they went down in the elevator, it occurred to Prosenjit that now was the perfect time to ask her to the movie. He searched her face, looking for a sign that she was enjoying herself. He reassured himself that she would never have come to his room if she didn't want to be his friend. The problem was, how should he begin? He believed that her response would depend entirely on how eloquently he phrased the invitation. Would it be better to jump right in with "Will you join me for a film?" Or should he gradually work his way up to it by discussing the history of American cinema? And if he asked her for next Saturday night, was a week enough notice? He decided that it wasn't. As he cleared his throat, the elevator door opened and he blurted out, "The folk dance is a monster good time."

She turned around. "Your friends don't seem to think so."

"No, no. They enjoy it too."

She shrugged and walked toward the auditorium, he trotting half a pace behind. When she turned around, he smiled and his dark eyes swam with feeling. He reminded her of a skittish deer, even more frightened and timid than herself. She was suddenly glad they were friends. Grabbing his hand, she pranced over to the dancers and made a place for them in the circle.

For a few hours, the shabby auditorium, with all the swirling skirts and rising body heat, made her forget the emptiness inside. As she moved around the circle, exchanging partners, she'd catch the Indian boy watching her, craning his neck back and forth so he could keep her in his sight. It was flattering to be the center of such attention, and she kicked her toes straight out in front of her in pert little jabs.

Later, as they stood on the sidelines, exhausted, watching the others dance, her arm brushed against his and she was conscious that he flinched and moved away. She glanced at him and saw that he was standing rigidly, as though at attention. It struck her as odd. Maybe he didn't find her attractive after all. She wondered how he'd react if she did something bold, like give him a French kiss. The idea tickled her. She allowed herself to imagine sticking her tongue in his mouth and wiggling it around. He was such a prude, she'd probably have to force the tip between his pursed lips. The thought oddly excited her. She gave him a sidelong look. He seemed oblivious to her presence. Mischievously, she let her arm dangle against his and rub against it very gently. He edged away and cleared his throat, continuing to stare straight ahead, as though he hadn't felt a thing. When she looked down at her watch she saw, with surprise, that it was time to leave. Moving closer to him, she said into his ear, "Well, I guess this is goodbye."

"Begging your pardon?"

"I've got to go."

"You're leaving?" He seemed almost frantic. "But I thought we would go for a coffee!"

"I'm sorry. My father's coming for me at eleven," she said, "and if I'm not standing outside, he'll let me have it." She began moving toward the door.

He tagged along after her, into the crowded lobby.

"Jesus, I didn't realize how late it was," she muttered.

He cleared his throat, but when he tried to speak, his voice broke. "Wait, I will go with you."

She whirled on him. "Don't be silly, it's cold outside. Anyway, he'll be here any second."

"No. I will accompany you. You can't stand outside alone," he insisted.

"Yes I can. I told you it's my father!"

"It is so dark. It is not for young ladies to wait by themselves."

"I'm going now. Goodbye." And she strode off through the lobby.

"Wait!" he blurted out. "The DasGupta boys are fine tennis players. Maybe someday you would like to see them play?" He was stunned to hear himself asking her to a tennis match, of all things. The last thing he wanted was for her to see the DasGuptas bounding across a court.

She turned around. "You mean those same guys who were in your room?"

"Yes, only they are champions. You would like the way Mr. Dilip DasGupta plays the net. He has a super drop shot." He trailed off, quite unhappy to hear himself chattering away about the DasGuptas.

"That sounds good," she said hesitantly, "especially since I know the guys who're playing. . . ."

"I will telephone you to fix it up." When she nodded assent, he wrestled a pen and a piece of paper out of his pants pocket and held them out.

A horn blew out front, and she dashed out the door. "I'm in the phone book," she yelled. "There's only one Tarasoff. Call me."

He stood clutching the blank paper as though it were a trophy. He promised himself that tomorrow, first thing, he would call her and switch the tennis match into an invitation to the cinema. Once that was done he would really have reason to rejoice. Secretly, in his heart, he knew that he would owe this great triumph to his friend Jal Mehta.

SHE awoke from a bad dream that still clung to her like the gooey film of a spider's web. The sun had pushed its way through the closed shutters and left a pattern, in slats of light, on the rug. In her semiconscious state she mechanically counted the slats until slowly, unwillingly, she began to rouse herself.

The unpleasant reality was upon her. She had agreed to go out with that Indian guy Prosenjit Poddar, and now she felt slightly panic-stricken. When she had accepted his invitation to the tennis match, two weeks ago, the appointed day was still so far in the future, it wasn't a reality. Then he had called and suggested a movie instead. She couldn't bring herself to hurt his feelings, so had said yes, not quite believing that Saturday night would ever roll around. Now it was Saturday morning and she was filled with a sick feeling. Somehow, she told herself, she had to get out of the date.

The smell of bacon drifted in from the kitchen, so she got up and dressed. When she walked into the room, Alex was sitting at the table with a half-finished plate of French toast in front of him. Her mother was standing over the stove, draining grease from the frying pan.

"Rise and shine," said Alex, when he saw her sour face.

She gave him a dirty look and slid in behind the table. She sifted through the pile of newspapers and found the pink entertainment section. Opening it, she held it up like a screen between her and her brother.

"French toast?" asked her mother.

"No thanks."

"How was your hen party?" asked Alex, referring to her evening, the night before, with Cindy and Janice. "I bet you girls got down to a lot of heavy-duty gossip."

"Listen, I'm minding my own business, so why don't you?" she said, and fixed him with a cold stare.

"What's the matter, on the rag again?" he said, through a mouthful of French toast. She ignored him and kept on reading. Her mother put a cup of coffee in front of her and asked, "Are you still taking Helen?"

"Of course." She had promised to accompany Helen to her swimming lesson in Strawberry Canyon. She enjoyed doing things with her little sister, and often spent her Saturdays taking her on pony rides or over to the El Cerrito shopping center. She spooned some sugar into her coffee and sipped it. "Where's Dad?" she asked.

"There's a garage sale down the block," said Alex.

"Oh, no." She grimaced and rolled her eyes. "Can't wait to see what he's coming home with this time." It was a standing joke in the family that Vitally was a sucker for flea markets and garage sales. Whenever he found a "bargain," he'd snatch it up regardless of whether anybody needed it or not. For a few days he'd foam at the mouth about his great find, bragging about how he'd driven down the price, and then, without reason, the item would be discarded or forgotten. They now had a garage full of junk furniture and used clothing they had never worn.

Mrs. Tarasoff sighed. "He took back half his paycheck." She looked imploringly at Tanya, as if there were something she could do.

"You didn't let him take it, did you?" Even though Vitally dutifully handed over his weekly check, he often tried to take part of it back, in spite of the fact that it left the family stranded for grocery money. When her mother didn't answer, Tanya groaned.

"What can I do?" said her mother, poking with a fork at the strips of bacon still lying in the pan, "He grabbed it from my hand."

Later that morning, Tanya took Helen to the Olympic-size pool in Strawberry Canyon for her swimming lesson. She sat on the grass, watching her little sister splash and kick in the shallow end. A vapor of chlorine rose from the turquoise water and dissolved into the sunshine. Tanya absently leafed through the new issue of *Seventeen*, occasionally looking over to give Helen a wave of encouragement. Every so often, she remembered that she still had to break the date with Prosenjit Poddar, but her mind veered away from it.

On the bus going home she thought about it seriously. She would call him the instant she got through the door. Then her mind went blank when she tried to think up the excuse. Everything sounded phony; a fight with her father, too much homework, a headache. Somehow she didn't believe she had the right to say no, that she had changed her mind. Finally she settled on her period. She'd blame it on bad cramps. A prudish guy like the Indian would be so embarrassed by the mention of female blood he'd never question it. As she imagined their conversation, she thought she felt a twinge of pain in her abdomen. Maybe it wasn't a lie after all.

When she got home, she looked up the telephone number of the I House. Suddenly the excuse about her period sounded lame. She'd better think up something better than that. Maybe it would help if she washed her hair. She got into the shower and sudsed her hair into a billowing foam. The prospect of going out with this stranger who idolized her made her squirm. It wasn't that she disliked him. He was harmless enough. It was just that he seemed so vulnerable and needy, as though with one harsh word she could cut him dead. She could tell that all he wanted was for her to love him; but she didn't, it was as simple as that. And so the date loomed as an ordeal. Polite conversation, cute smiles, and an obligatory kiss at the door. She could picture his brown eyes, moistening at sight of her, and his lips moving back and forth like the mouth of a goldfish in a bowl. By the time she had stepped out of the shower, she hadn't come up with an acceptable excuse. As she was drying off, the phone rang. It was the sound she dreaded. She listened as it rang one, two, three times and stopped. Somebody must have answered it. Like a criminal, she waited for the sound of footsteps coming down the hall. Nothing happened. Apparently it wasn't for her. A few minutes later, as she was sitting at her dressing table rubbing moisturizer into her legs, the phone rang again. This time Alex banged on the door. "Phone."

Tanya didn't answer. Maybe Alex could pretend she wasn't in and get rid of him. She kept spreading lotion over her legs.

"Hey, lamebrain. Phone for you."

She opened the door and said, "Say, if it's a guy with a foreign accent, tell him I'm not here."

Alex screwed his face up in disgust. "I'm not saying that."

"Please!"

Alex turned his back and started to trot down the hall, gleefully calling out behind him, "Tanya! Telephone!"

"You asshole." She bundled her terry-cloth robe around her and stomped after him, down the hall, to where the phone was waiting, receiver off the hook.

"Hello," she said, trying to make her voice sound normal.

"Hello, Tanya? This is Prosenjit Poddar calling."

"Oh, hi."

"It's all fixed up. The movie that you wanted to see? *The King of Hearts*? I have gone to the theater for two tickets," his words came croaking out. "You will come with me tonight?"

The thought crossed her mind to say that her mother was not feeling well, but she hated to use that as an excuse because she was superstitious and believed that her saying it might make it happen. "Well . . ." she said.

"It looks like a smashing film," he said.

"Okay," she said, feeling almost sorry for him. "But you can't come here."

"Begging your pardon? I am not understanding?"

"My father won't let me date. We'll have to meet someplace first."

"Oh . . ." He hesitated. "The Northside Theater Center?"

"Yes. I'll take the bus over."

They arranged to meet for a quick dinner before the show. After they hung up, Tanya hated herself for not being able to say no.

PROSENJIT arrived at Northside half an hour early and sat down on a bench. He was wearing the fancy dress trousers he had had made by a Calcutta tailor before he came to the States. They had never fit properly. The legs were too short and they rode up in the crotch. He kept shifting his position and tugging on the legs to pull them down. He waited while three buses came, deposited their passengers, and went. Tanya was not among them. The time she had fixed was past, and still there was no sign of her. He began to grow anxious and walked to the street corner to scan the horizon for another bus. He feared he had made a terrible blunder in allowing her to come to the theater in a public conveyance. He should have insisted on collecting her in a taxi. He looked at his watch and wondered if they would still have time to eat dinner before the movie. He was impatient and walked across the center to where *The King of Hearts* was playing. A sign, "North-side Cinema," hung over the entrance to an open-air patio. He peered in. Vines of ivy wound around wooden trellises, and rows of rough-hewn tables stood on the flagstone slabs. It looked like a German beer garden. He let his eyes wander over the faces.

His heart gave a great thud. She was already there, seated at one of the tables, reading a leaflet. He rushed up to her and burst out, "Oh, you are already here!"

"Hey, what happened to you?" she said.

"I have been waiting at the bus stop!"

"Why would you wait at the bus stop? We said we'd meet here for dinner."

He regarded her with glistening eyes. "I thought I would walk with you to the restaurant."

"Walk with me?" She shook her head in disbelief. "The restaurant's two doors down from the bus stop, for God's sake. Didn't you see the sign?"

He looked up and saw a painted sign with the name "LaVal's" gouged into the wood. He hadn't realized it, but the restaurant shared the courtyard with the Northside Cinema. He swallowed back his embarrassment. "For this I must apologize," he mumbled. "I didn't mean for you to wait alone."

"No big deal. Let's go eat," and she got up and walked ahead of him into the restaurant. LaVal's was a little dive that served Italian food, and was famous for its cold meatball sandwiches dished out on sourdough bread. While they were waiting to be seated, Tanya said, "If you like meatballs, this is the place."

"As a Hindu, I don't eat beef," he said apologetically.

"Oh, yeah, I forgot." The room was stuffy, and she began to work her way out of her pea jacket. "Allow me to help," he said and fumbled to assist her.

Suddenly they were caught in a tangle of arms and elbows, and she laughed. "Wait. It's easier if I do it myself."

He scrambled to pull out her chair before she sat down. Hovering over her, he made sure she was comfortable before he seated himself. "Now," he said, rubbing his hands together, "you must be hungry." He was worried they would be late for the movie unless they ordered immediately. Out of the corner of his eye, he saw a waitress moving about, and he leaned out from the table and began making great circles in the air with his arms.

"Relax." She laughed. "I'm not going to starve, you know."

"Only I must place the order," he said, too distracted to look at her. All he cared about was flagging down the waitress. "When you are out with me, you are my responsibility."

"That sounds good."

"That is how it should be." He worried that the evening had gotten off to a bad start, and was determined that from now on, things should go off perfectly. Jal had warned him that American girls loved to eat. They were not at all like Indian ladies, who waited demurely until their men finished eating before they permitted themselves to be served. It was hard to believe, looking at her slender arms, but apparently girls like Tanya had massive appetites and liked to fill up on garlic bread, pizza pies, and ice-cream cones. If he could just get a plate of food in front of her, he would feel better.

Just at that moment, the waitress trotted past their table without stopping. He watched her moving away and called out in a tense voice, "Miss, miss . . . could you please!" He did not relax until he had won her attention and motioned her back. When she came to the table she gave him a surly look and dropped two menus in front of them.

"What would you like for dinner?" he asked anxiously.

She ran her eyes up and down the page. "Hmmm . . . what're you going to have?"

"It is no matter. I will not eat."

"What? Are you kidding? You're just going to sit there and watch me?" She laid the menu down and shook her head in disbelief. "Forget it."

He sat very straight in his chair clutching the menu. They regarded each other in silence.

Finally she said, "Let's split a pizza. What d'you like?"

"Whatever is your pleasure," he said, too ashamed to admit he had never tasted pizza.

"Boy, you mean I'm the one who has to make all the decisions around here? Oh, all right. How about pepperoni and extra cheese? I don't think pepperoni has any beef in it." As she said this she put the menu aside and looked up. She let her eyes range around the room, checking out the other tables.

Prosenjit gazed at her face. Her eyes were a dreamy sea green. In India, women with light eyes were called *"Beral Chokh"* (Cat Eyes), and were believed to bring bad luck. He looked down at her hands and saw that they were working nervously, shredding a paper napkin into strips and rolling the strips into little balls. Her fingers were long and tapered, with mother-of-pearl polish on the nails. His heart swelled with happiness. He was content just to be sitting across from her, breathing the same air.

The waitress returned and stood over their table, tapping her pencil on her pad. Prosenjit ordered a medium pepperoni pizza, mispronouncing the word "pepperoni," and only barely aware that Tanya was giggling. His mind was already racing ahead to his next move. Now was the appropriate time to introduce one of the topics of conversation he had rehearsed. He stuck his hand in his pants pocket and stealthily took out a tiny sheet of paper and laid it on his lap. He snuck a look at the paper. On it was written, in his neatest penmanship, a list of topics which included Heredity vs. Environment, Family Planning, and The Poetry of Tagore. He cleared his throat and began, "Do you think it is a man's heredity that determines his fate, or what happens in early childhood?"

"What about a girl's fate?" she countered. "Doesn't that count?"

"Oh, yes, well, I mean that too."

"Well, I don't think it's genes or chromosomes, or whatever you call them, that matters. It's definitely what happens when you're growing up."

"That is quite different from the philosophy of my country. In West Bengal, where I come from, there is a belief that when the child is born he must become what his parents are, and the ancestors before them."

"But what if you don't like what your father does?"

"Generally speaking, one has no choice."

"How awful," she said with real feeling. "I don't think I could take it."

He smiled in satisfaction. Not only had his topic caught fire, but she had said just what he wanted to hear. "Yes, the life where I come from is very difficult. You would find our system cumbersome, I think."

"For sure."

"For my part, I do not adhere to the system. It is too restrictive. One cannot get ahead. It's not like it is here, where everyone has an equal chance. Here it is easy to mix with anyone."

The waitress slapped a tray of pizza down on the table, and Tanya began to cut out a piece. She used her knife to follow the outline of a slice, then scooped it out of the pan. A strand of cheese swung in midair, still clinging to the crust, and she pinched it off and popped it in her mouth. "Mmm . . . yummy," she said, and put the slice on a plate in front of her. Prosenjit was surprised that she had not offered it to him first. In India, such behavior would be considered an insult. He was obliged to cut his own slice.

"So, I've been meaning to ask you," she said between bites, "how come you came up and talked to me at the dance?"

"What?" He hadn't expected such a direct question from her and was quite taken aback.

"Yeah, I was really surprised when I saw you standing there, staring at me," and she fixed him with a teasing look.

He dropped his eyes to the floor. "You looked like someone I knew in India."

"Oh sure. Like a girl from a past life, maybe?"

He didn't understand what she meant and thought that he had offended her in some way. "No, no, like one of the girls from my village," he said, thinking about the playful girls who used to bathe at the riverbank.

"Well, maybe we did know each other in a past life, and I've come back to haunt you," she said, laughing.

Then it dawned on him that she might feel there had been a connection between them in a previous incarnation, and the blood rushed into his face.

"Do you know a lot of women back in India?" she persisted.

"No," he said, his face continuing to redden. "I do not know any. In India we do not mix freely before marriage."

"Don't you have any girlfriends waiting for you?"

"No." He shook his head.

"Not even one? I can't believe it, a cute guy like you." She sipped on her Coke. "Are Indian girls really that much different than American ones?"

"They show more modesty," he said, reflecting to himself that an Indian girl would never walk across campus with long masculine strides, stand with arms akimbo, or sit with her legs apart, the way so many of the ladies were doing at the restaurant. At least Tanya did not show such uninhibited behavior.

"How come they wear those red dots on their foreheads?"

"It is our tradition. It once meant the woman had been given in marriage, but it is now merely a beauty mark."

"And what about those saris? I really like the way they look.

But they seem so complicated to wear," she said. "I wouldn't know how to put one on."

"It is no problem," he said, thinking to himself that she would look beautiful in a sari. If they became engaged in marriage, he would buy her the finest silk sari from Benares. He could imagine her in rose-colored cloth, with a flowered border. He pushed back from the table and stared at her, taking her in. She had her legs crossed in a ladylike fashion. Then he noticed, to his horror, that a swatch of bare thigh showed under her skirt. It disturbed him greatly that her legs should be exposed in public.

"You're not eating your pizza," she said.

He looked down at his plate and eyed the half-eaten piece with distaste. The pepperoni made his stomach burn. He picked it up and bit into it, just to be polite. Looking out the window, he saw that a line was forming outside the theater; they really should be moving along. Then, to his dismay, she scooped up another slice and put it on her plate. Now they would certainly be late for the movie. He gripped the sides of his chair and clenched his jaw, not knowing what else to say to keep the conversation alive. Then he remembered the list of topics on his lap and looked down, but the paper was gone. He ducked under the table and groped around on the floor, and then he heard her say, "Uh-oh, I think the movie's about to start. We'd better hurry." He brought his head up in time to see her reaching for the check that lay on the table.

"What do I owe you?" she asked as she rummaged around in her purse.

"Please, please, this is my pleasure," he cried. The idea of her paying for her portion of the meal was unthinkable. Worse yet, her voice was loud enough to carry through the restaurant. "You are my guest," he insisted, whisking the check from her hand and scrambling up from his chair. He rushed to the cash register. He heard her say, "I'll meet you outside, then," and he turned to see her walking out the door. While he waited impatiently for the girl to ring up the bill, he watched her through the window. She had drifted over to the theater and was standing with her back toward him, reading the ads for coming attractions. As soon as he had pocketed his change, he dashed out the door and came up behind her. She didn't notice him, so he sang out, "Oh, Charlie Chaplin, what a jolly fellow. I like his films so much," and then danced around to get a look at her face to see if his comment had pleased her.

"Yeah." She was intent on reading the poster and didn't look up.

"If you're keen to see his film, we can go," he offered.

"Thanks, but I've already seen it," she said, still reading.

It was a damp night, and fog pressed into the courtyard. Hippies in shaggy sweaters and Army-surplus jackets stood in line, bunched together for warmth. A few had their dogs in tow, and the animals strained on their leashes. Finally there was a lurching movement at the head of the line and people started pushing forward. Prosenjit shepherded Tanya into the theater. Anxious that they get good seats, he called out, "Here, come this way." He bobbed down the center aisle, gesturing for her to follow. They were among the first to take their places. It was a small art house, and the room was quickly filled to capacity. Prosenjit breathed a sigh of relief that he had been able to secure good seats. Then, to his dismay, a hulking form with an Afro sat directly in front of them. A mass of frizzy hair zigzagged across the screen. "Bloody hell!" he cried and craned his neck to see if Tanya's view was blocked. "Here, let us exchange places."

"I'm okay," she assured him.

"No, no, it's useless. You can't see a thing," and he jumped to his feet and stood over her until she shifted seats. Then he remembered the refreshments Jal had coached him to buy.

"There is something you would like? Some ice cream, bonbons, or popcorn?"

"No, I'm fine."

"You would tell me?"

"Don't worry, I would tell you."

He settled back in his chair. The frayed upholstery gave off the odor of dog hair and stale popcorn. He felt disappointed he would not be able to feed her bonbons. When the light went out, he tried to concentrate on the images on the screen, but was too preoccupied with the warm body next to him. It was as though he could feel, through the very molecules in the air, an actual connection with her person. He imagined he could hear her beating heart and the gentle intake of her breath. He was conscious of every movement of her muscles. He looked over and saw that she had slid forward in her seat and had let her knees fall slightly apart. Her short skirt barely covered her thighs, which showed white in the flickering light. He tried to train his eyes to look straight ahead, but they kept straying back. He could feel the beginnings of an erection and quickly shifted the windbreaker that was draped across the back of his chair over to his lap. He was surprised when, a few minutes later, her arm brushed against his on the armrest. He quickly pulled his arm away for fear of being disrespectful.

Then the uncomfortable thought struck him that perhaps she expected him to touch her. He had heard that American women were free and easy with themselves and did not make an issue out of being touched. Maybe he should hold her hand or put his arm around her neck? He remembered a story that had circulated through the IIT during his senior year. One suave chap had returned from holiday in Darjeeling bragging about an American chick he had picked up in the lobby of the Windemere Hotel. He claimed she had flirted with him in the presence of his parents, suggesting they go for a stroll around the Mall after dinner. After two trips around, he had maneuvered her onto a park bench and fondled her over her clothes. Prosenjit had always thought the story farfetched, but now he wondered if there had been a grain of truth in it. Beads of sweat broke out on his forehead.

He looked over at her. She seemed completely absorbed in the movie, a zany comedy about inmates escaping from an insane asylum during World War I. At one point, she nudged him and whispered, "I wish I looked just like her," referring to the heroine of the film, a ballerina who was dressed in a pink tutu and ran around breaking men's hearts. Her hot breath against his ear made him shiver. He thought to himself that she was much prettier than the ballerina.

Her arm was still resting on the armrest, and he wondered if he should put his own next to it. He looked down at the silky white flesh. Gently, ever so gently, he positioned himself on the divider and leaned into her. All along the length of his forearm, his skin touched her skin. It tickled, and the hair of his arm stood on end. The sensation was too much to bear. He pressed his thighs together to stop the tingling in his groin. He glanced at her face, but she was engrossed in the movie. Surely she must be aware of the touch. Not only aware of it, but permitting it to continue. He kept his arm in place, afraid to move for fear she would withdraw herself. His heart was beating furiously, and he began to tremble. He was afraid she could feel him shaking in his seat. He fastened his eyes on the screen. The moving forms didn't register, but swirled in a mad, foaming sea of color. His whole being was vibrating, and he thought to himself that it was for this he had come to America.

A few nights later he sat down at his desk with a sheet of letter paper. He had managed to kill a few hours by reorganizing his tool chest and applying a second coat of varnish to his model ship, but now there was no more putting it off. He brushed the eraser crumbs off his blotter and carefully centered the paper. Then he wrote the words "Dearest Mother and Father," and stared at the page. He began a sentence, considered it, then tore it up. A half hour later there was a mound of crumpled balls flowing out of his wastebasket, and he was still staring at a blank page. Finally he began, "For me the question of marriage cannot arise until I have completed my higher studies."

There was one thought ever present in his mind. His mother had warned him that if he ever mixed with an American girl he would become dead for her. He was aware that the news he was about to impart would shake the very foundations of her existence. The break might be irreparable, but, because of his natural integrity, he felt compelled to tell her about Tanya.

He could envision her face as she read his letter. The widening eyes and the crease between her eyebrows deepening like the cleft from an ax. He remembered how she had encouraged him to make an early marriage before he pushed off for the States, saying that if he left home without a bride, she had a strong foreboding that he would never return. He had tried to convince her that her anxiety was groundless, but he could not altogether allay her fears.

She had always made him feel smug about his marriage prospects because she herself was so certain. In a country where a good match was determined by the prospective groom's earning potential, he was considered a superb catch. As a "foreign-returned" engineer he would be a more highly valued husband than a doctor, and only slightly less valued than a member of the elite Administrative Service. With such a career, not only would he be able to "marry up" to a higher caste, but he would bring in a substantial dowry, for it was the custom for the girl's family to provide money and goods in exchange for the son-in-law. The dowry might contain cash, household furnishings, and other "invisibles" such as foreign travel and education. It was no wonder then that in his village the birth of a girl was a gloomy occasion, one of the popular expressions for daughter was *pareya dhon* ("another man's wealth"), and marriage was referred to as "a man's market."

Prosenjit had often heard his mother brag about the huge dowry he would draw, saying it would equal ten thousand rupees and jewelry, maybe more. She viewed his marriage as a chance to secure the family's financial future. He remembered the time he had overheard her boasting to his aunt that they would not accept anything less than a brand-new Ambassador automobile. Even though he had made a great show of protesting that she had set her sights too high, inwardly he shared her expectations. He knew of a case where bidding had driven the dowry up so high that the father of the bride was forced to spend ten times his annual income to marry off his daughter. He felt certain that there would be a refrigerator, at the very least, when he tied the knot. No small achievement considering that refrigerators were unheard-of in Balurghat.

His mother loved to talk about the future day when the selection process would begin. It was part of the custom that ten, maybe twenty, girls would be looked over before one was chosen. They were on trial, and the criteria for judging included the fairness of the girl's complexion, her modesty and virtue, and, of course, the size of her dowry. Recently, his mother's letters had been full of pointed hints that he should begin thinking about "putting out the word" that he was looking. After all, he would be twenty-four years old on his next birthday. She had used the Old Bengali expression *Bhat chorale kaker awbhab hoi na*, meaning "There will be many crows if you scatter rice." In her last letter she had even included a clipping from the matrimonial section of the *Times of India* and a tempting proposal photograph of an eighteen-year-old Kshatriya girl named Sova Roy Chaudhury. She had praised Sova's fair complexion and demure smile, and ended the letter by asking for his permission to consult a *pandit*—an astrologer—about other candidates, promising that by the time he completed his higher studies and earned his Masters of Science degree, she would have located a dozen other young ladies, every bit as beautiful as Sova, for him to inspect. He need only fix a date for his return to India and she would have the interviews arranged.

His back stiffened. It was necessary now to restrain her from further action. He didn't want to dash all of her hopes and dreams, but he must tell her about the girl *he* had chosen. Not that he planned on doing anything so drastic as marrying Tanya; he only wanted to reveal to his mother that she was his friend. But explaining the notion of such a platonic relationship to his mother was impossible. What could he say to assuage her fears? Certainly he could never let her know that he had been alone with Tanya. There was an old saying, "Girls and boys are like fire and butter— when they come together, they burn." His mother believed that, and to a certain extent so did he.

But what made his confession an even more delicate matter was the fact that Tanya was white-skinned. In his mother's opinion, all memsahibs were promiscuous. They went dancing in public places and let boys touch their arms while crossing the street. They gave up their virtue in order to lure Indian boys away from their responsibility to family and country. And it was true, he knew of several boys who had gotten emotionally involved with American girls and had never returned home. His chums at the IIT had laughingly referred to this phenomenon as "the lure of the white thigh," but to his mother it was no joking matter. Memsahibs were evil-minded sirens, and every precaution had to be taken to guard against their seductive charm.

Prosenjit looked down at the page before him, pondering the least painful way of phrasing his news. With trembling hand he wrote: "I have met a nice religious Russian family and have been invited to their home for tea on Sunday afternoon. Their surname is Tarasoff and the father works as a car mechanic. He asks that I convey his respectful greetings to you. He is a good provider for the three children, ages nineteen, seventeen, and six. There is much to be said for their style of life. They are not so Westernized as other families one meets."

He paused. If only he could break off here, but somehow, this did not seem fair, so he continued: "The eldest daughter, named Tanya, has won a seat at the university and plays a musical instrument called the accordion, similar to our harmonium. Quite naturally, the family looks to me to express my intentions. I know you would caution me not to form an attachment with an American girl and I have honored your feelings."

He considered telling them that out of curiosity he had checked her horoscope. She had turned out to be an Aquarius, with Gemini rising and her moon in Scorpio, making her *raj-jotak*, or the most compatible astrological conjunction that he could hope to find. It seemed that their coming together was obviously *karma*, but he refrained from saying this. Instead he wrote: "In regard to your request to consult a *pandit*, I must ask you to wait. As I am the eldest son, and we are a low-income family, I have decided that I will not go for marriage until I establish myself and take care of my brothers. I must be frank.

"Your devoted son, Prosenjit."

When he finished writing the letter, he folded it and stuck it in an envelope, which he left, unsealed, on his desk. He dropped into bed, exhausted, and fell asleep instantly.

The next morning when he awoke he did not immediately remember the letter. It was not until he had pulled on his pants and rinsed his face that he spotted it, waiting, on his desk. His first thought was to destroy it. The fact that he was denying his mother the right to begin looking for his bride filled him with guilt. It was as good as saying that he no longer relied on her judgment. But when he picked up the letter, with tremulous hand, he heard Tanya's voice saying, "Maybe we did know each other in a past life, and I've come back to haunt you." He remembered how, while they were sitting side by side in the theater, she had permitted his forearm to rest against the soft flesh of her arm. Upon reflection, both seemed to be signals that she was encouraging his affections, that she loved him. Without rereading the contents of the letter, he licked the envelope and sealed it. Then he sprinted down the stairs and out to the mailbox. He closed his eyes and dropped it down the chute.

He walked back into the I House, haggard and shaken. If he had expected his guilt to subside, he had been mistaken. Instead, he felt ineffably sad. An image of his mother, washing clothes at the banks of the Atreyi River, singing a Bengali song, filled his mind. The thought occurred to him that if he ever did marry Tanya, he could never bring her home to his parents' house. He might never again return to the village of his birth. He might never speak another word of Bengali. Sending the letter to his parents was the first time in his entire life that he had ever acted in direct opposition to his family's wishes. He had outgrown their narrow world, and there was no turning back.

Without knowing how he got there, he found himself standing in the entrance to the cafeteria. The breakfast crowd was stampeding the food line, digging into vats of watery scrambled eggs and baskets of sweet rolls. He didn't feel like eating, but when he glanced around the room and spotted Jal, he felt the irrepressible urge to tell him about the letter home. He put a sweet roll and a cup of tea on a tray and headed for his table.

When he arrived at the table he made a great show of removing the items from his tray and setting them opposite Jal. He cleared his throat and said in an unnaturally loud voice, "I am here to thank you."

"To thank me? What the hell for?"

"Your advice in regard to Miss Tarasoff."

"Oh? Have you seen the young lady?"

He nodded yes and clearing his throat again said, "She has made me very happy."

"You don't say?" said Jal, looking skeptically at Prosenjit's inscrutable expression.

"I took her to see *The King of Hearts*. It was a super film."

"That's a start, at any rate."

"A start?" He squirmed in his seat, having half a mind to tell him that she had permitted him to touch her in the theater. "I'd say it's more than a start."

"You had better find out how many other guys she's dating."

Prosenjit looked at him, disconcerted. "What do you mean?"

"These American chicks play the field."

"Surely if she accompanied me to the cinema, she wouldn't accept another boy's invitation?"

"It's a dog-eat-dog world."

"But I like only her!"

"Well, she might like only you, too. I just don't want to see you make an ass of yourself." Jal laughed, between mouthfuls of egg. "It's very easy to do with these American chicks."

"Is that so?" said Prosenjit, rising from his seat. "That shows how little you know."

Jal raised an eyebrow.

"This much I can tell you," he said. "I would never expose what's in my heart unless the feeling was returned," and he headed out of the room, grateful that he had not mentioned the letter he had dropped down the chute.

A station wagon drove erratically down Shattuck Avenue and lurched to a stop for a yellow light. Christmas decorations blinked on and off, and a stream of after-dinner shoppers crossed in front of the car, on their way to Penney's. The driver of the station wagon, Natalie Gorlov, was more intent on making her point than paying full attention to the road. She was a high-strung, vivacious woman, with crow-black hair and hands that left the steering wheel and fluttered excitedly while she rattled on. Tanya's mother, Lidia, sat next to her in the front seat, soaking up her stream of chatter. A tattered cookbook lay open in her lap, and as she squinted down at the page, Lidia sighed, cutting Natalie off. "Twelve pounds of ground round. That'll come out to four dozen *pirogi*."

"That's way too much," exclaimed Natalie.

"Better too much . . ." Calculating out loud, Lidia recited all the ingredients they still needed to buy. The two women were responsible for baking the *pirogi*, special meat-and-cabbage pies, for the Christmas banquet at St. John's Russian Orthodox church.

Tanya sat in the back seat, gazing out of the window. She was bundled up in her trench coat, from underneath which the ruffled pink collar of her flannel nightgown stuck out. She had been reading in bed when her mother had proposed that she accompany them to the market, and she hadn't bothered to change.

Natalie's heavily ringed fingers clinked against the steering wheel as she talked. She was always weighted down with gaudy costume jewelry. In fact, everything about Natalie was bold and garish, like the oversized black and white checks on her wool slacks. Recently she had opened up her own Russian delicatessen in Walnut Creek. To Tanya's mind, that took real courage. She wished her mother had a tenth her spunk.

Lidia turned around. "Look at you." She shook her head. "You go out of the house undressed. What if the car breaks? We get a flat tire and get stuck on the road. Then what are you going to do?"

Tanya rolled her eyes. "We're not going to break down."

"How do you know?"

"Mama!"

Lidia sighed and faced front, as Natalie pulled into the parking lot in front of the Coop, an all-night market, and nosed the wagon into a space.

Tanya waited for the two women to get out of the car and walk some distance toward the market before she followed. It was embarrassing to be seen out shopping with her mother, especially at night. As she neared the entrance, a platoon of Hare Krishna freaks descended on her, waving twigs of incense and begging for spare change. They were swathed in saffron robes, and their shaved scalps shone under the neon lights. "Zombies," she said under her breath, and, ignoring the hot fervent eyes that bored into her, she marched through the automatic doors. Inside the Coop an air-conditioned breeze enveloped her, and she shivered, clutching her raincoat closer to her. Glancing around to make sure her mother was nowhere close, she yanked a shopping cart from the line and headed down an aisle.

Late every night, the Coop turned into a scene. It was barely nine o'clock, but already the place was teeming with dope smokers, their eyes bloodshot and vague, their appetites fueled by marijuana. Some lingered in front of the bakery shelves, gazing at the packages of Pepperidge Farm cookies. Others hovered over pints of ice cream, taking ages to select a flavor. More than once, Tanya nearly collided with a splotch-faced shopper who appeared stoned out of his brains, weaving down the aisle with a cart full of nothing but junk food.

She pushed her cart over to the dairy section and opened a refrigerator door. As she was reaching for a quart of milk, a soft voice from behind said, "Hey, Chiquita, grab one of those for me." She turned around and was stunned to see the unforgettable face of the guy she had flashed on at the Mediterranean Café when she was out cruising with Cindy. *The Musketeer.* She couldn't believe he was standing there, talking to her. She gaped at him, feeling herself turn scarlet.

He looked even better than she remembered. His angular face had a faraway look that reminded her of Bob Dylan. His shoulder-length brown hair was straight as a plank. She couldn't see his eyes because they were masked behind reflector sunglasses. It was unnerving to see her own image gawking back at her in the glass.

"Hey, I didn't mean to freak you out," he said. His voice came in a slow, insinuating drawl. She noticed that his front teeth were slightly splayed.

"You didn't."

"Man, you almost jumped out of your skin."

"I did?" She racked her brains for something interesting to say. Standing so close to him she caught a sweetish trace of marijuana wafting off his clothes.

"Yeah." He looked around with a furtive movement. "What's with these lights flashing on and off, like some weird strobe effect? They should put them on a dimmer." He took off his glasses and rubbed his eyes. Looking at her as if through a fog, he said, "This place makes me paranoid."

Bedroom eyes, the window to his soul. She thought she perceived a wisdom behind those eyes that was deep. He might be spaced-out, but he was definitely mystical. She was aware that she was sweating. The drenched patches under her arms felt cold. "The light hurts my eyes too," she managed.

"Fuckin' A."

Then she heard herself come out with, "I never thought I'd see you again."

"Hunh?" His detached gaze wavered back and settled on her in a puzzled look.

"That time at the Med?" she said.

"The Med?"

"Don't you remember we met at the Med?" Then it dawned on

her that maybe he didn't and she was making a complete fool out of herself.

"Jeez, did we meet before?" He gave her a lopsided grin and said with disarming sweetness, "I'm sorry. I'm so wasted half the time I forget where I parked my car."

"Oh."

"Yeah. Too much weed. Damage to the right lobe."

"That's okay," she mumbled, cringing at how she'd embarrassed herself.

"So we met before. What happened?"

"Nothing, really."

"I didn't do anything rude, did I?"

She shook her head and looked down at the floor.

"I'm a dumb motherfucker," he said. He reached out as if to lift her chin. The move was a sweet, affectionate gesture. When she raised her eyes he was staring straight at her, as if reading her mind. A lightning thrill shot through her, and suddenly she could see, stretching out in all its intimate details, a full-blown romance. She imagined them lounging around on Sundays watching football on TV, or going for picnics in Tilden Park, rolling around in a bed of pine needles and kissing until their lips were sore.

"What's your name?" he asked.

"Tanya Tarasoff."

"I'm Jeff Flanders."

Jeff Flanders, Tanya Flanders, she repeated to herself.

He reached out and tugged on her ruffled collar. "I like your outfit."

"Oh," she said, remembering that she was wearing her night-gown. "I didn't expect to be going out."

"I know what you mean."

Just then a girl walked over to them with purposeful strides and threw something heavy into his shopping cart. Tanya caught an impression of shimmering blue and silver, like a mirage. The girl was dressed in a powder-blue suede coat with soft white fur up around her chin. He platinum hair had been ironed straight and hung down her back. The Frosty Freeze Queen. She was much too pretty to compete with, and Tanya's heart sank.

An awkward moment passed. "My name's Marsha," she said, throwing the Musketeer a proprietary look. "A friend." This last was said with emphasis.

"Hi, I'm Tanya," she said, in a hollow voice.

"How do you two know each other?"

"From the Med." He grinned.

"That dive," said Marsha. Her blue eyes sized Tanya up in one cold sweep. Turning to the Musketeer, she asked, "What else do we need?"

He shrugged. "Salad stuff."

Automatically, Tanya surveyed the contents of their shopping cart. Packages of chicken, brown rice, granola, and raw milk. It sort of indicated they were living together. When she looked up she saw, to her complete horror, that her mother and Natalie were standing nearby at the meat counter. They were watching her and whispering. She pretended she hadn't noticed them and prayed to God they would have sense enough not to butt in.

"Let's split," said Marsha and turned away. Under her coat she was wearing a miniskirt that had hiked up around her thighs. She had great legs.

"Catch you later." He smiled at Tanya.

As they strolled off, Tanya heard Marsha say, "When are we going to feed skinny little me? I'm starved." She noticed that they each had a hand resting on the handle of the shopping cart. They stopped in front of the pet food, and he reached up for a huge bag of puppy chow and threw it into the cart. A wave of unhappiness swept over Tanya as she realized they were probably raising a dog together.

A few minutes later she ran into them over by the fruits and vegetables. She could tell by the sullen expression on Marsha's face that they were having a quarrel. She heard her strident voice asking, "Tell me what you want me to get. I don't know where anything is." It occurred to Tanya that Marsha wasn't used to shopping at the Coop. Maybe it was *his* market, not hers. They didn't live together after all. She still had a chance.

She hovered over the juice oranges, putting some into a plastic bag, trying to be inconspicuous. She strained to hear what they were saying to each other, but couldn't. Marsha was stuffing a head of lettuce into a bag, he was selecting some mushrooms. By the time they pushed over to the checkout counter, it looked like they weren't speaking. The thought flashed through her mind that maybe they had argued over her. Marsha might have picked up on the vibes and gotten pissed. She felt even more hopeful.

She skittered over to the glass doors to see what kind of car he drove. She saw him open the trunk of a battered Volvo and load the groceries in. Marsha was already plunked in the front seat, her platinum hair glowing under the parking lights.

At the checkout counter Tanya's mother said, in an offhand manner, "Who was that boy you were talking to?"

"Nobody."

"Someone you know from school?"

"No."

"He looked like a drowned water rat to me," said Natalie, her lips pursed.

Tanya decided she didn't like Natalie as much as she'd thought she did. She was a busybody. On the ride home all she could think of was calling Cindy up and telling her about the Musketeer. She ran through their entire conversation in her mind, savoring how he had called her Chiquita and how he had, ever so slightly, touched the tip of her chin. Clearly it was fate that had put him back into her life. She made up her mind she was going to keep coming to the Coop, every night if necessary, to see him again. Maybe she'd get lucky and end up with him—if Marsha wasn't a permanent fixture and if fate was on her side.

HIS adrenaline started to pump the moment he alighted from the bus. The sun had not yet gone down, and a thick mist had settled over the hills in the distance. He stood on the street corner, craning his neck, trying to get his bearings. In one hand he held a box of shortbread cookies, wrapped in scotch-plaid paper and tied with a festive red bow; with the other he shook open his map of Berkeley. In the early-evening gloom the print was impossible to read, so he moved under a streetlamp. When he found her street, he traced the line that twisted like a crazy hair across the page, until he pinpointed the location of her house. Keeping his finger in place and his eyes fixed on the spot, he groped forward, like a blind man searching his way, toward Tanya.

The idea of going to her house had occurred to him the night before. He had been in the cafeteria enjoying an after-dinner cigarette when Manuel Iturbe, a biochemistry student who lived on the fourth floor, had asked if he was eating Christmas supper with his "American girlfriend." Flushing red and mumbling something inaudible, he had excused himself from the table. Not only was he stunned that Iturbe, who was no more than a casual acquaintance, had heard about Tanya, but he was much too embarrassed to admit that he had not been invited. After he had retreated to the privacy of his room, he thought to himself, Bloody hell, what do I do now?

The truth of the matter was that ever since he had taken Tanya to the cinema he had been unable to suppress the urge to talk about her. Naturally, he had said nothing about how she had permitted him to touch her. And while he had tried to confine himself to a few gentlemanly remarks, describing how they had shared a pizza at LaVal's, he had to admit that perhaps he had been indiscreet.

While he did not specifically recall it, he had the uneasy feeling that he had referred to her as his "American girlfriend." Even worse, he was certain that he had repeated to one or two people what she had said about their connection in a previous incarnation. It was no wonder then that Iturbe was asking if he was eating Christmas supper with her family!

The problem now was that if Manuel Iturbe, or anyone else, found out he had never been invited to her home, he would become the laughingstock of the entire I House.

He stared at the telephone for a long while. It had been nearly one week since their date. He had phoned twice to thank her for the lovely evening, but both times a woman had answered and said that she was "out." He had assumed that this must be Tanya's mother, but he had been too timid to introduce himself. But now, telling himself that many days had passed and it was his duty to behave like a gentleman, he picked up the receiver and dialed. After three rings he heard Tanya's sonorous hello, and his heart leaped.

"Oh, hello," he sang out. "Thanks a pile for the jolly good time."

"Who is this?"

"Prosenjit Poddar," he said, disappointed that she didn't recognize his voice.

"You're welcome." Then there was silence on the other end of the phone.

"You're quite a stranger, now that there are no dances," he said finally, referring to the fact that the folk dances had been temporarily canceled, because of the Christmas break.

"I'm tired of those dances anyway," she said.

"No? Really?" It was a blow to his pride that she did not feel fondly toward the occasion where they had met.

"Yeah, I've decided they're full of losers."

"I was wondering," he mumbled, "if you would do me the honor of coming along with me to a harpsicord concert this Sunday, in Eshelman Hall."

"Oh, this Sunday? I'm sure I won't be better by then. I have this terrible cough," and she coughed loudly into the phone.

"You are not well?" He sank back on his bed, picturing her frail body and slender wrists, as delicate as twigs.

"No. I think it must be bronchitis."

"What can I do to speed your recovery?"

"Nothing. I'm just going to stay in bed and rest."

"No, please, it is no bother. If you are in bed I can get you something." He experienced a twinge of guilt as he realized that he rather liked the idea that she was confined to bed. After all, if he couldn't be with her, he was glad that no one else could, either.

She refused all of his offers and said goodbye. Her mind, occupied solely by the Musketeer, closed the Hindu out with finality. As for Prosenjit, after he hung up the phone, he found the stillness in his room unbearable. It seemed impossible that he would have to wait one or maybe even two weeks until he saw her again. He felt her absence like the withdrawal from a drug. Then he realized that he was in the States now and he was free to hop on a bus and visit her sickbed. He could go the next day, right after work, if he wanted. The bus from the towing tank made a stop on Solano Avenue, near her home. He might even take her some sweets to restore her spirits. By the time he turned out the light, the excursion had taken on the excitement of a pilgrimage to a national shrine.

The distance from the bus stop to Tacoma Street was only four blocks. All along the way, lights were switched on as people returned from work. He found himself walking under a row of trees, stripped bare of leaves and so gray and brittle that their branches jabbed the sky like fishbones. A soft drizzle came through the spiny boughs, and all around him piles of sodden leaves gave off the fetid odor of death-decay. Evening newspapers bundled in plastic were on the lawns, and car windshields were beaded solid with mist. Only his keen edge of excitement, as he hurried toward her home, cut through the heaviness.

As the street numbers got bigger, his heart raced, and he picked up his pace. The houses that he passed were square and low, slightly oriental in style. Their sloping roofs and overhanging beams made him think of mushrooms, sunk in the dankness of a forest. They seemed part of the earth, solid and old. And then he saw her street address painted on a mailbox: number 1838. He kept on moving, his eyes searching wildly for a place to hide. He scurried behind an oleander bush, directly across the street, and made a crevice for himself between the branches and a brick wall. Ever so quietly he crouched, balancing himself on his haunches, his heels sunk in the soft black mud, his arms clasping the package of shortbread cookies tightly against his chest. He remained there in the darkness, trying to catch his breath, aware for the first time that he was sweating profusely. And then he separated the leaves and peered out. He had a straight-on view of the house.

It was white cement with a chalky green shingle roof. Not much different from the ones on either side, but to him it seemed special. Steps led up to an enclosed porch, behind which one window looked out onto the street like a deep-set eye. The drapes were drawn, but a warm yellow light emanated from the front room. He was content to sit there for some time, watching the yellow light. In fact, the act of walking up the front steps and approaching it seemed nearly impossible.

He imagined that her mother was preparing the evening meal. Perhaps it was like one of those heavy English dinners of roast beef and potatoes that he had seen served at the Oberai Grand Hotel in Calcutta. Suddenly it occurred to him that she might react to his visit as an intrusion. After all, Tanya was unwell and would not be eating with the rest of the family.

He thought about how, when he was sick, his mother used to say, "*Jhal kheley boro hobi*"—"Only if a child eats hot will he grow to be strong." She'd mix flaming hot chile in with rice and knead the special mixture into *gollos* (egg-shaped balls she called "serpent's eggs"). Breaking off fingerfuls of rice, she'd coax them into his mouth. He loved the touch of her cool hand brushing against his cheek. He could imagine himself sitting on the edge of Tanya's bed, feeding her serpent's eggs. Then he saw his mother's face, stern and reproachful. He shuddered, thinking how displeased she would be that he was calling on his American girlfriend.

He wondered if Mrs. Tarasoff was as formidable as his own mother, whose rebuke was terrible. Worse even than the memory of her harsh treatment was his feeling that she had neglected him. He had had fits of temper as a child because she had paid too much attention to his younger brothers. Only when he had cried, and beat his fists against her sari, had she given him the affection he longed for. The memory still ate away at him.

His eyes moved to a side window fitted with pink shutters. Perhaps this was where Tanya slept. He pictured her lying in a bed heaped high with blankets. All she was wearing underneath was a diaphanous nightgown. When they married they would learn about the joys of physical lovemaking. On a rainy evening like this he would nestle up against her and fit his body into her curves. She slept soundly like a child and would not wake up, even when he touched her. Or maybe she would pretend not to wake up. She was a naughty girl and liked to tease him. He pictured slipping his hand up under the nightgown and stroking the flank of her leg. He became aware of his erection.

Suddenly his knees felt so stiff and achy that he could not maintain his crouching position for another second. He tried to shift his weight, but his shoes were wedged in the mud and he nearly lost his balance. He staggered out from behind the bush and stood in the open. Like it or not, it was time to mount her steps. Glancing around, he stole swiftly across the street.

He tiptoed up her driveway. A blue car with long fins blocked his passage. As he slid his body sideways, edging past it, he peered in through the car windows. Odd bits of junk were piled on the seats. He let his eyes roam over the contents, looking for something that might belong to her. A colorful tail of cloth was sticking out from underneath some boxes, but it was impossible to tell what it was. He moved on, along the side of the house, past a row of geraniums planted in a long wooden trough, until he came to cement steps that led up to the front porch.

As he climbed the steps he could feel his heart pounding. He rehearsed in his mind the introductory speech he planned to make to Mrs. Tarasoff, and smoothed down his hair. He stood on the welcome mat and stared at the doorbell. He could not bring himself to ring it. He cleared his throat. Finally he reached up and, ever so slightly, tapped the bell with his finger. He did not hear a chime go off, but he was loath to touch it again. After some minutes he realized that there was no sound coming from within. All he could hear was his own breathing and the thumping of his heart. He pushed the bell again, and this time, to his chagrin, a buzz sounded. He waited for less than a minute. When no one came to the door, with relief he placed the box of cookies on the mat and scurried down the steps.

As he was squeezing past the car, he remembered the colorful tail of cloth in the car, and a sudden impulse caused him to pause. Could it be hers? Quietly he pressed the handle and opened the door, wincing at the creaking it made. Reaching in between the boxes, he tugged at the cloth until it came free. He balled it up in his hand, stuffed it under his jacket, and gently shut the door. Then he took off down the driveway, and when he reached the corner, broke into a sprint.

It wasn't until he was blocks away, waiting for the bus to whisk him off to safety, that he took out his prize to examine it. It took him a moment before he realized it was the bottom half of a swimming costume, blue nylon, sprinkled with red polka dots. The predominating odor was chlorine, but he thought he caught her woman scent, and it intoxicated him. Smiling, he put it back in his jacket. All during the bus ride home, he put his hand to where it was and squeezed it, as though it were a part of her.

ON her way to meet Cindy, on the Sunday morning before Christmas, Tanya drifted through Sproul Plaza, taking in the lazy sounds of the street musicians who squatted on the steps of the Student Union. Although the campus had been peaceful through Christmas break, the acrid smell of tear gas hung in the air. A residue had settled on the fresh young leaves of the trees that lined the plaza, and when the wind blew, it was wafted like pollen, stinging her eyes, making her cough. She rubbed her eyelids to relieve the burning sensation and thought again about how she yearned to attend Berkeley and belong to this wondrous universe.

It was true that every time she heard about an upcoming riot, her ears perked up. Not that she knew anything about Eldridge Cleaver or the Third World Liberation Front; she never paid attention to any issues. But ever since Cindy had told her that a demonstration was the best place to meet men, maybe even run into the Musketeer, she had attended noon rallies as often as her schedule would permit. She had come to view the prospect of these confrontations with a certain glee. When she had heard battle cries like "On strike, shut it down" or "Ashes to ashes, dust to dust, we hate to burn it down, but we must, we must," the blood coursed through her veins. Like nearly everyone else, she wanted to be a part of the revolution. Now she was an outsider, just an interloper from junior college, a fact that she must keep carefully hidden. Looking up at the cold limestone facade of Sproul Hall, she promised herself that as soon as school opened, she would walk through those doors and pick up an application for admission. This time her father's derisive comments weren't going to have the slightest effect on her.

In the distance, the hypnotic beat of drums was a persistent war cry, pulling Tanya. She moved down the steps leading to lower Sproul Plaza. Ranging in a long line, with bongos straddled between their legs, were a half-dozen young blacks. Tanya sat down with the others who had gathered for the impromptu concert. She watched the ebony arms of the musicians, hard as polished stone and gleaming with sweat, come flying down on the skins. Their intensity was awesome. In their African garb and tribal beads they looked like an assembly of angry warriors. The beat rose and fell in waves of sound. From out of the crowd, Cindy appeared in her purple Pendleton and sat down next to her. The girls exchanged looks and sat in trancelike silence, mesmerized by the flailing arms. A few minutes later Cindy pointed off to a shallow fountain in front of Sproul Hall where two mongrels were now cavorting.

"I'm sick of seeing dogs fuck," said Cindy. "They always seem to do it when you're sitting there eating lunch or talking to a guy."

As they watched the dogs wrestle in the brackish water, the thought crossed Tanya's mind that if she sat there long enough, the Musketeer might walk by. After all, he had to pass that way to get to the library or the Bear's Lair. If only she could get into Berkeley, her chances of running into him would be greatly increased. Not only that, but she wouldn't feel so insecure about seeming dumb. Sighing, she said, "I can't wait to transfer here."

"I know," said Cindy, who shared her aspirations, though she was far from achieving even a mediocre grade point average.

"Imagine all those great classes," said Tanya, thinking about the times she had leafed through the catalogue. "Like the Hapsburg Monarchy or Native Peoples of South America."

"I'd be into something easy, like Speech 1-A."

" 'Course, the strike would probably shut everything down," said Tanya, remembering how, during the Third World demonstrations, some classes had been held in a Lutheran church on Dwight Street. She had seen students streaming inside and had wished with all her might that she could be with them.

"And all those darling TAs," sighed Cindy, who often fantasized about ending up with one of her teaching assistants. Then as an afterthought she added, "I've got to get a dress for New Year's."

"Oh? Where are you going?" asked Tanya. This was the first she had heard about a New Year's date.

"To the Fillmore, unless he stands me up. Last weekend when he didn't show, he told me some story about a term paper he had to write. So you never know."

"I'm doing nothing, of course."

"It's still early."

"Watch, I'll probably end up at the I House."

"What about the Musketeer?" teased Cindy, who had been subjected to Tanya's nightly reports after she had come back from cruising the aisles of the Coop, in hopes of getting another glimpse of him. "Maybe he's available."

"Oh, sure." Tanya gave her a look. "You know who he'll be with," she said and sighed, referring to the Frosty Freeze Queen.

"You never know."

"I still can't believe they're together. The way he called me Chiquita, and touched me."

Cindy nodded sympathetically, already having heard the story a half-dozen times.

"He wouldn't have come on to me if he wasn't interested, don't you think?"

"No way."

"He's got these faraway eyes that look so mystical."

"Was he loaded?"

"I'm sure he was."

"Well, still, he knew what he was doing. Probably if she wasn't there, you would have ended up with him that night."

"Do you think so?"

"Yeah," said Cindy, taking off her Pendleton. Underneath she was wearing a soiled T-shirt that had "Magical Mystery Tour" stenciled across the front. What did you say his last name was?"

"Flanders. Jeff Flanders."

"That's a good name," said Cindy. "What kind of a car does he drive?"

"A Volvo."

"Far out. I love Volvos."

"He lives on Arch Street, in one of those great old apartments."

"You mean you found out where he lives?" asked Cindy, incredulously.

Tanya nodded. "He's listed in the Student Registry."

"I can't believe you didn't tell me that."

"I thought I did."

"You've told me everything else fifty times." Just then a boy sitting to the other side of Cindy nudged her and held up a roach, asking if she wanted a hit.

"Thanks," she said, plucking it out of his hand. The roach was barely big enough to hold as she put it to her lips and sucked. She erupted in a fit of coughing.

"Yesterday I passed by his apartment," said Tanya, shaking her head no to Cindy's offer of the roach. "He lives on the second floor, in the back."

"Did you go up and knock?"

"Of course not."

"Why not? This may call for drastic measures."

"I could never do that."

"Why the fuck not? Guys do it all the time. Why shouldn't you?"

Tanya stared at her, speechless.

"For Christ's sake, how many times can you cruise the Coop?"

She shrugged.

Cindy threw her a disgusted look. "Let's go get a falafel."

Tanya followed as Cindy headed toward Sather Gate. "I can just see myself ringing the bell and *she* answers."

"He came on to you at the market, didn't he? If she hadn't been there he might have asked you out."

"Maybe."

"So what's wrong with taking matters into your own hands? I never would have gotten to first base with the Candleman if I hadn't made the first move."

"The thing is, he didn't remember meeting me at the Med and I recognized him instantly. It was so embarrassing."

"So what? He'll remember you now."

"Well . . . I might consider doing something if I never run into him again. But if I do call, what do I say my reason is?"

"Why do you need a reason?"

"What do you mean, why do I need a reason?"

"Tell him you want to fuck his brains out."

Tanya gave her a disgusted look.

"Why not?" said Cindy. "That would flip him out. No, really, if you're going to call him up, you can't do it with some half-assed excuse that he can see through. You have to be direct."

Tanya wondered if she could ever be that forward. Just recently, a girl passing out leaflets at Sather Gate had asked her if she believed in "women's liberation," an expression people were beginning to use around campus, and she had shaken her head no. The truth was that she really didn't know what the term meant. Now, contemplating her situation, she guessed that maybe it meant calling up guys and asking them out. Even though she had once taken the initiative with the Indian boy, in her mind he didn't count. Since he meant nothing to her, she had nothing to lose. However, the thought of making the first move with someone like the Musketeer made her tremble, especially when she considered that Cindy's "liberated" behavior had scared away most of the guys she had gone after. All she knew was that if Jeff Flanders rejected her, she would be devastated.

"Nothing good is going to happen unless you take a chance," goaded Cindy.

"But if I ever got him on the phone, I'd turn into jelly."

"You'd think of something to say."

"I'm going to wait a week, at least, and see what happens."

"Chickenshit."

As the days passed, Tanya grew more and more disconsolate at the prospect of having nothing to do on New Year's Eve. It seemed that her only alternative to being cooped up at home was the I House party. Normally, she would have found some small satisfaction in the prospect of dancing, which always lifted her spirits, but her longing for Jeff Flanders had erased even that. Besides, the idea of coming face to face with Prosenjit Poddar would be an admission of failure, and she found herself wishing he'd disappear off the face of the earth.

A few days before the gala New Year's Eve party at the I House, Prosenjit took the bus down University Avenue to an Indian emporium that was reputed to have a large selection of silks from Benares. He intended to take that first, momentous step toward marriage and buy Tanya a sari. But when he walked through the door and saw the round-faced Indian salesgirl sitting behind the counter and sucking on an orange, his courage deserted him. He dawdled by the counter, fidgeting with the tassels that hung from a tea warmer, too self-conscious to make his request. Finally she noticed him and asked if he needed assistance. He informed her in a stiff voice that his sister was coming from India and he wanted to commission the making of a sari.

The salesgirl raised her eyebrows. As it was the custom in India for the bridegroom to commission a sari for his fiancée, and as Prosenjit appeared to be of marriageable age, she immediately guessed his real intent. Averting her head to hide her smile, she led him to a dusty wardrobe and opened the door, revealing bolts of silk and colorful textiles piled high on the shelves.

He stood there deliberating until the salesgirl, sensitive to his difficulty, asked, "For what occasion will she wear it?"

Embarrassed, Prosenjit pointed to a swatch of deep aquamarine silk and said, "It is for nothing important, but I wanted to find something with a bright color."

The salesgirl handed him the bolt of aquamarine, and he ran his hand over it appraisingly. Then, unable to contain herself, she said, "Excuse me, but if this is a betrothal sari, the color may not be appropriate."

He flushed. "Are only certain colors appropriate?"

"Well, yes." She smiled. "Depending mainly on where the lady is from." He shifted uneasily from one leg to another and she added, "A girl from Bombay would never be happy with the same color that a Bengali girl would find pleasing."

"I see." And then he mumbled in a voice barely audible, "What if she is American?"

"Oh. . . ." There was a pained silence as a disapproving look spread across her face. She stepped back, hands on hips. "In that case, it does not matter so much."

He self-consciously replaced the bolt of cloth on the shelf. In the discomfort of the moment, the colors swam in front of his eyes. It took a minute before he could regain his focus, and then he pointed to a sheath of rose-colored organdy and said, "I am liking that one." As the girl took it down from the shelf, he wiped his hands on his trouser legs and licked his lips. It was an impossible decision to make, trying to guess what would please Tanya, but when he inspected the rose-colored cloth and saw that it had an intricate border of silver and gold embroidery, he felt that it suited her. He held a handful of the diaphanous material up to the light, and as he looked through it imagined her body swathed in the delicate pink. Turning to the salesgirl, he asked, "Is it possible for you to have it ready by New Year's Eve?"

"That's awfully short notice." She frowned.

"Could you make a special effort, on my account?" he pleaded, drawing in a deep breath.

"Oh, all right. We'll do our best."

Thrusting the bolt of cloth into her arms, he smiled, and let a giddy laugh escape his lips.

On New Year's Eve, he descended the steps to the auditorium an hour early, just as the kitchen staff were setting out cups and plates for the refreshments. The dreary room had been decorated for the party and seemed almost transformed by the crepe paper and balloons streaming from the walls. Two life-size dragons guarded the door like sentries, and orange-and-yellow piñatas hung from the ceiling, their burly papier-mâché bodies swinging to and fro.

He lingered while the room began to fill with people. Many of the I House residents came dressed in native costumes, which they proudly exhibited for one another, but Prosenjit was too preoccupied even to notice. He wandered into the lounge for a smoke. A chess game was in progress, and he stood over the board and lit his cigarette. Ten days earlier, when he had last talked to Tanya over the phone, she had promised him that if she had recovered from her bronchitis, she would see him at the dance. He prayed that she was well. He drew on his cigarette, but it tasted stale. In his mind he could picture her rapture when she opened the box and took out the sari. He could show her how to wind the shimmering material around her body and how to fasten it the way a Bengali girl would.

A few minutes later he snuffed out his cigarette and hurried back to the auditorium. The dance floor was jammed with partygoers. Rising up on his toes, he scanned the room. Suddenly he spotted her, standing by the refreshment table. He wondered how long she had been there. He was worried that she might feel slighted by his inattendance, and he rushed toward her, brushing past couples on the dance floor. As he approached, he could see that she was talking to that chap Manuel Iturbe. He waved to get her attention, but she didn't notice. Too polite to barge into their conversation, he hung back, trying to catch her eye. She didn't look his way. When Iturbe went for a refill of punch, he eagerly strode up to her.

"I've been waiting for you," he said happily.

"Oh, really?"

He failed to notice the note in her voice, cold and unrelenting. "You do not still have your cough?"

"No. I'm all better."

"I came to your house the other day, but no one was home."

"You mean it was you who left the cookies?"

"Yes." He smiled.

"That was really nice, but I think maybe you'd better not come over without asking."

"Not come over?"

"That's right. My father's really strict. He doesn't like it when guys show up at the house."

"I'm sorry," he mumbled. "I didn't have any idea."

Then she turned her back on him. Her eyes were on the ring of dancers, whirling around and around in the center of the room. He thought about the sari, wrapped and waiting upstairs. He girded himself to tell her about it, but the sight of her back, so straight and imposing, intimidated him. He racked his brains for something to say. Clearing his throat, he managed, "It's been very dull at I House, with everyone sailing off for Christmas break."

"Yeah," she said, barely turning to face him, "I'll bet it can get really dead up here."

"I had planned to go off on holiday myself," he said, explaining that Jal had organized a wine-tasting tour of the Sonoma Valley but he had forgone it in favor of attending the New Year's Eve party. He was anxious that she should know of his sacrifice.

She made no pretense of being interested.

He stood at her side like an obedient dog. In the uneasy silence he shifted from one foot to the other and cracked his finger joints. Finally he said, "Maybe someday you will visit my country."

"Maybe."

"The best time is wintertime, after the monsoons are over."

When she didn't say anything, he said, "If you go, you will be the guest at my family's house."

"Thanks, but that could be a long time off in the future."

"One never knows." He continued to stare at her, and she pursed her lips and looked off to the side. She seemed to feel restless under his gaze, as though some itchy material chafed her skin. He tried to stop looking at her, but couldn't.

Finally she said, "If you keep staring at me like that, it'll make me crazy."

"I'm sorry."

"Well, don't apologize. Just don't look at me like that."

As though following orders, he turned his head and looked away.

Suddenly, at sight of his abjectness, she made a show of checking her watch. "Oh, dear. I had no idea it was so late. Excuse me. I'm just going to make a phone call." When he made a motion to follow her, she said, "No, why don't you wait here, I'll be right back," and hurried off toward the telephone booths in the lobby.

He sat on a folding chair in the corner of the room and waited. She seemed like a moody girl, but he had heard that Cat Eyes were that way. Besides, her moods made her even more beautiful. After five minutes, he looked at his watch and decided she must be finished with her telephone call. He kept his eyes pinned on the doorway, waiting for her to return. Then it dawned on him that she might not be able to see him, seated in the chair. He rose and stretched himself up on his toes, to make himself more visible in the crowd. He walked back to where she had left him. He waited and waited. He strolled out into the lobby to check the phone booths. They were empty. He went down the hall and dawdled outside the ladies' room, hoping she might emerge. Then he headed back into the auditorium, worried that he had fouled things up and she would think he had deserted her.

After half an hour had passed he was filled with panic. Obviously she had come back into the auditorium while he was in the lobby and, not finding him there, had left. Or worse yet, he had done something to irritate her. Sick with apprehension, he dashed back into the lobby, but it was empty. He leaned against the Coke machine, thinking of the sari he had so carefully wrapped, and quaking with anger at himself.

PROSENJIT slept very badly. When he awoke the next morning and tried to concentrate on his calculus text, his thoughts kept going back to Tanya. It didn't help matters that the box with the sari in it was sitting on his dresser. It bewildered him that after his trying to be so agreeable, the evening had turned out unsatisfactorily. He didn't understand why, but she seemed to be angry with him. Again and again, he repeated the exact words of their conversation, trying to figure out what had gone wrong. Finally, he went out for a walk, into the morning gloom, and as he trudged across the patchy brown grass of the soccer field next to the I House, he rehearsed what he might say to put himself back in her good graces. He paused for a moment to watch some boys kicking a soccer ball back and forth, and the memory of what he had felt like as a child, when the older boys in his village had excluded him from their games, came back in a rush.

He returned to his room, determined to finish his calculus, but within minutes he decided it was useless. He could not go on without talking to her. His need was so great that it made him feel ashamed, and he struggled against it, as if exercising self-control would signify strength. He lay on his bed with clenched fists, staring up at the ceiling. Then, in an involuntary movement, as reflexive as breathing, he found himself grabbing for the receiver and dialing her number. Once he heard the sound of the telephone ringing on the other end, he experienced immediate relief.

The woman with the heavy accent answered and told him that Tanya was not at home. An hour later, he called again and was told the same thing. The remainder of his day was spent waiting for an appropriate interval of time to pass so he could dial again.

It was not until eight that evening that he reached her. When he heard her voice, he immediately began to apologize for losing sight of her at the party. His words tumbled out unconsciously. To his surprise, she casually dismissed what had happened as "no big deal," and explained that she owed him an apology, too. It seemed that she had run into an old friend in the I House lobby and had been forced to leave without saying goodbye. He couldn't help but wonder if the old friend was a male or a female.

"When can I see you again?" he asked.

"I don't really know. . . ."

"How about Friday night?"

"I'm sorry . . . I already made other plans."

"When, then?"

She hesitated.

"Why don't you meet me for a coffee tomorrow afternoon?" he urged.

"I have something important I have to do, at Sproul Hall."

"Why don't we meet there?" he persisted.

"Oh . . . I don't know."

"Please? It would be so jolly to see you."

At three o'clock, he was waiting on the steps of Sproul Hall when she emerged from the rotating glass doors, holding a large white envelope in her hand. He called out her name and waved. She shielded her eyes from the sun and squinted in his direction, descending the steps slowly.

"I'm so happy we could meet," he gushed.

She gave him a cool look.

He trailed along after her. "What was so important that you had to do here?"

"Pick this up," she said, holding up the envelope. "It's an application to get into Berkeley."

"Oh, I didn't know that you wanted to attend the university," he said uncertainly, as they began walking toward the wooded area of campus. He had been brought up to believe that a wife should have freedom of ideas, but not necessarily a bachelor's degree from a top university.

"Of course I want to go to Berkeley."

"The curriculum here is very rigorous, especially for a young lady."

"Why should it be any harder for a girl?"

"It's not that it's any more difficult," he said, surprised at her vehemence. "It's that women do not need so much education as men."

She stopped dead in her tracks. "I can't believe you said that."

He flushed. She turned and marched up the path toward Faculty Glen, where the waters of a little creek could be heard trickling over stones. He followed, upbraiding himself for saying the wrong thing again. She stopped at the base of a gently rolling knoll where a stone bridge spanned the creek. The glade, which was enclosed by bent cyprus trees and dark ferns, had the tranquillity of a Japanese tea garden. She leaned against the railing of the bridge, looking down at the water below. He came up behind her, his eyes on her half-turned face. He positioned himself next to her on the railing, pretending to watch the water below. All he could think about was how delightful it would be to slip his arm around her waist and pull her toward him for an embrace. While he was wondering if she would permit such an intimacy, she broke the silence. "You remind me of my father. He doesn't think I should go to Berkeley either."

He was surprised by the anger her voice held. "I only meant that you should be prepared for the difficult curriculum."

"That's what he says, too."

He smiled at her, but she continued to stare into the water. It seemed that once again he had managed to turn her good humor into a morose mood. It was a shame that she should be so unhappy on such a beautiful day. The birds were singing, the air was clear and crisp, and they were together. He tried to change the subject by pointing to a blue-breasted bird and asking, "What are you calling these birds in California?" To his chagrin, she ignored his question. Finally he said, "You seem sad today."

"Well, I'm not."

"You should be happy. Be smiling."

She turned on him. "I hate it when guys tell me to smile."

Her words punctured him. She seemed adept at humiliating him, and for each snub he endured, he was building a wall of resentment. He hated himself for loving her. "It is only that you look so pretty when you smile."

She took the application out of the envelope and spread it out on the railing. A few minutes passed while she studied it. Then he heard her ask, "You don't really think I'll flunk out, do you?"

"No. No. I didn't mean any such thing," he hastened to say.

"My grades are good enough," she said, more to herself than to him, "but I have to get three letters of recommendation."

"That shouldn't be so difficult," he offered.

"I just hate to go back to my high school and ask my teachers."

"Why? They are liking to write letters of recommendation."

"They might not remember me. I mean, one or two of them might, but I never opened my mouth in class," and she went on to explain how timid she had been in high school, and how her classmates had always treated her like an outcast. He listened sympathetically to what she said, quite pleased to be made the recipient of her confidences. He couldn't help but feel that they were very much alike. Doing his best to be consoling, he said, "It's clear as day that you have the aptitude."

"It's not my teachers I'm afraid of," she admitted. "It's my father. He doesn't want me to get into Berkeley."

The look of concern on her face made him feel powerful, and he launched into a story. "In my case, when I first spoke of pursuing higher studies in the States, my mother was skeptical. She said, '*Chataiye shue lakh takar swapna*,' meaning that I was dreaming about millions while sleeping on a reed mattress. But I persisted in spite of her objections. All you need is to be trusting yourself."

"Do you really think so?"

"Oh yes."

"Even though my father says I'm not smart enough?"

"He probably is afraid of losing you from the home. That's how it was with my mother. But in the case of your family, you need not go so far away, so there should be no problem."

"You don't know my father."

"Give him time. He will come around," he said, mustering up his courage and moving closer to her. In a jerky movement he reached around her waist and rested his hand there.

"You're a real friend," she said, momentarily bolstered by his words of encouragement. She threw her own arm around his waist and gave him a grateful little squeeze back, before she pulled away.

TANYA sat in front of the phone on Cindy's nightstand for a while before she had the nerve to dial his number. She knew it by heart because she had called it many times, just to hear the sound of his voice. This time when he answered, she didn't hang up. She had fortified herself by drinking one glass of chablis.

"Hello." There was a lazy twang to his voice that made her heart skip. She could hear the Rolling Stones blaring in the background.

"Hello, Jeff?"

"You got me."

She had him, but what to do? She looked over at Cindy, sprawled on her stomach across the mattress, filing her nails intently. "This is Tanya Tarasoff. You know, I met you at the market?"

"Tanya Tarasoff?"

"The girl in the flannel nightgown."

"Oh, yeah," he said, with some warmth. "How are you?"

She was overjoyed that he remembered her. "What're you doing?" she asked.

"Just sitting here, ripped."

She could imagine him with his matted brown hair and drooping eyelids. "I know you're going to think it's weird, calling up out of the blue, but I was wondering . . . well, somebody gave me tickets to the Elvin Bishop concert at the Bear's Lair and I was wondering if you wanted to go." She glanced over at Cindy, who gave her a nod of encouragement.

"I don't think I could deal with the Bear's Lair."

She was conscious of the tickets she gripped in her hand. She had purchased them that afternoon at the desk in the Student Union. They had cost her eight dollars. "Believe it or not, it's a good place to dance."

"Oh yeah?"

"It's true. They move the tables and chairs to one side . . ."

"When is it?"

"Friday night." She tried to conceal the tremor in her voice.

"Well, shit, what are you doing right now?"

"Basically nothing."

"Do you get loaded?"

"Yeah, sure."

"Yeah? Well, 'Star Trek' is coming on at nine. Why don't you come by and we'll smoke a number?"

"Now?"

"Yeah, but hurry, cause I'm going to crash early."

He gave her directions, and she hung up. In one wild, ecstatic motion, she bounced off the bed and shrieked, "I'm going to his house! I'm going to his house!"

"Tonight?"

She was jumping up and down, shrieking with excitement. "Yes, yes, he invited me over!"

"Calm down and tell me what he said."

"Can I tell my mom I'm spending the night with you, in case something happens?"

"Yes. What did he say?"

"He wants to watch 'Star Trek' with me."

"See what happens when you take my advice?" said Cindy triumphantly. "Now maybe you'll get off my case about being too up-front."

Tanya ran over to the record player and put on Janis Joplin. "Do you realize what this means? He doesn't live with her after all." She turned up the volume. Janis's rasping voice, singing "Get It While You Can," swelled out of the speakers. She skipped over to Cindy and threw her arms around her neck. "I'll always listen to you from now on."

"I'll remember you said that," said Cindy, who was now applying polish to her nails.

"What a mess," said Tanya, as she surveyed herself in the mirror, making a face at the old jeans and baggy sweater.

"Borrow anything you want," said Cindy.

Tanya opened the closet door, peered in, and began yanking clothes off their hangers and holding them up to her body.

"What about your diaphragm?"

"What about it?"

"What are you going to do?"

"It's a safe time. Anyway, probably nothing will happen."

"Be serious."

"Just wait. We'll be just about to get into something and Marsha will come waltzing in."

"I'll bet you she's out of the picture."

"Oh . . . I don't know. I don't know. How could he like me after he's been with her?" She gave Cindy a searching look. "Anyway, he said he wants to crash early."

"That means with you, dummy."

As Tanya slipped into one of Cindy's turtlenecks she asked, "How many guys do you think you've slept with, if you were to add them all up?"

"I don't know . . . a dozen. It's hard to say."

"Well, I've only been with a half."

"You mean that jerk from high school?"

"It was the first time, and I couldn't really tell if it happened."

"Here," said Cindy. "I'm going to make up a fuck list," and she reached for a yellow legal pad lying on the floor. "I can get a mental picture of where we were when we met, what song was playing, and how it happened."

"Look at my stomach, it's sticking out," moaned Tanya, standing in front of the mirror, zipping up her jeans. "How could I ever let him see me undressed?"

"Oh, please, don't talk to me about stomachs. Here I'm up to eight guys already."

"Jesus Christ."

"I'm sure Janice's got twice as many."

"At least," said Tanya, as she tucked in the navy turtleneck. "Janice is a mooch. It's a good thing she's not around, or she'd try to snake him away. Oh, my God. I forgot to shave under my arms."

"Forget it. He'll never notice."

She looked at Cindy, unsure whether to trust her judgment on such a vital matter.

"Hurry. You're going to miss 'Star Trek,' " said Cindy, turning her attention back to the list. "God, I almost forgot about that flake I met at Kip's. He was the worst."

"Who was the best?" asked Tanya as she clipped her hair back in a barrette.

"The Candleman. We're really in sync. But then I always tend to think the one I'm with now is the best."

"Mine was the guy I almost ended up with at the Russian River," said Tanya, thinking about the boy who had never called her back after their one evening together. She prayed that Jeff Flanders wouldn't be like him.

"Ugh, here's one I'd like to forget," said Cindy, hoisting herself off the mattress and waving the paper at Tanya. "I picked him up inside Shakespeare Books and went back to his apartment. The minute I looked through his record collection, I wanted to puke. He had all these sappy Neil Diamond records. But I didn't know how to say no. I'll never do that again."

"It's hard to say no when you know you're going to hurt someone's feelings."

"The guy even sang along with that dumb Neil Diamond song 'Solitary Man.' It gives me the creeps to think about him."

"Maybe the Musketeer won't even be interested."

Cindy rolled her eyes. "Give me a break."

In fifteen minutes Tanya was on her way, gliding unseeingly down Durant toward the grungy part of town, south of Telegraph. Before she rang his bell, she ran a comb through her hair and smeared on some lip gloss.

The room was dark except for the light from the television, and a candle that had been melted onto an orange crate and gave off a weird glow. He was sitting on a frayed sofa with another boy, and motioned her in. She looked down at her hands, and her nails shone iridescent pink.

"You look different," he said. She wondered if he meant better or worse.

A German shepherd puppy bounded over to her and nuzzled her. "That's Trotsky," he said. "Just push him away if he bothers you." She sat down on the couch.

The other boy was engrossed in the program and didn't bother to introduce himself. He had a thick beard that he absentmindedly played with as he laughed at the show.

"Here, take a hit off this." Jeff handed her a joint and turned back to the TV. She put the joint to her lips and inhaled, the way she had seen Cindy do. The smoke seared her lungs, and she coughed, looking quickly at him to see if he thought she was being stupid. He was watching Mr. Spock and didn't seem to notice. She had forgotten how good-looking he was. She sat there in silence and pretended to watch.

When the commercial came on he looked at her and said, "Do you feel anything?" He indicated the joint. She bobbed her head up and down. "It's good stuff, isn't it?" And she nodded again in agreement.

Her eyes roamed around the room, looking for a trace of Marsha. Happily, she could see no evidence of a feminine touch that would signify her existence. There was a poster of Jimi Hendrix and beneath it, propped against the wall, an electric guitar, with mother-of-pearl inlay on the front. Loads of paperback books were stacked on the floor, with intimidating titles like *The Origin of Totalitarianism* and *The Birth of Tragedy*. He must read all of these, she thought to herself. He was so much smarter than the guys who went to Merritt. Then she remembered that she had never told him that she went to junior college. Sooner or later he would find out, and then she would really be ashamed. Somehow she would have to tell him the truth.

"It's good weed," he was saying to the guy with the beard, "but you're charging too much a lid."

The Beard drew on the joint and gave him a shrug. "What do you think, I'd rip you off?" He passed her the joint, and she felt obliged to take another hit.

"Hey, man, relax. I never said that." The Musketeer opened the plastic bag that held the grass and sniffed it. Then his friend sniffed it. Their noses were bent over the bag, twitching; their faces were very solemn.

"Mexican Red," said the Beard, "from Oaxaca."

"It's good shit, but *très cher.*"

They looked like anteaters, Tanya thought, with their quivering noses. Mexican Red, Acapulco Gold. She told herself not to laugh or else he'd think she was laughing at him.

When "Star Trek" was over, the Beard got up to leave, and the Musketeer followed him to the door. "Hey, man, stay in touch."

She thought, Finally we're alone together and I'll be able to talk. The Mexican Red had come on in a rush and the room was spinning. She was glad when he switched off the set.

"Where do you live?" he asked.

"With my friend Cindy," she lied.

"Oh, yeah? What's she like?"

"She's great. She'll try anything."

"What about you? Will you try anything?"

"No, I'm too scared," she said, loving how he looked her in the eye while they talked.

"Scared of what?"

"Lots of things. I'd be scared to take acid, for instance. I might do something crazy. I always have nightmares, and it might be like that on acid."

"Not if you're with someone you can trust." When he said this she melted. "What do you want to hear?" he asked, getting up to put on a record.

"Anything you like," she said. She wanted him to come back to the couch. She looked at him kneeling by the stereo. He was thin and agile, like a thief.

"Organic mescaline is some good shit," he said. "Maybe I can get us some."

If he was talking about taking mescaline with her, he definitely wanted to see her again. At least one more time. He put on "Let It Bleed." She was sure he had a great record collection, with all the albums she loved. When he sat back down, he leaned his body against hers and propped his legs up on the orange crate. She wanted to ask him about Marsha but didn't dare.

"So, have you been thinking about me?" he asked, a mischievous glint in his eye.

"What makes you think that?"

"You called me up, didn't you?"

She blushed.

He nestled closer. "What were you thinking?"

"At first after the market, I was real happy. Then I got depressed, thinking I'd never see you again." She looked at him. "Did you ever think about me?"

"Yes."

"Well, what did you think?"

"I'll tell you later." He grinned.

"Oh, come on," she pleaded. "I told *you*."

He just laughed. Then he said, "One thing about you, you've got great lips," and he touched them lightly with his finger tip. "They're so full. That's the first thing I noticed about you, at the market. Before I saw your nightgown. You looked so lost, bundled up, with your raincoat over that nightgown." And then he started kissing her, and she remembered how the boy at the Russian River had told her it was all in the kiss and that she didn't know how to French.

She felt giddy and twisted her head to the side, burrowing herself into his neck. He was warm and smelled like a man.

"You act so innocent, but I don't think you are," he whispered. "The way you put on lip gloss, I think you know all about those lips of yours," and he pulled back and grinned at her.

She got up from the couch to find the bathroom and opened one of the doors. "Oh, it's a bedroom," she said, her voice going high.

"Come on," he said laughing. He stood up and reached for her hand. Tanya laughed too, because she felt that was what she was supposed to do.

He led her into the other room and dropped down on a mattress, pulling her with him and kissing her again. "You taste good," he said, rolling her over on her back. Her arms lay awkwardly by her side, like dead limbs. She didn't know him well enough to speak a single word. It was as if she were straitjacketed. "What do you like?" he asked. She couldn't find an answer, so she kissed him back. "Relax," he said. "You're too uptight." She wanted to say, "No, I'm not," but she knew he was right. He said, "Before when you asked me did I think about you, this is what I thought," and he started to unfasten the waistband of her jeans and lift up her turtleneck. She felt she should say, "No, don't," but then she decided it was too late.

When she woke up in the middle of the night her mouth was dry. She tried to swallow, but it felt like cotton. She became aware of him sleeping heavily next to her. Under the tangled sheets, the whole bed smelled like sex. She wondered if her mascara was smeared all over her face, and she searched for her purse by the side of the bed. When she found it, she crept up and groped along the wall with her hand until she found the bathroom, closing the door gently behind her and switching on the light.

The blotchy face that looked back at her in the mirror made her wince. She opened his cabinet, and the first thing that caught her eye was a vial of Lily of the Valley that Marsha must have left. It figured that she wore such a cloying scent. She closed the door softly. On the sink was one sliver of soap, floating in its dish, which she used to scrub away the dark smudges under her eyes. She combed the snarls out of her hair and fished for the miniature flask of Binaca at the bottom of her purse. When she opened it, the bottle had a ring of grime and sand around its neck. She took a quick swig and gasped, shooting her breath out like a dragon. Now she was at least prepared to wake up next to him in the morning. She turned out the light and tiptoed back to bed. Crawling under the covers, she lay there for what seemed like hours, listening to him snore, wanting to snuggle up next to him, but afraid to disturb his sleep.

Sunlight came streaming in through the venetian blinds. He rolled over and opened his eyes.

"I've got to go," she said, because she felt he might want her to leave.

"What time is it?" he said, yawning.

"Eight-thirty."

"Wait for a minute. I'm just going to take a shower," and he climbed out of bed. She saw his naked body for the first time, although she was too shy to take a really good look. He was so slender his ribs stuck out.

She lay in bed listening to the water running, wondering what he thought of her. Then she got up to put her clothes back on so she wouldn't have to dress in front of him. She had to search for her underwear, which she finally found tangled up under the sheets. The rest of her clothes were wadded up in a ball on the floor. After she was dressed, she perched stiffly on the edge of his bed. A black leather phone book lay open on the floor, and she leafed through it. There were lots of girls' names, written in a loose scrawl. When she heard the water stop and the shower stall snap shut, she quickly put it back where she had found it.

He walked back into the room with a towel tied around his waist. She was bent over, lacing her shoes, hiding the guilty flush on her cheeks. "Do you want some breakfast?" he asked.

She didn't know whether he was just being polite. "I don't really eat much in the morning," she said, looking for a signal of how he felt.

"Well, have some juice, at least." He began to bustle around in the kitchen, pulling boxes of cereal from the shelf and cutting fruit.

All she could think of was, did he want to see her again.

"So what are you doing today?" he asked. He had arranged a big bowl of granola for himself, heaped with slices of banana.

"Going to class," she said, before she remembered that she had never confessed about junior college. She cast her eyes down and hoped that he wouldn't know she was lying. She noticed how shapely his forearms were, as he spooned up the cereal. "Everytime a new semester starts, I get all psyched out. . . ." Her voice trailed off. He raised his eyebrows quizzically. She wondered why she had bothered to say anything, she sounded so lame.

He read the sports page while he ate, and didn't look up to talk to her once. When he finished, he said, "Here, let me lay some of this on you," and he dipped into the plastic bag and portioned out some grass.

"Hey," she said, "I really want to try mescaline with you," groping for any thread that would connect her future to his.

"I'll see what I can do." He walked her to the front door. She waited for him to ask her for her number, but all he said was, "Thanks for last night." Then he kissed her lightly on the lips and opened the door.

She blurted out, "Hey, I forgot to give you my number."

"Oh Jesus, that's right," he said and went to get a pen. While he was writing it down, he said, "I'll give this guy a call who knows where to get some good shit."

She moved uncertainly down the stairs. "That would be great," she said, looking up at him, standing in a splotch of sun, with a grin on his face.

"Talk to you later," he called, as she turned and went off.

ON Saturday morning, Prosenjit took the bus down to the Berkeley Community Theater to buy tickets for the Buffy Sainte-Marie concert. He had never heard of this singer, but Tanya had mentioned that she was so popular, it would be impossible to get good seats. He had been looking forward to the date with painful eagerness, and was unable to relax until he had secured tickets. He could not help but think that in the dark of the theater, he'd be able to take her hand in his and perhaps even steal a kiss. Lately the thought of physical contact was very much on his mind, even though he admonished himself for thinking of her so freely.

Upon his return to the I House, he telephoned her to confirm their arrangements. When she heard his voice she said, with real distress, "God, I'm sorry, I won't be able to go to the concert with you."

"Not go with me?"

"I think I'm having a relapse. I woke up with a sore throat."

"By tonight maybe you will feel better."

"No," she said, "I'm definitely not going to risk getting sick again. So why don't you go ahead and invite someone else?"

"I don't want to go with anyone else."

"Don't be ridiculous." She laughed. "It'll be a great concert."

"I will wait until I can go with you," he said sullenly. "You're the only reason I wanted to go in the first place."

"But you've already bought the tickets."

"It is of no consequence," he replied, in a piteous voice, and no matter what she said to persuade him to go without her, he stubbornly refused.

*　　*　　*

Later that morning he went over to her house. It wasn't that he suspected her of lying; he just wanted to be certain that she was at home, nursing her sore throat. It meant skipping a tutorial session with Dr. Wehausen, but he convinced himself it didn't matter. He hid across the street, behind the oleander bush, for what seemed like a long time. Then her front door opened and she walked out. His heart pounded violently in his chest. She was dressed in tight jeans, her hair pulled back in a jaunty ponytail. She did not look as if she was suffering from a relapse of bronchitis. He watched as she headed down the street on foot, waiting until she turned the corner before he followed.

He trailed her four blocks to where the bus to the university stopped. Then he hung back in an alcove. She was standing reading a paperback, mouthing the words to herself. When he thought enough time had elapsed, he stepped out of the shadows and went up to her. She did not hear him approach. "Good day," he said, a slight tremor in his voice. "I am happy to see that you have recovered."

She whirled around. "What are you doing here?" It was quite clear she was not pleased to see him.

"I was close by paying a visit to the hardware store."

"All the way over here?"

"Yes. It is not so very far. Besides, I needed a particular tool that is difficult to find."

"You shouldn't go sneaking up on people like that."

He flushed. "It's a jolly good piece of luck that I even spotted you." His voice trailed off. He was surprised at how the scowl on her face changed her appearance so dramatically. She looked almost fierce. "You do not still have your sore throat?"

"Yes. It still hurts."

He blinked. "Do you mind if I stand with you for the bus?"

"It's a free country."

He kept looking directly into her eyes, but she wouldn't return his look. Finally he said, "I thought you were too sick to leave the house."

She turned on him. "I'm too sick to go hear music tonight, but that doesn't mean I don't have some errands to do." They stood in silence for a few minutes, then she lifted her book to eye level and began to read. She acted as though he weren't there. He shuffled over to the newspaper stand and pretended to read the headlines through the glass. He believed that if only he were more charming, he could talk her out of feeling sick. It was his fault she wasn't going to the concert with him that night. Then he heard the bus pulling up and he saw her mounting the steps. He ran to the curb and called out, "I will ride with you if that's all right?" Before she could answer, he scrambled up the steps. He followed her to the back and slid in by her side.

"I hate to take you out of your way," she said. "I'm in a rush to meet a friend."

"I understand. I'm on my way, too."

The bus lurched forward, climbing up Solano Avenue into the hills. She kept her face turned away from him as she stared out the window, with the book open in her lap and her finger marking the place where she had left off reading. They rode along in silence. He let his knee bounce against her leg, but still she refused to look in his direction. He chose his words carefully, afraid of saying the wrong thing. "We're still friends, aren't we?"

"Of course."

"Then why aren't you going out with me tonight?"

She threw her arms up in exasperation. "I've already told you. I don't feel well."

He could stand it no longer. "Who is your friend you are meeting?"

"No one you know."

"A friend from I House?"

"What makes you think everyone I hang out with lives at the I House?"

"Is it a boy or a girl?"

"What difference can that make to you?"

A bitter retort leaped to his tongue, but he restrained himself. He thought about the sari he had purchased for her. The least she could do was to treat him with civility, when he was sacrificing so much for her. He had a great desire to hurt her as much as she was hurting him. He pouted in silence, his face filling with anger.

Finally he said, "I have something urgent to talk to you about."

"Urgent?"

"Yes. I have been wanting to tell it to you since a few days back."

"Well, what is it?"

"My mother has written to me urging marriage."

"Marriage?" Her face brightened for the first time. "Who are you marrying?"

"I do not know. It will be arranged. Here, look at this," and he reached into his jacket and took out a folded wad of paper. Shaking it open, he thrust it under her nose.

She spread the paper out on her lap. It was the matrimonial section from the *Times of India* that his mother had sent. The page was filled with long columns of fine print. Some of the items were circled in red ink. She picked out one and read aloud in an amused voice, " 'Beautiful, convent-educated East Bengali girl, eighteen years, for well-established electrical engineer. One hundred and seventy-seven centimeters long. Fair complexion. Write Box 65221.' " She looked up from the page. "Is *she* one of your possibilities?"

"Yes, only there are so many to choose from."

"How bizarre."

He went on, expecting her to be impressed. "My mother has made some selections."

"Your mother?" she said, incredulous. "You mean you let your mother decide for you?"

"Parent-planned marriage is the custom in my country."

"How dumb," and she turned away.

He snatched the paper out of her hand. "It's not for you to speak disrespectfully of my mother."

"I'm not saying anything against your mother. I don't even know your mother. It just seems like a weird custom, that's all."

He sulked.

"Oh, don't be so sensitive. I wasn't putting down your mother."

"In my case there will be no problem fixing up a match. I will be much in demand."

"I'm sure you will," she said. "But what about love? Don't you ever think about that?"

"Love comes after marriage."

"Well, if that's what you believe, I think you should go back to India and do it."

"You do?"

"Yes. Go back and get married, if you can't make up your own mind."

He wanted to tell her that it was she he intended to marry, but he couldn't find the words.

When he didn't say anything she said, "I'd never let my parents choose for me. They'd pick someone I couldn't stand." There was something about her expression, so righteous and emphatic, that bore into his soul. She went on, "Love is the only thing that counts. It's the only thing I ever really think about." Suddenly she rose from the seat and yanked the cord above her head. "This is where I get off." He got up to let her pass and then, to her growing irritation, followed. When they were out on the street, she walked at such a fast clip that he was forced to run to keep up with her.

She stopped short and turned on him. "This is where we say goodbye. I'm meeting my friend."

"Yes, yes, I know." He stood staring at her. "Please, is your friend a boy?" he asked miserably.

"I can't believe you keep asking me that question."

"I want to know it."

"It's really none of your business."

He blinked as though a cat had scratched him in the eye, quick and searing. "But you don't understand," he cried. "For me the question of an arranged marriage can no longer arise."

"What are you talking about?"

"I have committed myself to you!"

"But you don't even know me," she exclaimed.

"I know you well enough."

"No you don't."

"It's you I want to marry," he said, hanging his head.

"Listen," she said, not really taking his declaration seriously, "we're still friends. Good friends. But right now the last thing that's on my mind is getting married."

"If it's not romance, it's nothing," he said, feeling more debased by the moment.

"Don't say that," she said, reaching out toward him. "I really like you."

"I can't go on like this," he mumbled.

"I really don't know what else to say," she said, growing more uncomfortable.

"Just say goodbye," and he turned and headed down the block, hoping that she would beckon him back, that it had all been a bad dream. He kept listening for her voice, but when he reached the far corner and stole a glance over his shoulder, he saw that she had disappeared.

WHEN she awoke it was still dark. She knew she should go back to sleep. A clock ticked away at the side of her bed, and she grabbed it to look at the time. She had hours to wait before dawn. It seemed impossible to her that she could lie in place through the night. She shut her eyes, and immediately cold cement walls enclosed her. Soon the noise of the clock took over. It was like being caught underground in a mining accident, listening to a shovel clinking away, far, far above her. Her mind groped for a way out, but she was helpless, just as she was helpless to make him love her, helpless to find a release from the obsession that gripped her.

She remembered how he had cradled her in his arms, and wrapped them around her waist. "We fit so well together," he had whispered. His soft breath against her ear made her shiver. That tenderness in his touch had left her believing that he had never loved anyone else as he had her. How could he not call after that night? She tossed over on her side and wrapped her arms around her pillow, pretending it was he. It seemed impossible that what had been such a magic moment in her life was nothing special for him. But it had been six days since she had slept with him, and not a word.

Every night she had waited for the telephone call. She had stayed home on purpose because she didn't trust either Alex or her father to give her the message. Her entire life revolved around that phone. When it rang, her heart leaped with excitement, and she prayed, "Please, God, let it be him." Her future was played out in those few seconds before she learned the identity of the caller. More often than not, it turned out to be Prosenjit, pestering her again.

She lay on her back and stared up into the dark. The other day in the cafeteria she had said to Cindy, "I'm positive he'll never call."

"How much do you want to bet?" said Cindy.

"I'll bet you a dinner at an expensive restaurant."

"All right, if he calls, you're taking me," said Cindy. "Any place I want."

"Don't worry, you'll be buying."

"No I won't. I already know just where I want to go."

Cindy's optimism had made her feel much better. But the relief lasted only for a few hours, until she was back at home.

At first, when she was still filled with hope, she had been full of the energy of a pole vaulter. She felt like running and springing and hugging everyone on the street. She barely slept, and meals were taken in a few hasty bites. She was certain that her days of loneliness were at an end, and she smiled to think how much difference one little meeting at the market could make. If she hadn't gone to the Coop with her mother, she might have missed the great love of her life. Fate was working for her, there was no doubt.

She had passed his apartment every day after school, riding the bus from the Merritt campus over to Telegraph and Dwight, and walking the three blocks to his corner. She knew all the landmarks along the route and came to think of them possessively. She couldn't resist calling his house several times a day. Most of the time he wasn't home and the phone just rang and rang. The few times he did answer, she hung up. It was a struggle, but she rationed herself to only one hang-up a day.

The other night when she had discussed the problem with Cindy, Cindy had encouraged her to be aggressive. "What difference does it make if you call him or he calls you? It's all going to come out the same in the end."

"I don't want to seem desperate," Tanya said.

"Who's desperate? You're just expressing your feelings."

But Tanya was afraid that if she came on too strong now, she'd chase him away. Why was it that the person she loved didn't love her? She thought about the times it had been the other way around, like with Prosenjit Poddar. The fact that he was infatuated with her made her want to run. Yet just when she wished he would fade out of the picture, he had become even more persistent. He clung to her like a barnacle. She knew she was going to have to extricate herself from that situation, but she postponed giving him the brush-off. The thought of confronting him and hurting his feelings was abhorrent, and somehow she believed if she just ignored the problem, it would disappear. Still, she was experiencing some guilt, and she believed that what was happening to her now was her punishment for treating him so shabbily.

Obviously there was someone else in Jeff Flanders's life. Maybe it was Marsha; maybe it was somebody new. He had an animal magnetism that would make him attractive to any girl. Somehow Marsha didn't threaten her as much as a new love. When she had ventured the theory of a new woman to Cindy, Cindy had scoffed. "Oh, sure. He met the perfect girl, and now he's reciting poetry to her and weaving daisies into her pubic hair."

"Maybe he has."

"Be serious."

"I'm in love," Tanya moaned, "and he's never going to call me again."

"Listen. If the relationship is meant to be, it'll be," Cindy said. "In the meantime, I can't take hearing about it anymore."

The sounds of morning came through the window, birds chirping in the bush. There had been something so discouraging about Cindy silencing her. It was as though suddenly she was involved in a hopeless cause. It was a dreadful thought, but it occurred to her that the fight might be all one-sided. She might be alone, reaching and striving and suffering for someone who didn't even care. If this was true, all that was left was for her to give up and admit that it was over. But she was unwilling to do that. Incapable, in fact. She got up to face the day, already exhausted by her struggle, and cowed into a state of self-loathing.

EARLY in January, Jal Mehta drove back from the Sonoma Valley with his new American girlfriend, Alice Cross. They had taken a leisurely ten days to explore the northern California grape country, meandering through the vineyards and stopping for a few days in an enchanting little inn which had been built during the Gold Rush. Jal, usually so cool and collected, was still reeling from the success of his holiday with Alice. He arrived at the I House eager to tell someone about his vacation. The DasGupta brothers would have been the perfect audience, but they were away for the Pac-8 playoffs at Washington State, and that left only Prosenjit, a poor second choice. He considered his friend, no doubt studying in his room at this very moment, and decided to roust him out for a pizza dinner at Giovanni's. Quickly showering and changing into fresh clothes, he dashed up the stairs to the sixth floor. He thought he heard conversation coming from inside Prosenjit's room, and when he knocked and got no answer, he burst through the door.

The sight that met his eyes jolted him. Soiled clothes were heaped on the floor, and components of electronics equipment were scattered about the room. There was a stereo receiver that Prosenjit had been assembling, lying belly up, a ganglia of wires sprung from its insides.

Jal stepped into the room. The shutters were closed tight, the air close and fetid. In the midst of the wreckage, Prosenjit was sitting, hunched over his tape recorder, fingering one of the dials. He didn't even turn around to see who had entered.

Jal was mystified. In all the years of their acquaintance, Prosenjit had always taken a bos'n's pride in running a tight ship.

Tanya, Lidia, Alex, and Vitally Tarasoff, 1952

Prosenjit's village: Balurghat, West Bengal, 1982

People's Park demonstration: Berkeley, May 1969

Tanya (left) *and Lidia* (at her side) *at family party*

Tanya, age seventeen

NAVAL ARCHITECTURE & MARINE ENGINEERING SOCIETY
ANNUAL GROUP PHOTOGRAPH

Prosenjit Poddar (seated first row, second from left), *student at IIT.: Kharagpur, West Bengal, 1966*

Dr. Larry Moore, 1974

Dr. Harvey Powelson, 1969

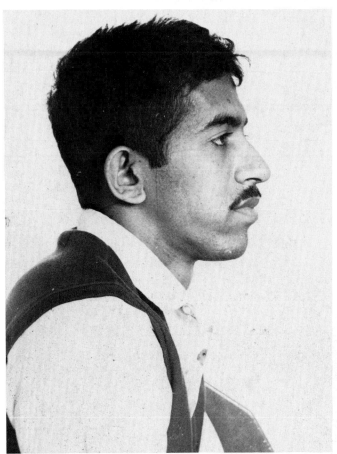

Prosenjit Poddar, police mug shot: October 28, 1969

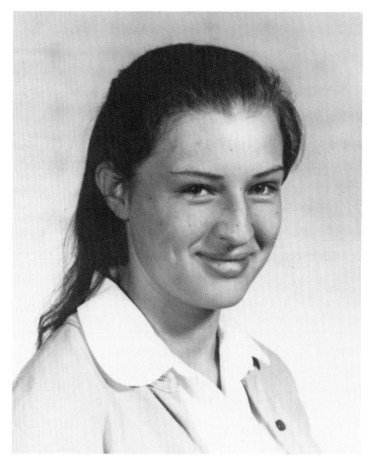

Tanya, high school graduation photo

Something had obviously snapped. "What's going on here?" Jal asked, as he waded through the litter and made a place for himself on the bed.

Prosenjit met his eyes for the first time and uttered a doleful sigh.

"Are you ill?"

He mumbled a response that Jal didn't quite catch.

"No? Well, how about going down to Giovanni's for a pizza?"

"No, man, what's the point?"

"A change of scenery and some fresh air. This room's stifling."

"I will stay in the room, without dinner."

"What's got into you?"

"If she's going to be so much trouble, I can just give her up."

"It's Tanya, isn't it?" he asked, with considerable irritation. Wasn't it just a few short weeks ago, over breakfast, that Prosenjit had burbled something about how happy the girl had made him? Jal, in spite of his skeptical attitude, had assumed that for some reason the pretty American had succumbed to the Bong's overtures and the courtship was going smoothly. "All right, start from the top," he commanded, "and tell me what's gone wrong."

Prosenjit related the events of New Year's Eve in a dull, listless tone, explaining how she had disappeared without saying goodbye. He repeated, word for word, his phone conversation with her the next day, in which she apologized for leaving with someone else. As he talked, his listlessness seemed to fall away, and, in order that Jal get an accurate picture of what had happened, he became more and more intent on capturing each nuance of feeling. He did not, however, reveal to his friend that he had purchased a betrothal sari that was at this moment stashed away in his closet; nor did he confess to him how he had hidden outside her house, behind an oleander bush. When he got to the part about their "chance meeting" at the bus stop, he began to stammer violently.

"Hang on," said Jal, waving his arm to make Prosenjit stop. "You mean to say that just by coincidence, you met her at the bus?"

"Yes, a very remarkable occurrence. She was on her way to meet someone else."

"But I don't see what your problem is."

"Why didn't she keep her date with me that evening? Why did she say she was sick?"

"She may very well have had errands to do that day, and then chosen to stay in at night. It's a well-known fact that sore throats become more pronounced on wet, rainy evenings."

"But her manner was rude!"

"Perhaps she did not enjoy the surprise of finding you at the bus stop."

"Is that good enough reason for her not to tell me who she was meeting?"

"So she was meeting a friend. No big deal."

"What if it was the same gent who she went off with on New Year's Eve?"

"Rubbish. Don't surmise anything about a lady unless you have absolute proof."

"It's very strange, you know, because previously her father came to the dance to pick her up. He always retrieved her before midnight, but he must have made a special allowance."

"Will you please stop? You don't even *know* there is another gent!"

"In that case, why didn't she let *me* escort her home?"

"Just as you said—you were nowhere to be found when the time came." Jal rose to his feet and kicked aside a mound of soiled clothes. "The important thing is to take it easy. American girls are sometimes hard to understand." It annoyed him to see Prosenjit, the boy who had always been so aloof and diffident, wallowing in self-pity. He began to pace back and forth. "Did I ever tell you about the fiasco with the girl from Wheeler Auditorium?"

Prosenjit shook his head.

"She was in my section. Physics 10. You know, the course that's an excuse for mentally deficient freshmen to fulfill their science requirement? The one where they view *Space Odyssey 2001* as homework? Well, she was in my section, but it wasn't until the lecture that I noticed her, smiling at me in the most inviting way. Her name was Carole, and she said she was raised in Los Angeles. I was quite surprised, but she invited me to her apartment for an authentic Mexican dinner the very next evening." He broke off. Prosenjit was sitting with his head buried in his hands. "Don't you even want to know why?"

Prosenjit gave no sign.

"When I walked into the room, she had the rock 'n' roll up so high that conversation was impossible. She herself was draped across her couch in a revealing outfit. The so-called dinner was not forthcoming. She offered me a marijuana cigarette and then came right out and suggested sexual intercourse."

It took a minute before this filtered through to Prosenjit. Jerking his head up, he cried, "It's not possible!"

"I'm telling you the truth!"

"What did you do?"

"Far be it from me to refuse a lady."

Prosenjit said nothing, but the disapproval showed on his face.

"Afterward she brought out our meal. A mishmash of Mexican food, burned and totally inedible. I left shortly, and didn't see the lady until two days later, in the lecture hall. I felt it was only proper, of course, to invite her to the cinema. And so I behaved as a gentleman and did."

"Of course."

"The shocking thing was, when I went up to her, she acted as though she didn't know me."

"How do you mean?"

"She ignored me. I did not exist. You never can tell what these American girls are up to."

"Are you saying that Tanya is this way?" cried Prosenjit, now worked up into a fretful state.

"Not at all. From everything you've told me I can see that Tanya's had the right kind of upbringing. I'm sure she's just the opposite of this Carole, who's into, what would you say—free love."

"Free love?"

"Yes. The kind of love that is here today, gone tomorrow. Generally, partners only exchange first names so that they can't even find each other again. I'm just telling you all of this as a warning. You have to take it very tentatively to be sure how the young lady really feels."

"But I have already written home," Prosenjit blurted out, "and told them not to fix up a match. I have said, right out, that I am committed to an American girl."

Jal was stunned. "You told your mother?"

Prosenjit nodded miserably. "I posted the letter a few weeks back."

Jal walked to Prosenjit and put his arm around his shoulder. "Don't worry. You haven't done anything that can't be rectified. You wait and see, the next time you speak to Tanya, you'll clear up the misunderstanding." But even as he attempted to soothe his friend's hurt, the thought flashed through his mind that while Tanya appeared to be naive and innocent, there was something feline in her nature that made her suspect. Perhaps she was not as blameless as she seemed.

All the next week, Prosenjit brooded over Tanya. He had wanted to tell Jal about the sari stashed away in his closet, but his pride prevented him from doing so. Now, alone and stewing in his misery, he savagely cursed himself for making an ass of himself before her. He had revealed his love in the most degrading way. Worse yet, he had given her the ultimatum that she must commit herself to him or else they couldn't continue as friends. Of course she had rejected that flat out. He couldn't understand it; one moment she permitted him to slip his arm around her waist and the next she said she wasn't "interested" in romance. At all times, she seemed coolly indifferent to his suffering. He felt humiliated and could not suppress a desire to somehow hurt her in return. He imagined all the cutting remarks he could make to get back at her, but none of them seemed adequate. He was ashamed of himself for having such base thoughts, but he felt he could not rest easy until he had punished her. "She's an ill-mannered slut," he muttered, wondering again who the person was she had been meeting that afternoon. He was obsessed with learning the identity of this mystery man, for he was certain that it was someone of the opposite sex. He was sure, too, that she was laughing behind his back;

maybe they were both laughing behind his back. It was absurd to care what they thought of him, but he couldn't help himself.

Finally, in what he considered the ultimate blow, he made up his mind not to go to the next folk dance. Certainly she would notice his absence and feel chastened. If she wanted to see him, she would have to seek him out in his room. Then he would snub her. He could see her standing in his doorway, hanging her head, mumbling an apology. He would tell her how rude she had been and take his time to decide if things could be made right. He was proud of his resolution.

But on the day of the dance, he began to feel agitated. He was so restless he couldn't sit still. He wondered if she planned to show up at the dance with her mystery man. If she did, she would no doubt make a spectacle of herself, dancing with the man in public. He tried to think of other things, but he had no command over his own thoughts. An hour before the dance, he came to the conclusion that it would be easier to go than to endure the pain of not seeing her. As he stripped off his clothes to jump into the shower, he said to himself, "Why shouldn't I go if I want to? It's my dance, too." He was more than a little ashamed of his weakness, but the thought of seeing her came as a great stab of relief, like a narcotic gushing through his veins and pacifying him.

He concocted a pretext for going to the dance. He had recently repaired a camera for Lynne Caporale, an I House acquaintance, and he decided to return it to her that night. He spruced himself up, borrowing a dash of cologne from his next-door neighbor and slicking back his hair with oil. Camera in hand, he padded down the stairs to the lobby. It was almost ten o'clock when he entered the auditorium. He scanned the dance floor, his eyes searching out every corner. Tanya was not to be seen. He loitered by the refreshment table, engaged in a halfhearted conversation with Lynne Caporale. The minutes passed, and Tanya never showed. By eleven-thirty he had to acknowledge she wasn't coming. Dejected, he climbed the stairs to his room, rationalizing that she must be ill.

The following week, Prosenjit was so preoccupied with Tanya

that he could not concentrate on his work. It was mid-January, and winter-quarter classes had just begun. Under normal circumstances, he would have used this time to dig in and get a head start on his colleagues. Instead, he skipped both sessions of his seminar with Dr. Wehausen, and when he bothered to show up at the towing tank, he paid only halfhearted attention to the sea-keeping experiment and broke a half-dozen of the platinum gauges. He seemed to be losing interest in the things that just a few months earlier had been the center of his life.

Jal observed all of this with growing concern. It seemed to him that the obsession had grown into a monstrous fish, gobbling up Prosenjit as if he were a little minnow. Finally, deciding that it was time to intercede, he persuaded Prosenjit to take a walk into the Berkeley hills, above the I House. They headed up a winding path past the recreation center in Strawberry Canyon. It was a clear day, and the sun beat down on the students who sprawled on the grassy knoll overlooking the Olympic-size swimming pool. It was the same pool where Tanya sometimes took her sister, Helen, for swimming lessons.

On the long climb up, Jal thought about how he would rather be taking this walk with Alice on his arm, and as he glanced over at the sullen face of Prosenjit, he felt a surge of exasperation. When they reached the top, where the path ended and fire roads fanned out into the brush, he cleared his throat and demanded, "Do you remember the first day we met? Back in school?"

"Very clearly. I gave you a hand on the Hydro exam, and you passed with flying colors."

"No. That wasn't it at all. That chap was raking you over the coals in mess hall and I was the only one in the room to come to your assistance."

"I am not remembering it that way," said Prosenjit, feeling the old antagonism. "Only it's true, you were always liking to play the white knight."

"Well, there are some who need rescuing," said Jal, responding in kind. "Even though one hates like hell to admit it."

"What of it?"

"Do you know why I did it?"

"Just as I said," said Prosenjit. "You're the kind of chap who likes to think of himself as a hero."

"No. It was because you had the superior intellect. It was quite obvious from the start that you, an Untouchable, were the topper in our batch."

Prosenjit winced at the reference to Untouchable.

"Do you know how much hostility that brought on against you?"

"I lived through it, didn't I?" said Prosenjit, with some bitterness.

"And now you act like an ingrate and risk it all. Over a silly girl. You don't seem to realize you have bigger fish to fry."

Prosenjit said nothing, but jammed his hands in his pockets and gazed out over the landscape. Below them, the Bay and Golden Gate Bridge were in silver relief.

A moment later Jal said sharply, "Forget the girl."

"But just last week, you told me she was a nice girl and that I had jumped to the wrong conclusions."

"That was before I realized what was happening to you. You've come unhinged."

"I don't see how you can say one thing one week, and the very opposite the next."

"You're bunking class like some deranged hippy, and before you know it, you'll be sacked from the program."

"I can always make out all right," said Prosenjit stubbornly.

"The girl is driving you crazy."

"I've heard enough."

"For God's sake, man, you were born an Untouchable! You're blowing your one chance to break free!"

Prosenjit whirled around. "Shut up, you self-righteous bastard!"

Jal pressed on. "Think of the thread of your existence. Everything you went through, just to get to Kharagpur. Not to mention the States."

Prosenjit turned and trudged off down the path.

As Jal watched him disappear into the shrubbery, he called out, "You've achieved something that is unheard-of in our country. Get hold of yourself!" Then he was left alone. He turned and looked down at the Bay, far below. It shimmered back in a thousand silver pieces, like the tesserae of a giant mosaic. As Jal stood there in the silence of the sunset, he became aware that it was not quiet at all, but that the air was full of a faint, crepuscular noise. It was a myriad of insects, fretfully rubbing their wings back and forth like matchsticks. Somehow the image of one spindly bug, hanging by a thread, enmeshed and thrashing, isolated itself in his mind. Suddenly he felt a great sense of foreboding. And he strode heavily down the path, wondering what would become of Prosenjit Poddar.

ALL the way back to the I House, Prosenjit raged against himself for confiding in Jal. It was only out of weakness that he had opened his heart to that self-righteous bastard, who, no doubt, was now getting a good laugh at his expense. The nerve of him telling me to forget the girl, he fumed. What makes him such a know-it-all?

He stomped down the dirt path, blind to passersby, kicking aside stones that lay in his way. The altercation with Jal excited so much fresh anger against Tanya that by the time he had reached his room, he was determined to put her in her place. Although he couldn't believe she was anything like that girl Jal had described as a practitioner of "free love," he did not for a moment doubt that she had flaunted herself before other men. She was rude and vulgar, and the way she had spoken disrespectfully of his mother was unforgivable. He would have found her character defects easier to bear if he thought she could be made to show some remorse. As it was, she seemed to enjoy his discomfort. He believed that she had behaved rudely, in part, just to provoke him, and he sorely regretted that he had given her the satisfaction of having lost his temper. Most of all, he reproached himself for having laid down that ultimatum. Suddenly, on an impulse that he could not control, he made a decision to retract the ultimatum and reached for the telephone. When he dialed the number it rang three times before the woman with the heavy accent answered.

"Madame," he said, "my name is Prosenjit Poddar and I wish to speak to Tanya."

"My daughter, she not home."

The fact that this might be the mother registered itself again. "I am her friend, and I am honored to speak to you," he said.

"You are a friend to Tanya?" Lidia Tarasoff inquired. She seemed delighted that he had at last introduced himself over the phone. A rare occurrence these days, when boys didn't seem to have any manners.

"Yes. It is very important what I want to say."

"Wait, let me write down your name," said Lidia. He could hear her rustling about for a pad. When she returned to the phone she panted between heavy breaths, "I don't know when she returns."

An hour later, when he hadn't heard from her, he called again. Once again Mrs. Tarasoff was full of kindness, but he began to suspect that Tanya was avoiding him. He even imagined that he heard her whispering in the background, coaching her mother to say she wasn't in.

By eight that evening Tanya had not returned his call. Surely the mother had given her his message and said that it was important. He decided to inform her parents that she was insulting him. The next time Mrs. Tarasoff answered the phone he politely explained that Tanya was a rude girl and that he wanted to speak to Mr. Tarasoff.

"You want to talk to my husband?" Lidia sputtered. "Please, that no good!" Her voice rose to a hysterical pitch.

"It is not for a young girl to be rude. Your husband should know that she has insulted me."

"Please, I will talk to her."

"I am wanting to speak with Mr. Tarasoff," he persisted.

Lidia Tarasoff whimpered. In the background, Prosenjit heard an angry masculine voice thunder, "Ma, shut the door!" and fainter yet, the sounds of a television sporting event.

Mrs. Tarasoff cupped the mouthpiece of the phone and whispered to Prosenjit, "Please, it is no good to speak to my husband."

Prosenjit heard the masculine voice yell, "Who is that?" Then there was a whooshing sound, as though the woman was covering the receiver. He could barely hear her muffled voice in the background. She came back on the phone and hissed into his ear, "I told you, Tanya call when she gets back."

"Only I am most anxious to talk to your husband," said Prosenjit.

Still in the background, but much louder now, the masculine

voice demanded, "Who keeps calling?" There was a scuffling noise and then the man himself said into the phone, "Who is this?"

Prosenjit cleared his throat and said crisply, "Mr. Tarasoff? This is Prosenjit Poddar."

"Who the fuck are you?" demanded Tanya's brother, Alex.

"A friend . . ." he stammered.

"Listen, asshole. Lay off Tanya and quit calling the house."

Prosenjit reeled with embarrassment. "But, sir—" he started to say.

"Do you understand, fuckhead?"

"I, I . . . am only, I mean to say . . ."

"You call here again, and I'm going over to where you live and beat the shit out of you." He slammed down the phone.

Prosenjit's hand was trembling as he put the receiver back on the hook. For a moment he thought he was going to gag up his lunch, and he leaned over the sink bowl, steadying himself with both hands. After the nausea had passed, he crawled into bed, fully dressed, and lay there for hours. He tried to blot out the sound of the man's voice, but the words "beat the shit out of you" kept reverberating through his brain. With a cry of anguish, he threw off the covers and ran from his room. He lunged down two flights of stairs and rapped on Jal's door.

"I have made a decision," he blurted when Jal opened the door.

At sight of Prosenjit's contorted features, Jal recoiled in outrage. It was all he could do to keep from throttling the lovesick Bengali.

"I am going to give the girl up," said Prosenjit, standing squarely in front of him.

Jal held himself together as best he could. "Good man," he said in an even, restrained voice. "I will be glad to act as an intermediary for you. Give me her telephone number and I will inform her that you are forever out of her life."

"No, no. She has insulted me and I want to tell her off myself."

"Ah," said Jal. "That won't do. It's not for a gentleman to be rude to a lady. If you allow me to manage it, I will terminate it in a courteous fashion."

"No." Prosenjit was obstinate. "She has behaved like an ill-mannered slut."

Jal, his impatience mounting, pushed the phone into Prosenjit's hands. "Call the lady now. Put me on. I will tell her you are terribly sorry, but you have brothers back in India to support, and she is disturbing your studies."

"But I can't even get her on the phone! Her father won't let me speak to her!"

"All the better. I'll tell the father precisely the same story."

"No. I want to put her in her place."

"You don't want to terminate, you want to insult her."

"But she has insulted me!"

"Hang on to your self-respect, man. Your object is to rid yourself of the girl, not play a game of one-upmanship. Do this with dignity, and you will come out feeling all the better for it."

Prosenjit hesitated.

"Promise me you'll behave like a gentleman."

Prosenjit swallowed hard and for the first time allowed his eyes to meet Jal's.

"Write her a note. Put it on good stationery." Jal slapped him on the back. "It's the best way. You wait and see. Soon you'll feel better."

After Prosenjit had left the room, Jal felt pleased with himself. No one could say that he hadn't acted as a friend and done a good deed. And he had a fairly good expectation that he would never hear another word about Tanya Tarasoff again.

"IT'S no good feeling sorry for yourself," said Cindy, sipping on a vanilla Coke and checking out the room at the same time. They were sitting at a booth inside Kip's, a dimly lit pizza parlor just south of Telegraph, where all the waitresses wore dirndl skirts and billowy white blouses.

"I don't know what's wrong with me."

"Nothing. The guy's a flaming asshole."

"He said he wanted to take mescaline with me. I thought for sure he'd make a plan."

"How did you leave it with him?"

"He said he'd be in touch."

"Right. Well . . . you'll just have to find someone new."

"I don't want anyone new."

"Listen, he's not in the same league as you. How can you expect him to appreciate who you are?"

Tanya picked at the slice of pizza on her plate. It had been over three weeks since her night with Jeff Flanders, and she hadn't heard a word from him. From time to time, on the street, she had seen a boy who looked so much like him that her heart had started to pound. She had hurried to catch up to him, only to find herself facing a total stranger. And yet, in spite of these momentary flurries, she was beginning to acknowledge that it was finished. She no longer derived pleasure from the pastimes that had filled so many waking hours—the frequent journeys past his house, the telephone hang-ups, the trips to the Coop Market. There were even hours that passed when she forgot to think about him, and for this she was thankful. The shame of giving herself so completely and then being rejected had somewhat diminished. Now, in place of the anguish, what she felt was just a general soreness, almost like a bruised feeling, such as one might expect to feel after a high fever had subsided.

Still, she did not regret the experience. Looking back on her one-night stand, she told herself that if she had it to do all over again, she would make the same choice. She prided herself on having been able to fling herself into the moment and feel so much passion. The problem was that she had been left with a gaping hole in the center of her life. During the heat of her infatuation she had been foolish enough to push aside all her other interests and friends.

When she surveyed the wreckage, she felt some remorse. There had been that formal note from Prosenjit Poddar, written on expensive stationery, declaring that he could no longer be her "friend." At first she had been relieved that he had finally dropped all the fantasies he had about her. But now that he was out of her life, she had to admit that she missed his attentions. If nothing else, he had appreciated her, worshiped her even. He had proved himself to be constant in his devotion, and in these times of fly-by-night affairs, a friend like that wasn't easy to find. She used to be able to say, "If no one else ever loves me, there's always Prosenjit Poddar." But as the weeks went by and there was no word from him, she feared that she had snuffed out even that meager acquaintance. She was curious to know if he still cared about her.

"Listen, sometimes you take a chance and you lose," Cindy was saying, in reference to the Musketeer.

"It's so weird," said Tanya, "but I really thought there was something special between us."

"He might have felt the same way, and then got scared. Guys are that way, you know."

"I know."

"Anyway," Cindy said, "I think that guy over by the door is checking you out. He just gave you the eye."

"Who?"

"The one with the big beard."

"Oh, please."

Just at that moment a masculine voice said, "Slide over," and Tanya looked up to see a boy she recognized as Cindy's boyfriend,

David, the Candleman. She and Cindy made a place for him in the booth.

"So what's going on?" he asked, taking off his sunglasses. He had a rugged face and a long nose.

"Tanya's depressed," said Cindy. "That schmuck never called her back."

"Don't be depressed." He grinned. "I've got something that'll make you forget all about him."

"What?" asked Cindy.

"They're freeze-dried, brown, and wrinkled."

"Peyote buttons!" squealed Cindy.

"I know you're up for them," said the Candleman, laughing, "but what about Tanya?"

Feeling their eyes on her, she shifted uneasily in her seat.

"Let's go somewhere real pretty to take them," said Cindy. "Like Tilden, so we can get off on the flowers and the trees."

"I'm going to see if I can borrow a car," said David, and he got up from the table to make a phone call.

When he was gone, Cindy said, "It's a perfect day to trip around in Tilden."

"If you're going to eat those peyote buttons now," said Tanya, "I think I'll just go home."

"What are you talking about?"

"I'm not going."

"Oh, come on! You can't pass these up!"

"You know I'd just be in the way," she said, thinking that if she could get Jeff Flanders to come along, it would be perfect. He'd love to trip around in Tilden Park. Now she had an excuse to phone him. She wanted to suggest inviting him, but was too embarrassed to bring up his name. Hoping that Cindy would mention him first, she ventured, "It would be different if I was with somebody."

"For God's sake, we're not going to do anything while you're around!"

"That's not what I mean. It's a different experience when you're with someone you care about."

"How would you know? You've never even tripped."

"I mean, it would be different if I was with Jeff."

"Jeff? You've got to be kidding," said Cindy. "I thought you were trying to forget that asshole."

"I am."

"Well, it doesn't sound like it."

By the time the Candleman returned, the girls were sitting stony-faced, no longer speaking to each other.

Tanya remained at the table long after Cindy and the Candleman had taken off. She couldn't help but imagine herself walking through Tilden with Jeff Flanders, following trails of velvet-green moss, deeper and deeper into the redwood forest. She calculated that if she called him now, there would still be time to catch the others. Her fingers itched to dial the number. She even began to formulate her opening line, but finally some last vestige of pride prevented her from making the call.

How could she get through the afternoon without succumbing to the despair that dogged her? She might use this time to study, she reasoned. With tears forming in the corners of her eyes, she hauled out her spiral notebook and absently flipped through it, pretending to read. Stuck between the pages was a loose sheaf of paper, crisp and brittle, like parchment. She looked down and saw that it was the letter she had received from the Indian, Prosenjit Poddar. She stared at it for a moment, amused by his disjointed sentences and awkward use of the English language. She was reminded of how rude her brother Alex had been the last time he had called. In spite of her morose mood, a laugh rose inside of her as she thought about all the phone calls he had made to her house. For days she had had to listen to Alex rant on about that "wimpy foreigner" who had called a dozen times, and how he had told him where to get off. Poor Prosenjit! She felt bad for him. No wonder he had written this pathetic letter. Suddenly she longed to see him again. Driven by a perverse impulse she didn't stop to question, she rose from her seat and headed for the phone booth.

PROSENJIT hung up the phone, seething with indignation. She had chirped away so blithely, as though nothing had changed between them, suggesting they meet at the Union 76 station on Solano Avenue. Why she had picked a gas station he did not know; nor did he care. He was thankful that his days of trying to read her mind were over.

He looked back on the last few months with disgust. He couldn't understand how he had allowed himself to stoop so low. When he thought about her it was with anger, because he believed she had gone out of her way to hurt him. She had entered into a serious relationship with him, one that implied a long-lasting and sacred commitment, and then had discarded him like some used tissue. Even more humiliating, she had done all of this in front of his dorm mates at the I House. It must have been that she had been pretending all along. Otherwise how could a lady behave so heartlessly? Lately he had fallen into the habit of cataloguing her defects of character, and then speaking of them with exaggerated effect to acquaintances on his floor. It was important to him that the others share the same low opinion of her; somehow this restored his self-image and strengthened his resolve to stop loving her. The miraculous thing was, it was working.

Over the course of the last four weeks, he had regained his energy for his schoolwork and was once again absorbed in the project at the towing tank. He had come to realize how since he had met her he had allowed the focus of his universe to narrow down to a grain of sand. He was experiencing almost a child's pleasure in being open to the world once more.

He had been so surprised when he heard her voice on the phone that he lost his composure. "What are you wanting?" he sputtered.

"I just wanted to say hello."

"Hello."

"It seems like such a long time since we've talked," she said. "I didn't like the way we left things."

"There is nothing to talk about."

"How can you say that? Haven't you missed me?"

"I've been busy with other things."

"Why don't you come down and meet me at this gas station where my brother works?"

"I'm not interested," he said.

"I could meet you there in twenty minutes," she said.

"No . . ." he managed. "There is too much I have to do here."

"Oh, come on."

Almost against his will, he found himself agreeing. When he hung up the phone, he was conscious that his heart was pounding violently.

The point was that now he had the opportunity to put this ill-mannered girl in her place. It had been only four weeks since Jal had told him that there should be no rancor in their parting, but now that she had taken the initiative and called, he felt justified in telling her off. He wanted to let her know how much pain she had caused him. Perhaps when she was made to understand how he had suffered, she would give him the apology he deserved. Then he could wash his hands of her forever. He reached for a sheet of letter paper and heatedly jotted down a list of the ways in which she had insulted him. When he was done he copied it over in neat block letters. Foremost on the list was his suspicion that she had betrayed him for another man.

He had just enough time to polish his shoes and press his new seersucker shirt before he took off. Within fifteen minutes, he was on his way. As he hurried down Bancroft, he was oblivious to the broken glass and tear-gas canisters scattered about the street, unaware that there had been a riot on campus earlier that day.

When he arrived at the gas station, the only person in evidence was the attendant, a big, raw-boned youth in a grease-smeared uniform. He was holding a wrench in his hand like a club, and was swearing violently at an inanimate object on the ground. Prosenjit approached him gingerly. "Excuse me, sir, can I trouble you?"

The boy looked up, scowling. "What do you want?"

"I am looking for a young lady with dark hair. Have you been seeing any such person?"

"There's no lady here."

Prosenjit took out a slip of paper and studied it. "Where is the Union 76 station on Solano?"

The boy grinned. "You're standing in it, mister."

Just then, from the street corner, he heard Tanya's voice. "Yoo-hoo, Pro-shen-jeet. Over here."

He turned to see her, waving gaily, hurrying toward him, with a stack of books clutched to her chest. At the mere sight of her his heart turned over.

When she arrived at his side she said, her eyes dancing, "I see you two have already met."

Prosenjit and the boy looked at each other. The boy shrugged and said, "Who is this guy?"

"Prosenjit Poddar, my friend from the I House," she said, and then, inclining her head toward the boy, "My brother, Alex."

"Oh, it's that one!" exclaimed Alex.

Suddenly it dawned on Prosenjit that this Alex might be the one who had cursed at him over the telephone, and all the indignities he had suffered flooded back. He flushed crimson. This was yet another offense to be logged against her. He reached into his pocket for the list.

Apparently Alex also felt uncomfortable, because after a moment of awkward silence he muttered, "Yeah, well, I've got some work to do," and turned, ambling off into the garage.

"Hey, wait a minute," cried Tanya, skipping after him and grabbing his arm. Prosenjit watched them whispering in the corner of the garage. He strained to hear what she was saying, but all he could make out was something about being rude. When she returned she smiled and said, "I'm sorry. I really wanted you to get to know my brother, but now's not a good time. He bought a used car a while back and he can't get it to run."

"You are the one who is impolite. It is not so much your brother."

"God, I didn't realize you were still mad at me."

He felt the lump rising in his throat.

"What did I do that was so terrible?"

He fixed his eyes on the ground, studying a crack in the cement.

"No, really," she said, "I want to know."

"I don't know why you bothered to call me."

"I thought we could at least be friends."

"How is that possible, when you have thought only of yourself?"

"What do you mean?"

"There are so many things." He pulled the list out of his pocket and then, making sure they were not within earshot of Alex, cleared his throat. "You smoke cigarettes without offering me one. You serve yourself food before offering it to me."

"What's wrong with that?"

"Back at home, it would not be done."

"But this is America you're in," she said, smothering a giggle.

He went on, doing his best to ignore the smile on her face. "You left the folk dance without bothering to say goodbye."

"Hey, you've done some things yourself. It's not fair to blame it all on me." She tossed her head. "Sometimes it's not so easy dealing with you and all of your hangups."

What did she mean by that? Hadn't he made every attempt to behave in a courteous fashion? "For my part," he said, "I could have accepted it all, except that you have not kept your appointments with me."

"What appointments haven't I kept?"

"Last month, when we were planning to go to the concert."

"You're impossible. How do you expect me to remember that far back?"

"You know the time," he mumbled, fixing his eyes on a tool that was lying on the ground some ten feet off.

"Come on," she said soothingly. "I think we should at least give it another try." Just then, from within the garage, there was the noise of metal hitting cement and Alex's "Oh fuck!" Tanya said, "My poor brother," and moved to the edge of the dimly lit garage.

The Dodge Charger was jacked up a few feet in the air. Only Alex's shoes protruded from underneath. Prosenjit brushed past her and squatted down next to Alex. "What's the problem?" he asked.

"Fuck if I know," came Alex's voice from under the car.

"I don't know why you bought this crate in the first place," said Tanya.

Prosenjit straightened up and, not allowing his eyes to meet hers, circled the car. He ran his hands admiringly over the custom metallic paint job and murmured, "It looks really super."

"Yeah," said Alex, wheeling first his torso and then his head out from under the car. "It looks great, but it's all fucked up."

"Maybe I can be of assistance," said Prosenjit.

"Oh, come on," said Tanya.

Alex hoisted himself up and slid in behind the wheel. "Here, listen to this," and he started up the motor. It sputtered for a moment, then went dead.

Prosenjit leaned in for a closer look at the engine. From the corner of his eye, he could see Tanya standing with her hands on her hips, shifting impatiently from one foot to the other.

Alex came and stood by his side. "It's not the timing, that's for certain," he said.

"You have cleaned the carburetors?"

"Twice."

"Then it must be the distributor cap," said Prosenjit, loosening the cap and blowing hard on the inner surface. He could feel Tanya's eyes on the back of his neck, and the sensation was not unpleasant.

"Hey," said Tanya, suddenly stepping forward and addressing herself to Alex. "I didn't invite him over here to work on your car."

"No, no," said Prosenjit, waving her off. "I'm glad to be of service," and he reinserted the distributor cap. Motioning to Alex, he said, "Start it up again."

Alex jumped into the front seat and turned the ignition key.

"Come on," said Tanya, tugging on Prosenjit's sleeve. "Alex can figure this out for himself."

"Hey," called out Alex. "Why don't you lay off?"

"Oh, fuck you," she muttered and withdrew to the small office at the front of the station.

Alex jammed down the starter, and sure enough the engine caught. "Wow!" he cried, gunning the motor. "Unbelievable!"

Prosenjit beamed. This was the kind of acclaim he normally got only from his younger brothers. He glanced toward the open door of the office to make sure Tanya was within earshot.

"Let's take her for a test drive!" cried Alex.

Prosenjit slammed the hood shut and slid in by Alex's side. They pulled up next to the office, and Alex tooted the horn. "Hey, lame-brain," Alex called. "We're going for a ride. Back in a minute."

"I want to go too," she cried.

"There's no room."

"Oh, come on!"

When she opened the door and squeezed in next to Prosenjit, his spine tingled. Alex laid a patch of rubber behind them. As he shifted into second, he glanced over at Prosenjit and said, "Fuckin' unbelievable. It runs perfect." Prosenjit smiled. Having Tanya there to witness his achievement was remarkable luck. He felt happier than he had in months. As they drove along, Alex filled his ears with talk about the relative merits of Porsche transmissions compared to Corvette transmissions. Tanya sat in silence, but Prosenjit could feel her arm pressing against his. He wondered if she was still miffed, but when he turned and glanced at her, she smiled, and all the anxiety he had been feeling vanished. He settled back into the car seat, wondering how he ever could have endured their separation. Before he knew it, Alex had pulled up by the entrance of the I House and was saying, "Hey, come back anytime. We can hang out."

Reluctantly, he opened the car door and climbed out.

Tanya leaned out of the window and waved. "See you soon!"

"When?" cried Prosenjit. "Maybe at the next dance?" But before she could reply, Alex had peeled away from the curb.

PROSENJIT basked in a feeling of well-being. He had been reconciled with his love, and along with that happy state flowed all the attendant fantasies of marriage and raising a family. Even though he had failed to elicit a formal apology for the way she had treated him, he rationalized that it no longer mattered. What happened was a lovers' spat, so common in the States. She would never have called him back into her life if she had not all along recognized their commitment.

It was at this point that he made the decision to secretly tape-record their conversations. Tape recordings would provide concrete and indisputable proof that she loved him. Over the next few days he worked out a bugging system to equal that of any FBI agent. With money earned at the towing tank, he purchased an old Nagra tape recorder, the kind used by documentary-film makers. Its microphone was capable of picking up any sound within a radius of twenty feet, including ambient room tone. He placed the reel-to-reel recorder behind some books on a shelf, out of view, with buttons within reach to switch it on or off. He planted one tiny microphone under his work table and another behind his bookshelf. He even tested the system on an unwitting visitor, just to be sure that everything worked.

On Friday night, at eight o'clock, he was waiting in a dark corner of the lobby. She had promised that she would see him at the folk dance, but this presented a sticky problem, because he had not yet found the courage to confess to Jal or any of the others that he had resumed his friendship with her. Somehow he would have to intercept her before she went into the dance. Every few minutes he crept silently to the front entrance and peered out to the street. When he saw her walking up the path, he rushed to greet her.

Feigning a sprained ankle, he explained that he was unable to dance. He was pleased to find that she was sympathetic to his injury and didn't seem to mind missing the folk dance.

"Wait, just one sec," he said, as he walked into his room, groping his way through the darkness until he reached his desk. He flicked on the recorder switch and then turned on the overhead light.

She followed him in. "I don't feel that well anyway," she was saying. "It'll be good to just sit here and talk."

He noticed that there were dark circles under her eyes and that she looked thinner than he remembered. When she sat down on his bed, her arms hung limply at her side.

"What's the matter then?" he asked.

"Nothing." She hung her head, studying the polish on her nails. "Oh, by the way, I meant to tell you, my brother really likes you."

"Really? What did he say?"

"He said you're a great mechanic."

He beamed. "Only what I fixed was such a simple thing."

"Well, he didn't think so. You should go back there and hang out sometime."

He pulled out a chair and sat down. He glanced toward the bookshelf that hid the reel-to-reel recorder. He had left a tiny space open on the shelf, through which he could see the numbers that indicated how much tape was left on the reel. He was relieved to see that the system appeared to be working without a hitch.

"What Alex really needs is a friend like you," she was saying. "You would be a good influence on him." She paused, picking at a fleck of nail polish. "You know, I'm sorry if I was mean to you," she said, looking up at him with great, mournful eyes. "It's just that lately I've been really depressed."

"Tell me what is it that has happened."

"It's hard to explain."

"You can tell it to me," he coaxed, moving forward on his chair. "I'm your friend."

She breathed deeply and let out a sigh. "Oh, I don't know. There was this guy I really cared about, and he never called me back."

"What are you saying?"

Tears welled in her eyes. "A guy I liked, who acted like he really liked me too." She hung her head and began to tell him about the first time she had seen Jeff Flanders drinking coffee in the Mediterranean Café.

Pain, more intense than he had ever known, surged through him. He rose from his chair. Averting his face, he moved his hand over his eyes to hide his own tears. "We spent the night together once," she was saying, "and I never heard from him again."

He felt shamed and humiliated, but instinctively fought it down. He knew he should get up and leave but he could not bear the thought of it. "I would have taken you anywhere you wanted," he managed, in a strangled voice.

"That's not the point," she said, starting to cry. "I wanted to be with him."

"Only I was always good to you."

"I know. I should never have gone to his house." Her shoulders started to shake, and then her entire body was racked with sobs.

Fighting back his hurt pride, he felt he wanted nothing more than to take her in his arms and cover her face with kisses. As he stood there, numbed with his own emotions, he kept saying to himself that, at least, there was some relief to be found in having his suspicions confirmed. She had been a bad girl and now would have to be taught how to be good. He reached out and put his hand on her shoulder. "It was no way for a gentleman to behave."

She leaned her body against his and burst into hysterical crying. He had had no idea that she was capable of crying like that. He held her to him and gently stroked her back. It seemed to comfort her.

"I just wish I had never met him."

After a few minutes her crying subsided. "You're really a friend," she said, extricating herself from his embrace and reaching for a Kleenex from her purse. She blew her nose. "I knew being with you would make me feel better." She lifted her swollen lids and looked him in the eye.

In that instant he forgave her utterly and loved her as he had never loved her before. "I have something for you," he said. "A present I think you will like." He went to his closet and took down a box. He had been waiting for this moment for a long time. He watched while she unwrapped it and spread the shimmering pink fabric out across his bed.

"It's beautiful . . . but what is it?"

"A sari," he said proudly.

She smiled. It was good to see her happy again. "You have to show me how to wear it. Should I take off my dress?"

"No, no. You can try it on over your clothes."

"That's not going to work. Here, close your eyes," and she began to unbutton her dress.

He sat on his chair, with his back facing her and his hands covering his eyes. He couldn't help but imagine the supple white flesh of her breasts. She called out that she was ready. He turned around. She had the folds of cloth draped around her neck, like a Roman tunic.

"No, no," he said, moving toward her. "This is all wrong," and he wound the material around her chest. The contact with her body was thrilling. "There. This is how the women in West Bengal tie their saris." He fastened the tail of cloth tightly at her waist.

"But how can I move around in this? It's so hard to walk," she said as she took mincing steps around his room, laughing. "It's like being bound up like a mummy!"

He stood back to admire how she looked. Her little-girl body was slender as a reed; her arms were almost too thin. He thought to himself that she really did seem quite helpless, as though she needed to be cared for.

She twirled in front of the mirror. "I feel so feminine," she said. "How do I look?"

"Very nice." He sat down at his desk, squinting at the row of three tiny numbers on the recorder that were counting out the tape. There were about fifteen minutes of tape left.

"Maybe we should go down to the dance so I can show it off."

"I'm not in the mood for those people," he said, thinking that by this time Jal had surely returned from the cinema with his American sweetheart and would be breezing through the dance with her on his arm.

She glanced at him, suddenly concerned.

"You're not still mad at me, are you?"

He shook his head.

"Then why are you so quiet all of a sudden?" she said, gathering up the skirt of her sari and walking over to him. "Did what I told you about that other guy upset you?" She plunked herself down on his lap.

"It is not pleasant to contemplate." Overwhelmed, he let his arms hang limply at his sides.

"You made me feel so much better," she said, really meaning it.

He kept his eyes fixed on the ground.

She went on, "You remind me of a character in my favorite book. *Siddhartha.* Do you know that book?"

"No." He gently shifted his position so that his arm hid the recorder buttons.

"Well, Siddhartha is this saint from India. He's very mystical and pure. He gave up all his worldly possessions and went on fasts, and things like that. My favorite part is the early part when he goes to bed with a prostitute to experience the dirty side of life."

Prosenjit stiffened with embarrassment.

"Have you ever gone to bed with a prostitute?"

"In India, there is no physical relationship before marriage."

"But men do go to prostitutes, don't they?"

"Not responsible men. Only those who are not mindful of their families or professions."

"Then how did they ever come up with the sixty-nine positions of the *Kama Sutra*?"

"The *Kama Sutra* is a religious text that refers to the pleasures of love after marriage," he stammered. "Excuse me, but I am unacquainted with it," and he pushed her off so that he could get up from his chair. She walked to the other side of the room. With a sigh of relief, he lit a cigarette.

"You know, sometimes I can't believe you. Does that mean that you're going to wait until after you're married?"

"Chastity before marriage is a virtue. For both a man and a woman."

"At least you don't discriminate." She moved closer to where he was standing. "Well, if you're not going to go down to the dance,

I'm going home." To his shock she put her arms around his neck and pulled him to her. "Thank you. I'm not so depressed anymore."

Then she kissed him. Her mouth was wide open and her tongue pushed against his lips, prodding them open. He resisted for a second, but then he responded by allowing his tongue to play back and forth against hers.

Long after she had left the room, he sat at his desk playing the tape over and over. His mind dwelled on the events—analyzing her every action, interpreting each word. He had been correct all along; she had betrayed him for another man. But if he was to believe her, that unfortunate episode was over. More important, he had presented her with the sari and she had accepted. In his mind, this act symbolized their betrothal. It was the most sacred commitment he had ever taken in his life. And if he had any doubts at all, he had recorded her acceptance on tape, and could listen to it to his heart's content.

In the dark he thought about how she had glided across the room to kiss him. She was like the demonic goddess Kali, the destroyer, who seduced men and then led them to their death. As he began to fall asleep, he pictured the Kali festivals that took place every October in Balurghat. In order to placate the temper of Kali, the people of his village carried a carved wooden image of the goddess through the streets, banging on drums and chanting her name. The goddess had nine poisonous snakes coming out of her head, and a blood-red tongue. According to legend, there had been many who had been devoured by that mouth.

She had kissed him and he had felt the flick of her tongue! It was the first kiss he had ever received from a girl. A wet kiss. Their bodily juices had commingled. He wondered what he had done to make her love him so. As he drifted deeper and deeper into sleep, he dreamed first of the mouth, then of the darting tongue that had touched his own.

ONE night in March, Jal found himself on the brink of winter-quarter finals, unprepared and facing disaster. There had been so many immoderate evenings at Giovanni's, so many jolly cookouts in Strawberry Canyon, that he had neglected his real purpose for being at the university. Ship Hydrodynamics, in particular, seemed a lost cause, and as the night wore on, he came to the conclusion that only that bastard Prosenjit could save him. It was a dependency he hated to acknowledge, but by the time he arrived at his friend's door he had reconciled himself to it. To his surprise he heard a ripple of female laughter coming from within, then a voice that could only be Tanya's. Bloody hell, he thought. That vixen's caught him again. I'll clear her out fast enough and give him a solid firing he'll never forget.

He pounded on the door. The tinkle of laughter stopped abruptly.

"Yes, please, who is it?" came Prosenjit's voice.

"Jal!" he hollered, unable to control his annoyance.

Prosenjit opened the door and stepped aside so Jal could enter. The room had a musty odor, and soiled laundry was heaped on the floor.

"What the devil is going on here?" demanded Jal, looking around for the vixen.

"Ah," said Prosenjit. "I'm glad you've turned up. I need your advice."

"My advice!" Jal threw up his hands. "Where is she?"

"I'm sorry, but there is no she in the room, unless you mean a ghost."

Jal marched to the closet and yanked open the door. "I could have sworn I heard Tanya's voice," he muttered, as he slid the clothes to one side of the rack.

"Here she is." Prosenjit grinned triumphantly, patting his tape recorder.

Jal looked at him, dumbfounded. "Have you lost your mind?"

Prosenjit pressed the play button, and suddenly the room was full of the throaty voice of Tanya, laughing and cooing in a provocative way. She was saying, "When I say we're friends, that doesn't necessarily mean I'm in love with you. I mean, I might love you as a friend but not be in love with you. There's a difference."

Jal exploded, "You're making a bloody fool out of yourself!"

Prosenjit lowered the volume. Quite innocently, he asked, "Can you explain to me what she means?"

Jal was shaken. It was as though nothing beyond the sound of her voice mattered. With a jerk of his wrist, he snapped off the machine. "Two months ago I washed her out of your life! Have you forgotten?"

"But I want you to listen. To help me interpret."

"Interpret my ass! Do you think I'm going to put off studying for my exam to listen to some silly tape you have made with Tanya Tarasoff?"

"There is one part here where she says one thing, and then contradicts herself again in another."

Jal could see now that Prosenjit was possessed. He hadn't heard a word he'd said. Stepping up close to him, Jal demanded, "I don't suppose *you've* even studied for the exam?"

Prosenjit waved him off. "I will make the marks."

"The hell you will. You'll flunk out is what will happen. And I'll be glad to see it."

"I'll still land up ahead of you." Prosenjit laughed as he fast-forwarded the tape.

"You keep this up and they'll sack you from the program and ship you back to West Bengal." As Jal said this, he couldn't help but wonder what would happen to his own future at Berkeley, without Prosenjit to guide him through the rigorous exams.

"Here, please! I want you to listen to one section. Then I will help you for tomorrow."

Jal sank down on the bed, exasperated.

Prosenjit's brow furrowed as he wound through the tape, searching for a specific section. "When we are done listening," he said, "I will hand all my notes over to you, and you can carry on. Ah, here it is," and he hit the button and Tanya's voice came out of the speakers. "I think you were just using me," she said. "That's what ticks me off." Then Prosenjit's voice: "I don't see how you can say that." And Tanya's response: "You were. All the time you were just using me to make yourself look good."

He hit the pause button. "Jal," he asked, "do you think that I have used her?"

Jal threw up his hands. Although he knew it was a mistake to let himself get sucked into this pond of quicksand, he was at a crucial juncture, facing three finals over the next two days. It was easier to address the question and be done with it. "I can't say because I don't know what context she is speaking in."

"I was always a gentleman, even when I said I couldn't see her anymore."

"Yes, yes, I know," said Jal testily. "But how did it come about that you two were making this recording?"

"We weren't," admitted Prosenjit. "She never knew that I was doing it."

"You mean you were secretly taping her?"

"Yes, and it required a bit of ingenuity on my part."

"That's contemptible."

"Not at all. I was doing it to clarify her contradictions."

"How long has this deceit been going on?"

"I have this many tapes," said Prosenjit, and he held up three boxes, representing more than a dozen evenings that he had spent in his room with Tanya.

It soon became clear that Tanya had a different notion of what their reconciliation meant than did Prosenjit. While there were times when she submitted to his attentions with seeming compliance, accompanying him to his dorm room and allowing herself to be served tea and cakes while he unburdened his soul, there were also moments when, for no apparent reason, she snubbed him with an icy stare.

What bothered her the most was the way he idolized her. It drove her crazy that whenever they met, he greeted her with a nervous giggle and his eyes became moist and adoring. She made attempts, however ineffectual, to let him know that she did not share his feelings. She often confided in him as she would to a girlfriend, telling him details of her latest crushes and bemoaning how she had "blown it" with Jeff Flanders, the "love of her life." While she knew that the truth hurt him, it seemed like the best way to make him keep his distance. His response to her confessions was to sulk. He'd cast his eyes to the floor, twist his hands in his lap, and sit in abject silence for long stretches of time. Invariably, the spectacle of his sullen face would cause her to erupt in impatience, yelling, "I don't know what your problem is! You're not my boyfriend!" and stomp out of the room. For days, she would keep him on tenterhooks by avoiding his phone calls. Then she would grow restive and bored and would turn up at the next folk dance, where she would "accidentally" run into him. By that time he would be so desperate to have her back that he would beg her forgiveness.

The fact was that she did not for a moment consider him her "boyfriend," and would have been horrified to think that anyone else did. Unfortunately, the signals she gave him were crossed. While she did not find him in the least bit physically appealing, she had such low self-esteem that if a man paid for her dinner or the tickets to a movie, she believed she "owed" him a kiss goodnight. Consequently, she occasionally gave Prosenjit an openmouthed kiss. But these wet kisses were bestowed out of a sense of duty, nothing more, and they always exacted a heavy toll.

Naturally Prosenjit did not understand any of this, and often complained that he did not see enough of her. In order to prove his point, he showed her parts of a diary that charted their time together. The diary was organized with a detailed table of contents that included section headings like "Taking My Girlfriend to *The King of Hearts*," and a diagram of where she was standing on the night that they first met. When she saw the diary she became so alarmed that she yelled at him that he was crazy and ordered him to throw it out. And yet having this kind of power over him was not an entirely unpleasant sensation.

As the weeks passed, Prosenjit's condition deteriorated. His eyes were glazed over and his posture was stooped. He skipped full days of class and often did not show up at the towing tank. Not only Jal but others in the I House became aware that he had withdrawn to his room, where he remained most of the day, either lying in bed or listening to the tapes, with a "Do not disturb" sign tacked outside his door. He rarely went down to the dining hall for meals, and when he passed an acquaintance in the corridor he often walked past without showing any sign of recognition.

On one occasion, Jal, who was in the habit of spending his Friday evenings at the computer center on campus, and returning to the I House around ten o'clock, ran into Tanya and Prosenjit coming out of the elevator, Prosenjit tagging along at her heels. The next morning he decided to look in on his friend. He knocked, but there was no answer. Ignoring the "Do not disturb" sign, he opened the door. The blinds were drawn, and Prosenjit's electronics gear, normally stored in a particular location, was strewn about the floor. Prosenjit was hunched over the recorder, listening to a tape.

"I have not seen you down in the dining hall," said Jal.

Prosenjit seemed annoyed that Jal expected him to break away from the tape, even for a minute. He drummed his fingers on the desk, his eyes darting around the room.

"Have you eaten?"

"Very little."

Jal noticed tins of food stacked in the closet and a few empty cans discarded in the wastebasket. When he attempted to engage Prosenjit in a conversation about their Offshore Structures class, his friend's responses were disjointed, as though he was having trouble following a thought. It was only when Jal nodded toward the tape recorder and asked, "Still Miss Tarasoff?" that Prosenjit showed any interest in talking. Looking accusingly at Jal, he said, "I thought you saw only ridicule in the tapes?"

"That's true. It's not an activity one approves of."

"Then why do you ask?"

"I want to know what you're doing with your time."

"I am listening to the part where I have spoken to the girl about marriage."

"You asked her to marry you? Actually?"

"Why are you laughing?"

"I'm not laughing."

"Don't tell me that. I can see you're enjoying this."

"What did she say?"

"Her reply is no matter. What is important is that I have given her a sari. A girl does not accept such a gift lightly."

"What makes you think she knows the significance of a sari?"

"I expected you to say as much."

"Well . . ." Jal threw up his hands. "I can see there's no use trying to talk to you." He left the room, swearing never to return.

It was only three days later that Professor John Wehausen, Prosenjit's graduate adviser, pulled Jal aside and inquired after his charge's health. "I'm concerned about Poddar," said Wehausen. "He's not attending class and his performance in Offshore Structures is barely above failing. The few times I've seen him, he's looked almost seedy. Unwashed."

"Yes, sir. I know what you mean," said Jal.

"Why's he having such a hard time?"

"He's homesick, I suppose."

"Well, he may not be homesick for long." Wehausen ran a hand through his faded red beard. Something told him that Jal was covering up for his countryman. "I'd hate to do it, but I may have to flunk him."

"Sir!"

"To be quite frank, I'm acting on the basis of a report from Gunnar Stanfil, out at the tank. The boy's gone to pieces out there. He doesn't show up for work, and when he does, Stanfil says he's so shaky he's busting up the gauges."

"Somebody's got to do something, I suppose," said Jal. "Personally, I can't get through to him."

Wehausen fixed him with a hard look. "Weren't you two in school together at the IIT?"

Jal nodded.

"I was out there myself in '64, on a sabbatical," Wehausen said, thinking that India was the most depressing place he'd ever visited. "It was my impression that you students clung together quite closely. Stuck up for each other."

"Poddar and I have never exactly been birds of a feather—"

Wehausen cut in brusquely. "Because if he doesn't shape up, he'll be out of the university and on his way back home." Having delivered his ultimatum, he walked off.

Jal hung his head. The last thing he wanted was further involvement in this debacle. Now it seemed that in spite of his strenuous efforts to remain detached, the burden had been put squarely on his shoulders, and by the head of the department.

Angry and shaken, he went to dinner that evening with the DasGupta brothers. During the meal all Jal could think of was how he could best discharge his duties toward Prosenjit, with the least amount of upheaval in his own life. He was so unlike his usual convivial self that Dilip DasGupta remarked on it. Jal grimaced. "It's Poddar again."

"So Casanova's at it again," said Dilip, who liked to be kept abreast of all the gossip. He chuckled. "More trouble in paradise?"

"It's even worse than you think." Jal cursed. "Now Wehausen's saddled me with the whole shebang, as if I could do anything with that crazy Bong."

Dilip exchanged looks with his brother, Amit. "You asked for it," he said.

Jal ran his hand over his face. "The other morning I went by his room to haul him to class, and I found him under the covers with the tape recorder going."

"A new form of erotic pastime?" inquired Dilip.

"Miss Tarasoff really knows how to put the screws to him, let me tell you," said Jal. "You should hear how she sweet-talks him."

"Can you get us tickets?" said Dilip, and they all laughed.

"If he doesn't buckle down, he's out on his ear."

"Another Untouchable bites the dust." Amit smirked.

"And you're the one who always believed in him," said Dilip. "You and your enlightened point of view."

The remark, tossed off so flippantly, stabbed Jal like a dart. "Well, I'm through with him now, let me tell you," he snapped. "I want nothing more to do with Poddar and his memsahib."

As the days dragged on it became quite clear to Jal that if Prosenjit was sent home in disgrace, there would be many, like the DasGuptas, who would delight in his ruination. And there was little doubt that some of this unpleasantness would wash back onto Jal himself. As the self-appointed spokesman for the rights of Untouchables, he had antagonized many of his classmates back in India with his noble speeches and his championship of Poddar. If Prosenjit was cashiered from the university and given a return trip ticket to Calcutta, his humiliation would be taken as a failure for Jal too, and on a grand scale. He would be held up for ridicule in front of the entire Good Old Boy Association of the IIT and labeled a loser. If there was one thing that Jal could not tolerate, it was a stain on his immaculate reputation. All during dinner he considered various ways in which he might drop Prosenjit, but by the time he got up from the table, he had to admit that that was impossible.

The truth was that he believed Prosenjit was a genius, and considering his background as an Untouchable, perhaps the most deserving boy in all of India. And beyond that, Jal had to admit that he loved him. Despite the stormy nature of their friendship, Prosenjit was his friend of the heart. Jal felt that his only choice was to take command of the situation and exert whatever influence he had left.

It was not until a few weeks later, in mid-April, that Jal made his way, with grim determination, up to Prosenjit's room. He was aware that the Untouchable had given up going to class entirely. When he arrived at his door, he was irked to find the "Do not disturb" sign hanging outside. Ripping it off, he barged in.

Prosenjit was at his work table, cleaning his tape recorder. When he saw Jal he exclaimed, "Don't come too close—you'll stir up dust." He dipped a cotton ball into a bowl of alcohol and gently swabbed the magnetic heads.

Jal said, "I thought we'd walk to class together."

"Can't you see that I'm in the middle of a project? In any case, I'm not going to class." Prosenjit jerked his head up. "So carry on without me."

Jal noticed that he had pouches under his eyes, and his hair was damp and unkempt. He said, "Come on. Wehausen paid me a visit. I'll tell you about it on the way over."

"Professor Wehausen came to see you?"

Jal nodded. "He thinks you're that important. He said if you're not able to catch up with the work, he'll arrange for you to drop out for the quarter."

Prosenjit hung his head. "He never liked me in the first place. He wants to see me sacked from the program."

"What makes you think that? The chap's understanding and wants you to succeed."

Prosenjit put his head in his hands. "I can't get her out of my head. It's like the real person inside of me is being suppressed. I no longer know who I am."

"Come on, get up. We'll go talk to Wehausen now."

"Tanya has told me that she has known the other man."

"What do you mean?"

"She has admitted physical relations."

"That settles it," said Jal, knowing that Prosenjit's Victorian sensibilities made him value chastity in a woman above anything else. "What more do you need to know."

"I have it on tape," said Prosenjit, starting to ready the recorder.

"Please, please! It's the last thing I want to hear. Something so intimate should not be played for me," said Jal, feeling a surge of revulsion. "The main thing is, you must teach yourself to forget her."

"How can I? I can't control myself."

"I will go to her," said Jal. "I will tell her to leave you alone."

"If I can't be with her, I'll plug myself into the electrical system."

"Don't be silly."

"I'm serious. I've written as much to my father."

"You didn't!"

"Yes I did. I have the letter right here."

"Give me that letter," said Jal, standing above him. Prosenjit handed over the letter, and Jal tore it up. "I think you should give me the tapes, too. Put them in my custody. They're not good for you. They're driving you crazy."

Prosenjit began to sob. "I have lost my self-respect. I have lost myself."

"Do what I say," commanded Jal. "Hand those tapes over. You have the key to my room, and if you feel you need to listen to them, just go into my room and take them from the closet."

"Let's talk about it tomorrow."

"Tomorrow isn't good enough. We must start today to help you regain your self-respect." Jal began gathering up the reels of tape and boxing them up. "I'm a layman, and I don't really know how to help you get it back. But there are others who do."

"Who is that?" asked Prosenjit.

"A psychiatrist."

"No," Prosenjit said, with vehemence.

"I can get you an appointment and you can judge for yourself," said Jal.

"Please, please, do nothing. Don't try to help me," he said, as he grabbed away the stack of reels Jal held under his arm. "It's no use."

"I'll be back tomorrow," promised Jal, as he strode out the door, "and we'll talk about it then."

DURING the spring quarter, Tanya jumped at every opportunity to immerse herself in the Berkeley scene. Her father's disapproval made this difficult, but she found ways to evade his watchful eye. During the day he was at work, so she was free to join the mob that gathered under Sather Gate or, if nothing was happening, to loiter around the lunch tables in the Bear's Lair. At night, if he had passed out, she could sneak off to a mixer in the recreation room at Cunningham Hall, or down to a rally on Telegraph. But when he sobered up, he monitored her closely, and she was forced to content herself with the folk dances at the I House. These he permitted her to attend only because she had convinced him that the I House was the one place she could "practice her languages."

She was obsessed with the idea of transferring to Berkeley. She had excelled in her courses at Merritt and had even managed to land a job grading papers for her Portuguese teacher. These successes had finally caused her to question her father's pronouncement that she was "too dumb" to get through a semester at the university. She hungered for the intellectual stimulation. But more than that, she had been seized by the overwhelming urge, experienced by nearly every young person within close range of Berkeley, to be a part of the action. Only as a registered student would she truly *belong*.

Late in April, unbeknownst to her father, she filled out Berkeley's application for admission for the fall quarter, and hand-delivered it to the registrar's office. The secretary behind the desk informed her that a decision would not be made for another four to five months. To Tanya, the months of waiting seemed like a lifetime.

* * *

One Friday night in early May, when the buds were coming out on the trees, Tanya was on her way to meet Prosenjit at Swensen's Ice Cream Parlor on Durant Street.

Earlier in the week, she had received a call from him asking if she was going to the folk dance. "I'm not sure," she had said, knowing that her indecision would drive him crazy. This had been greeted by a long silence, until she could stand it no more and had snapped, "Hello? Are you there?"

He had responded in a sullen voice, "Yes, well, I suppose you have more interesting things to do than to be with me."

"You're not going to start that again, are you?"

"No."

"If you do, I'm definitely not coming."

"I promise I won't."

"All right," she had said, "but there's got to be something better than going to that folk dance all the time. Why don't we meet at Swensen's and we can figure out what to do later." After they had hung up she wondered why, when he bent over backward to please her, she found him so irritating.

It was still light, but the sun was sinking fast, as she stepped out of the bus at the corner of Telegraph and Ashby and pressed on, in the direction of campus. As she neared Shakespeare Books, she heard the plaintive wail of a guitar playing "Hey Jude" and sounds of laughter. When she reached the next corner, she looked up, toward the hills, and spotted the crowd that was gathered in People's Park.

People's Park was three acres of parched earth at the corner of Dwight and Haste streets, a stone's throw from Telegraph Avenue. Tanya had passed this intersection numerous times, on her way to and from campus. Actually, the so-called park looked more like a junk heap. During the day it was filled with cars parked willy-nilly between the dust and crabgrass; at night it took on a more sinister aspect as a crash pad for itinerant street people and stray dogs. But on April 18, an anonymous rabble-rouser calling himself the Robin Hood's Park Commissioner had announced in the underground newspaper the *Berkeley Barb*, "Hear ye, hear ye.... A park will be built this Sunday between Dwight and Haste. The land is owned by the university, which tore down a lot of beautiful houses in order to build a swamp. . . . We want the park to be a cultural, political freak-out and rap center for the western world. . . ." The park had been proclaimed the symbol of the revolution. For three weekends in a row, a motley assemblage of students and street people had converged at the site, dragging trees, plants, and rolls of sod. With a thousand dollars raised among themselves, they installed benches, and a sandbox and swings. So it was that People's Park had become a haven for nursing mothers and dope dealers alike.

But the land belonged to the university, and to make matters worse, irate neighbors circulated a petition demanding that the authorities put a stop to "all-night bongo drumming, lovemaking, and dope-peddling" at the park. Rumors began to spread that the police planned to move in with bulldozers and cement and erect a chain-link fence around the site.

In the grainy early-evening light, Tanya could make out children frolicking on the swings. A bonfire blazed in a central pit and flames licked a red sky. Someone was ladling free soup out of a garbage can, and the aroma of lentil beans wafted toward her. She paused to watch three girls dancing in a circle around the fire. Their tie-dyed shirts flared out like translucent sails. It was an eerie sight. Somehow the silhouettes darting past the flames reminded her of a Bosch painting of hell and damnation.

Others were beginning to gather around her, anonymous faces, some haunted, some laughing. She searched their eyes, hoping to make contact but not knowing how. Something held her apart from the others, almost as though she were encased by an invisible wall. And so she moved through the crowd like a sleepwalker, wishing that someone would prick her skin and get her back into life.

As she left the crowd and walked on, toward Swensen's, the thought of spending an evening with Prosenjit only increased her agitation. He was so open and vulnerable, and while there were times when she found she could accept his neediness, there were other moments, like tonight, when it repulsed her.

What's more, he was an outcast. Not only did he not fit into the world she so desperately wanted to belong to, he barely knew it existed. Accepting a date with him only confirmed her fear that she was an outcast, too. She was so ashamed of him that she had not told Cindy she was going out with him that night. In fact, she rarely admitted her visits to his dorm room, even though she was in the habit of going there once or twice a week. She didn't fully understand why, but whenever his name came up, she dismissed it with a derisive comment, like "Oh God, that creep won't leave me alone."

Sometimes she wondered why she bothered to see him at all. It seemed to her that he had grown unreasonably suspicious. He accused her of crazy things, like offering to have sex with the Das-Gupta brothers for money. He repeatedly searched for ways of tricking her into confessing that she had spent the night with Dilip DasGupta, almost as though he wanted to be proved correct. When she denied his accusations, he became so angry that his face turned purple. During one of these episodes, he told her that he wanted to build a radio-controlled bomb and hide it in her purse.

"I will pull a switch and blow you up," he warned.

"Go ahead," she sneered. "I dare you to do it."

"I am planning it, only that I am afraid to injure an innocent person."

"You're really sick," she said, in a voice full of scorn, and she stormed out of his room.

It was impossible to take these threats of his seriously. She knew that he worshiped her, and this only inflamed her all the more. There was something about taunting him that she seemed to enjoy. She hated herself afterward, but time and time again, she found herself doing it. Perhaps the cat-and-mouse game that they played gave her a sense of power, perhaps it created the illusion of drama in her life, but whatever the motivation, she seemed to be driven by an impulse she couldn't control.

When she was halfway up the block she spotted him, waiting in front of Swensen's, pacing back and forth. Even from a distance she could see that there was a look of stern disapproval on his face. He kept glancing at his watch. She supposed she was a few minutes late. Rather than hurrying up to him, she stopped and ducked into an alcove.

She had been debating, ever since a recent letter had arrived, what to do about her summer vacation. The letter, from her mother's sister living in Brazil, had renewed the invitation for Tanya to spend two or three months at her aunt's home in São Paulo. Tanya remembered São Paulo, the city where the Tarasoff family had lived while they waited for their visas, as a vast, dusty wasteland. They had all been overjoyed to leave. And yet, both her parents were urging her to go back, especially her father, who was concerned about her "unhealthy involvement" in the Berkeley scene. Tanya was of two minds. While she suspected that life at her aunt's house would be dull, the prospect of a journey to South America still held some vague promise of adventure. Besides, it was the perfect way to escape her father's surveillance. Now, as she stood there in the shadows of the alcove, it struck her that another good reason to accept the invitation was to escape Prosenjit. It wasn't so much that he frightened her, really, but she had become increasingly aware that she had gotten herself into a real mess. Lately she found herself wishing that he would just disappear. Short of that, going to Brazil for three months, and putting eight thousand miles between them, seemed like the easiest and most effective way to extricate herself from the situation. But the fact that this wimp, whom she claimed to feel nothing for, had any influence over her summer plans filled her with irritation. She peered out from the doorway and watched as he paced back and forth. She could imagine that thin sheen of oil that always seemed to cover his skin, giving his face an unnatural intensity. The notion that she was causing him some discomfort was strangely gratifying.

Prosenjit glanced at his watch once again, and calculated that she was forty minutes late. It was just like her not to show him any consideration. She had probably taken too long at her dressing table and missed her bus. No doubt she was now on her way, sauntering up Telegraph Avenue. Then it dawned on him that she might have stopped to observe some of the reckless activity of the student demonstrators. The thought made him fume, and he considered walking down Telegraph to intercept her. His pride, however, prevented him from doing so. It would be better to remain at the appointed spot so that when she arrived he could scold her for keeping him waiting.

He reached down and picked up a leaflet that sat atop a stack of more leaflets. On it was written, in wavy black letters, "Pigs Run Amuck." He tried to occupy his mind by reading the print beneath it, but he couldn't concentrate.

Two minutes later he walked to the corner to check his watch against the clock on the Campanile Tower. When he returned to his post in front of Swensen's, she was still not there. Now, at last, he was overcome by the anxiety that she would not come at all. His left eye began to twitch, and his hand flew up to cup the eyelid. At that moment, he didn't know how he could get through the night without seeing her.

Then it occurred to him that perhaps if he bought her an ice-cream cone, she would turn up. It was a superstition that dated from his childhood. Back at home, when his younger brothers had been late for supper, his mother had laid their food on the table and then, miraculously, they'd appear, falling on their plates like hungry crows on rice. Even though he thought about how ashamed he would be if anyone discovered him buying her the cone before her arrival, he was tempted to try it. He glanced into Swensen's, at the girls working behind the counter. He reasoned that if he bought a single cone, they would assume he was buying it for himself. He fought with himself for a few minutes and then turned on his heels and walked into the ice-cream parlor.

From her alcove, Tanya watched Prosenjit emerge from Swensen's. In his hand he held an ice-cream cone. He stood in the middle of the sidewalk, holding the cone stiffly in the air, away from his body, like an upheld torch. Soon the ice cream began to melt down the sides of the cone, but he made no move to lick it, even as the milky fluid began to drip down his hands.

Suddenly, in a flash of understanding, she realized that he had bought that cone for her. She recoiled from the sight. Backstepping into the crowd, she turned and rushed down the block, her heart beating violently. In the madness of that moment, she despised him more than she ever had before.

Despise him or not, she had, as yet, been unwilling to let him go. She had convinced herself that he was someone to hang out with as long as she did not have a real boyfriend. From time to time, she had toyed with the idea of breaking it off, but something had always told her that it wouldn't be so easy. Besides, the thought of having no one at all was terrifying. She had reasoned that if he was unhappy with their relationship, it was his responsibility to end it. Yet deep within her heart she knew that he didn't have the strength. He was under her spell. She felt an excitement in that knowledge, and at the same time a fear. But now, for the first time, the fear became more powerful, and it enveloped her. The notion of escaping to Brazil not only seemed like a good solution, it seemed like the only one.

She ran through the darkness, her heart still pounding, until she reached People's Park. The disorderly mob had swelled in size. People were dancing wildly around the open firepit as blood-red flames shot into the sky. Their faces, part human, part animal in feature, rushed past her, chanting and shouting. She stepped into the circle of dancers. It was as if she had been seized by a chthonic force, pulling her downward into a chasm, and in that chaos she found relief.

IT was three weeks later, on June 5, 1969, that Jal Mehta shepherded Prosenjit down the path that led to Cowell Hospital. Holding him lightly at the elbow, Jal made passing comments about the handsome stand of pine trees that were growing on this side of campus, trees that reminded him of the hill stations he had visited, like Simla and Darjeeling, in the foothills of the Himalayas. Prosenjit walked as if in a trance, making no sign that he was listening. Suddenly, through the pines, the cold gray facade of Cowell came into view, and Prosenjit froze.

"Come on, old boy. You've come all this way, you can't stop now," said Jal, pushing him through the hospital doors.

It had taken Jal weeks of cajoling to convince his friend to consider therapy. The battle had been all uphill, because Prosenjit, like most traditional Indians, had a built-in suspicion of psychotherapy, which was unheard-of in remote villages like Balurghat. There the afflicted ones looked to the head of their family for guidance. Guidance, when given, was laid down like a decree, meant to be carried out with unquestioning obedience. While this means of dealing with problems had the effect of robbing the individual of his free will, it also took away the agony of indecision.

"For God's sake, man, you're twelve thousand miles away from home and you don't have anybody," Jal had said, knowing that his friend had received a letter of stern condemnation from his father, upbraiding him for wasting his time with a memsahib.

"I do not want electroshock treatment," Prosenjit had replied.

"That's your misconception about what the psychotherapist does. Open your mind." But Prosenjit had remained unbudgeable until, finally, Jal hit on what he thought would be the perfect ploy. "He will talk to you and explain the girl's behavior."

"You mean he will tell me why she says one thing a few days back and then the opposite today?"

"Yes. These doctors have much clinical experience in the laboratory and can give you fresh insight."

Still Prosenjit was doubtful. "He is a complete stranger to me. How will I know he will keep what I say secret?"

"Rubbish! Every word you say is kept confidential. They take a sacred oath to guard your secrets to the grave."

Prosenjit had then nodded, indicating that he would give the suggestion serious thought.

But in the end, Prosenjit's decision to seek psychiatric counseling had nothing to do with Jal's arguments. It was only after he had received the startling news from Tanya that she planned to go on summer holiday to Brazil that he agreed to go.

Tanya, it seemed, had informed him that she had saved enough money from her job grading exams for a professor of Portuguese for an eight-week vacation in Brazil, including airfare and spending money.

It seemed to him that it was unbecoming for a single woman to travel by herself. Besides, the notion kept running through his mind that if she wanted to see the world, she could wait until after they were married. As a naval architect, he would have many opportunities for travel, and they could do so to her heart's content. But it was not so much the news itself which left Prosenjit pale and shaken, it was the blithe way she had delivered it. In the first place, she had not bothered to show him the consideration of discussing her plans with him before she had made the decision. It had been presented to him as a *fait accompli*. She had given him only two weeks' advance notice before her departure. Even worse, she had acted as though their separation would have no impact on her life, let alone on his own. Her manner had been so flip that when he had told her in a solemn tone that he would miss her terribly, she had laughed and urged him to "find somebody new." That evening, after she had left his dorm room, he played back the tape of their conversation, listening to it over and over and measuring every inflection in her voice to try to glean her real feelings. Finally, he had broken down into convulsive sobbing and crawled into bed, where he spent a sleepless night. The next morning, he had presented himself haggard and hollow-eyed before Jal at the breakfast table. In simple, direct words he told Jal he was so upset that he wanted to "physically hurt the lady."

Alarmed, Jal put down his fork. "Yes, but what can be done?"

"I will kill the girl," said Prosenjit.

"But that's not right."

"What would you do if I killed her?" demanded Prosenjit.

"What else? I would be questioned by the police and I would tell them what I knew and the rest would take care of itself."

"In that case, I'll have to kill you, too. What will you do about that?"

"There's nothing I can do. I rely on my faith in human nature."

"I am no longer a human being," cried Prosenjit. "I'm like an animal. There is no longer anything in me. I can no longer help myself."

The next day, when Jal was again breakfasting, Prosenjit came to him full of remorse. He explained to Jal that he had made those threats against him and the girl because he could no longer control himself. He assured Jal that he didn't really want to hurt anybody, but that he might not be able to stop himself. He told Jal that the attack would not come in the daytime, when he would have to look into Jal's eyes, but at night, while Jal was asleep. He advised him to lock his door. He then began to cry. It was at this point that Jal begged Prosenjit to let him arrange an appointment for the two of them to see a psychiatrist at the student health center, and Prosenjit finally agreed.

THE waiting room of the psychiatry clinic was down two flights of stairs, in the basement of Cowell Hospital.

Founded in 1945, the clinic had become internationally renowned as a treatment center, specializing in brief but effective psychotherapy for young adults. The current chief of the clinic, Dr. Harvey Powelson, supervised a staff of more than forty psychiatrists, psychologists, and psychiatric social workers. Over the course of the last few tumultuous years, hospital administrators had recorded a steady increase in patient visits, jumping from two thousand in 1965 to more than twelve thousand in 1968. A corresponding rise in the use of marijuana and psychedelic drugs had also been reported, with the number of attempted suicides more than doubling. But at no point in the history of the clinic was the demand for therapeutic counseling more apparent than during that first week in June 1969, in the wake of People's Park, and just at the time when Prosenjit decided to seek help.

Although Prosenjit was nearly oblivious to the violence that swirled around him, the events of the last few weeks had had an impact on almost everyone living in Berkeley. On May 14, a rampaging crowd had raised the cry "Let's go down and take the Park!" and more than two thousand demonstrators had surged down Telegraph, hurling bottles, bricks, and steel pipes. It was then that helmeted law enforcement officers had opened up with a new anti-riot weapon—twelve-gauge shotguns that fired low-velocity birdshot. By the time the melee was over, city officials reported that forty-three persons had been hit by gunshots. One, James Rector, a twenty-five-year-old carpenter, was taken to Herrick Hospital in critical condition.

Within hours, Army jeeps and trucks had rumbled through the streets, carrying two thousand National Guardsmen. Loudspeakers blared the news of a curfew from ten at night to six in the morning ordered by Governor Reagan. The city was under siege. The Guardsmen enforced a tense peace through the weekend. Then Rector's death, from shock and multiple hemorrhage, was announced, and the rioters took to the streets. The response was lightning-fast. From out of the sky, green Army helicopters swooped down, spraying tear gas as if to wipe out a pestilence. It was the first air attack ever launched against domestic disorder in the United States.

During that last week of May, officially designated as finals week, university students went to class watched by National Guardsmen carrying gas grenades, rifles, and unsheathed bayonets. The ominous noise of helicopters was ever-present. Not surprisingly, the numbers of students seeking psychiatric treatment jumped sharply. From the moment the clinic doors opened at eight in the morning until they closed at five, students could be seen filing into the neoclassical-style hospital with the gray stone facade.

Inside the clinic's windowless waiting room, the lemon-yellow walls were streaked and peeling. The only decoration was a bouquet of dried leaves punctuated with scraggly cattails, arranged in a ceramic bowl. Jal Mehta stood in front of the magazine rack, flipping through an issue of *Ramparts*, while Prosenjit waited obediently on the orange Naugahyde couch, staring down at his feet. After a few minutes, Prosenjit reached out and snapped a dried twig off the arrangement and crumbled it in his hand.

Glancing at the others who were waiting, Jal hissed, "Don't do that," and scooted in next to him on the couch.

A few minutes later, the door of the clinic opened and a chunky figure with brick-red hair surveyed the room. "Mr. Poddar?" he said, looking back and forth between the two Indians.

"Yes." Jal leaped to his feet. "I'm here to represent the patient," he said, indicating the hunched figure of Prosenjit. "I am the one who phoned you. My name is Jal Mehta."

"How do you do? I'm Dr. Gold," said the redheaded man, extending a hand. He looked uncertainly at Prosenjit, who still had his eyes on the floor. "Mr. Poddar? Would you like to come down to my office?"

Prosenjit looked up and nodded weakly.

"I think it would be a good idea, doctor," said Jal, "if I accompanied him."

"That's rather unusual," Gold hesitated, "but I'll leave it to the patient. Mr. Poddar, how do you feel about having your friend join us?"

"Yes," mumbled Prosenjit, "I would like Mr. Mehta to speak for me."

"All right, then," said Gold, and Prosenjit and Jal followed him down the gray linoleum corridor to his office.

Dr. Stuart Gold was one of three staff psychiatrists in charge of inpatient services, the division of the Psychiatric Department where students were referred if they were demonstrating signs of extreme emotional distress. In contrast to the outpatient clinic, where students saw therapists for fifty minute sessions, once a week, the treatment in inpatient services required hospitalization. Many of the patients admitted to this ward had been diagnosed as psychotic. Others were casualties of experimentation with mind-expanding drugs. In almost all cases, the symptoms of their mental disorders were considered severe enough that psychiatrists routinely prescribed antipsychotic agents like Compazine and Thorazine, which had a powerful sedative effect. So powerful, in fact, that patients taking these medications were sometimes referred to as "chemical zombies".

Dr. Gold made himself available two hours a day, at eleven in the morning and at four in the afternoon, to handle urgent appointments, such as the one arranged for Prosenjit by Jal Mehta. On such occasions, he provided crisis-intervention therapy in an effort to determine whether or not hospitalization was necessary. If he concluded that the case did not warrant such serious action, he would recommend that the patient be treated on an outpatient basis, and assign him to one of the other therapists on staff.

For a man who had joined the clinic only two years earlier,

Gold's position was considered a real plum. Some of his colleagues ascribed his success to favoritism and accused him of "sucking up" to Dr. Harvey Powelson, Chief of Psychiatry. Indeed, within his brief tenure at the clinic, he had managed to become one of Powelson's minions, and was often seen padding down the corridors after the formidable Chief. In an environment where competition was cut-throat, Gold's success did little to ingratiate him with his colleagues. Some accused him of being a "mama's boy," while others circulated the story that Gold was so insecure that he had needed his own analyst's "stamp of approval" before he decided to marry his wife.

Ushering Jal and Prosenjit into his office, Stuart Gold settled himself into the leather swivel chair that he had had designed for himself. He groped in his pocket for his pipe. "So, Mr. Poddar," he began casually. "Why don't you tell me what I can do for you?"

Prosenjit didn't respond.

Jal cleared his throat. "Doctor, it was my idea that he come and talk about his problem with you. We are both from India. Old school chums. There the practice of psychiatry is virtually unknown." He smiled. "But since we are in the States, I thought he should at least take advantage of it."

There was a rapping sound as Gold knocked the ash out of his pipe. "Is he here of his own free will?"

"Oh, yes!" exclaimed Jal. "Only he did not want to come alone."

"In that case"—Stuart Gold's eye rested on Prosenjit—"you will please continue." But Prosenjit said nothing, and an awkward silence settled over the room.

Jal shifted uneasily. Looking first at Prosenjit and then at Dr. Gold, he began to talk about the conditions Prosenjit had had to face, growing up as an Untouchable, in a traditional village two hundred miles north of Calcutta.

Dr. Gold idly jotted notes on his pad and snuck a glance at his watch. However impressed he was by Jal's aristocratic bearing and British accent, he couldn't help but wonder how details about the caste system in India were pertinent to this case. It was an unstated fact at the clinic that foreigners were "bad news." Like many of the other therapists, Stuart Gold held the belief that foreign students, especially ones from the Middle East and Asia, did not respond readily to Western-style therapy. By the time they showed up at the clinic they were depleted and confused. They were always looking for a substitute parent to tell them what to do, and in most cases it became appropriate to abandon the therapeutic process and do just that.

As Gold strained to concentrate on Jal's monologue, he couldn't help but notice that his intended patient, Mr. Poddar, was scrunched into the fetal position.

"He is very, very brilliant, as his scholastic record will attest," Jal was saying. "Both as a naval architect and as an inventor."

To Gold, just to look at the boy, this seemed hard to believe. His eyes were glassy. He seemed dull, blunted in affect, as if he wasn't aware of what was going on. Gold scribbled a note on his pad.

"Doctor," Jal went on, "a relationship with a young lady has overwhelmed him. Because of her hold over him and the fact she blows hot and cold, he no longer can function in his normal way. His work at school and at the research facility has deteriorated. He has been unable to concentrate, and he has had difficulty sleeping and eating. I am very concerned."

Gold turned to Prosenjit. "This is why you're here?"

Prosenjit nodded.

"How long have you been dating this girl?"

Prosenjit hung his head, and Jal answered. "It's not a thing like dating really. The relationship has been more casual, with them meeting at the folk dance."

Dr. Gold listened with growing incredulity as Jal went on to explain about the tapes, and how Prosenjit had hidden microphones in his room so he could ask questions of the girl, trick her into saying something complimentary to him, and then play the tape back later to get some corroboration that she loved him. As Jal described it, Prosenjit treated the tapes like a spy story. Just recently, he had actually spliced together sections of tape to make her say "I love you," which he played over and over for himself.

It struck Gold that there must be something about the cultures of the Middle East that made the young men susceptible to wild and inexplicable infatuations. He remembered the boy from Iran he had treated on an outpatient basis. That young man had gone bananas over a girl just because she smiled at him in the library, and in spite of Gold's disapproval, he had followed her around for months.

"The girl, whose name is Miss Tarasoff, is going away for summer holidays," said Jal. "It is a great chance for him to escape the hold she has on him, and resume his studies."

"Yes, well, Mr. Mehta, I've got a pretty good picture," said Gold. "If there's nothing critical you want to add, I think it would be better if I spoke to the gentleman by myself."

"Yes, certainly," said Jal, rising from his chair. "If you need me again, don't hesitate." As he walked from the room he felt enormously relieved that he had at last discharged this most distasteful duty.

After Jal left, Prosenjit barely stirred. He remained hunched in his chair, his eyes cast on the floor.

Gold gazed out of the window, unsure of how to begin. "So . . ." He hesitated. "It seems you have a very good friend in Mr. Mehta." He fumbled in his pocket for the comfort of his tobacco pouch. When Prosenjit didn't respond, he asked, "Would you say that he accurately described your involvement with this Tarasoff girl?"

"No," replied Prosenjit in a bland voice. "He wants to steal her away from me."

Gold stared into the Indian's dull, strangely opaque eyes. "If you feel that way about him, why did you let him bring you in?"

"He's been bossing me around, that's why."

"He seems to be only trying to help you."

"No, no. At the folk dance he came up and introduced my girl-friend to this boy named Dilip DasGupta, so Dilip could later call her and make a date."

"How do you know that?"

"The girl told me about it."

"Are you sure she's telling you the truth?"

"All I know is that they are all laughing at me."

Stuart Gold fidgeted with his pipe while Prosenjit described Jal's "plot" to steal Tanya away from him. He noticed that as the boy spoke, an all-knowing smile curled the corner of his lips. It was clear that he believed that Jal and a number of the others living at the I House were in cahoots against him.

It was then that Stuart Gold made his diagnosis. The inappropriate smiling, the utter preoccupation with the girl to the exclusion of everything else, the history, as reported by Jal Mehta, of withdrawal from society, an eating disorder, and the loss of sleep. Not to mention the delusional aspect to his relationship with both Mehta and the girl. It all added up to one thing: paranoid schizophrenia. The boy was clearly psychotic. Gold considered the possibility of hospitalizing him, but decided that it would be better if he could get him into the outpatient clinic. That way he could carry on with the normal course of his life. The girl would be out of town for three months and they could see how things went. Of course, the attending therapist would have a hell of a time treating him, but it just might work.

Prosenjit was saying, "She is playing with me. There are times she makes a date to see me and doesn't show up."

As Gold jotted his conclusions down on the pad, he couldn't help but feel relieved that in just moments he would be able to assign this case to someone else.

"Just two weeks back I waited over an hour outside Swensen's Ice Cream Parlor."

Gold looked up. "The next time that happens, you might consider giving her ten minutes and then leaving."

"I was going to take her to the cinema—"

"Did I understand correctly," asked Gold, cutting him off, "that the girl is leaving town for the summer?"

"Yes," said Prosenjit. "She will be out of station for three months." He twisted what was left of a dried twig between his fingers. "She has promised to write me letters. The thing is, I am sure that she loves me, but she won't admit it."

"What gives you that impression?"

"I can't say. I just know it."

"Well," said Gold brusquely, glancing at his watch, "time's up. I'm scheduling an appointment for you with another therapist and giving you some medication that will help you sleep." He wrote out a prescription for the antipsychotic agents Thorazine and Compazine, and then added Cogentin, a drug to counteract the side effects of the first two medications, which often produce muscle tremors. He handed the slips to Prosenjit. "If you experience any side effects, report them at once to your therapist."

Prosenjit stood up slowly. "Is this person going to help me?"

"He's certainly going to try." Gold looked over the list of available therapists, a gleam of satisfaction slowly coming into his eye. He picked up the phone and buzzed the receptionist on the intercom line. "Please set up an appointment"—he squinted at the Indian's name on his yellow pad—"for Prosenjit Poddar," he said, spelling out the name. He glanced at Prosenjit. "Make it with Dr. Moore. Dr. Larry Moore." He listened for the confirmation and hung up. Turning to Prosenjit and rising, he said, "Turn to your left, and follow the yellow line."

Prosenjit bowed slightly and walked out. After the door closed, Gold breathed a little sigh of relief. As he sank back into his chair, he couldn't help but wonder what Larry Moore's reaction would be to his new patient.

At thirty-four years old, Dr. Lawrence Moore was considered the rising young star of the psychiatry department. He had earned his Ph.D. in psychology from the University of Oregon two years earlier, and had come to Cowell on a postdoctoral fellowship from the National Institute of Mental Health. Since his arrival, Gold and some of the other trainees had been taken aback by Moore's success in the clinic. Perhaps it was his youthful assurance or his melancholy good looks, but he had quickly become the darling of a coterie of middle-aged female social workers, mostly Jewish, whose maternal instincts he seemed to arouse. This clutch of ladies gave him the nickname Young Dr. Moore and hovered over him at the lunch table in the Cowell cafeteria. Gold had often seen him there, surrounded by his doting entourage, eating tuna sandwiches and airing his theories on the nature of the human psyche.

As far as Gold was concerned, the young psychologist tended to take his own insights much too seriously.

But Moore's clique, who formed a powerful faction within the clinic, were convinced that the young therapist possessed the ability to engender that rare and indefinable phenomenon known as instant transference, and they touted him for a brilliant future. Their praise was so persistent that it reached the ears of Dr. Harvey Powelson, who took notice of Moore and began to treat him like a favorite son, much to the consternation of the other trainees and ambitious young psychiatrists.

Just recently, Gold had heard the startling news that Dr. Powelson had offered Larry Moore a permanent position on staff, making him the first trainee in twenty years to have received such an invitation. Naturally, this distinction had done little to increase Moore's popularity among the staff, even causing some to react with open hostility.

Stuart Gold was not certain why he had assigned the Poddar case to Larry Moore. Perhaps it was because he thought that the young psychologist was always a little more willing to play counselor, priest, or parent to a troubled patient than some of their other colleagues. Although Gold found this aspect of Moore's personality hard to take, it seemed to him that in the case of the Indian, it was precisely what was called for.

The longer he considered it, the more Gold thought that if anyone could break through to a psychotic foreign student, it was Young Dr. Moore. Smiling contentedly, he put on his cardigan and sauntered down to the cafeteria for coffee and a Danish.

NESTLED high in the hills overlooking the Bay is the Berkeley Rose Garden. Planted at the turn of the century, the garden was originally conceived as a classical Greek arboretum. Gravel paths wind through scented bushes, and stone benches have been placed here and there in shady nooks. Over the years the flowers have gone untended and overtaken the trellises in a wild effusion of color. In the midst of this unruly fairyland sits one estranged clay tennis court. Although pitted and scarred, it has long remained the favorite of a few diehards who care more about atmosphere than about the sport.

A lanky young man in tennis whites moved across this court with casual grace. From a distance his long stride seemed effortless, his stroke smooth and sure. Yet his game was off today, as anyone who knew him would attest. His concentration was erratic. As he watched his powerful backhand deflect off the net, he thought, I'm going to blow this set.

Larry Moore was over six feet tall, with an elongated, lean face. There was something about his expression, dark and brooding in the manner of an El Greco painting, that let one know that at age thirty-four, he had lived close to the edge. It was as though his life experiences had been cut in deep shadow or bright sunlight, full of suffering and exaltation. Perhaps it was this quality that put his patients so quickly at ease, made it possible for them to confide their innermost demons.

Moore took a ball from his pocket and walked to the baseline. As he raised his racket to serve, an unsettling image flitted across his mind. He saw his new patient, the Indian boy, Prosenjit Poddar, sitting rigidly in a chair, his fists clenched. He remembered the sudden tremor that had passed across the boy's face, causing his eyes to bug out and his mouth to twist into a distorted shape. Moore tossed the ball into the air and double-faulted.

"Set," called Neal Ross, his regular partner and close friend. As the ball rolled across the court, Moore's six-year-old daughter, Karin, scampered to retrieve it. Ever since his divorce, Karin had accompanied him to his tennis matches. In fact, she went with him almost everywhere, whenever he was off work.

"How about another?" exulted Ross, who was used to being trounced by Moore.

"No, that's it for me," said Moore, walking to the bench. He mopped his face with a towel and slipped his racket into its cover. As he stood on the court watching his daughter bounce a tennis ball high in the air, a breeze rustled through the leaves, carrying with it the balmy fragrance of summer. He turned to the stone steps that led to the garden, calling over his shoulder, "Karin! Come on. I'll buy you an ice-cream cone."

As Moore strolled down one of the gravel paths, it occurred to him that he had never lost a set to Neal Ross before. Then again, he had rarely had such an unsettling session. He recalled the wild look that had come into Prosenjit's eyes when he had talked about the girl, Tanya. The Indian believed himself to have been gravely injured by the girl. She had betrayed him and violated his honor. He was manifesting a compulsion to get even with her, to effect some kind of retribution. There was no doubt in his mind that the boy was crazy as hell.

The feelings that had been triggered off in Moore that morning were disturbingly familiar. Larry Moore was no stranger to violence and high drama. Although he kept his personal problems to himself, the stormy events of his life were well known at the clinic. Prior to his decision to become a psychologist, he had gone off to the University of Stockholm to pursue a career in mathematics, more specifically the study of the mathematics of waterfalls. While in Sweden, he had met and married a woman named Inger, who returned with him to the United States one year later. It was at this point that Moore decided to apply to graduate school in psychology, which was something he had always wanted to do. He earned his master's from Stanford University, and entered a Ph.D. program at the University of Oregon. Inger became pregnant, and their daughter Karin was born in 1963, while Moore was completing his doctorate.

When Moore received his postdoctorate fellowship to do his training at Cowell Hospital, he considered himself doubly blessed. Not only did the clinic have a reputation as one of the best psychiatric training centers in the country, but also the San Francisco area promised to be the perfect place to live. He and Inger moved to a house on Santa Barbara Road in the Berkeley hills, and at first, life seemed idyllic. But his case load was heavy, and not long after his arrival at Cowell, Moore found himself working sixteen hours a day, coming home only to eat and sleep. It didn't take long for Inger to realize that for her husband, the practice of psychotherapy was all-consuming. His absence was unnerving, and she began to feel increasingly isolated and abandoned. By the time Karin was two years old, she had taken to calling her husband at his office and threatening suicide. Finally, in February of 1967, she carried out her threat by feeding a critical dose of sleeping pills to their little girl and swallowing the remainder of the bottle herself. Moore returned home to find the mother and daughter unconscious. He rushed them to the hospital, where Inger was revived, but Karin remained in a coma for eight days, and only barely survived.

Since the incident, Larry Moore had been raising the child on his own, and had severed all communication with his ex-wife. Inger retained a powerful attorney and instigated a custody suit. This was something Moore couldn't fathom. He viewed Inger's act of violence against their daughter as attempted murder, and failed to understand how she could refuse to take responsibility for what she had done. He hired his own lawyer and was anticipating a long and ugly court battle.

Although Larry Moore claimed that being both father and mother to Karin was rewarding, his nerves were frayed and he was still working sixteen hours a day. His circle of women friends at the clinic were concerned that he was taking on too many responsibilities, both at work and at home. They pointed out that even though he had hired a full-time housekeeper, it was obvious that Karin needed a proper female role model. These well-meaning women urged him to remarry and frequently tried to fix him up, but after a few unsuccessful blind dates, he rebuffed their efforts by saying that he was "gun-shy." He even confided to one friend that the recent events of his life had left him so traumatized that he had made the conscious decision *not* to find a stepmother for Karin.

Now, as Larry Moore gazed out over the vista, shrouded by fog, he couldn't help but think about how during the session with Prosenjit an alarming, almost acrid odor had filled his office. It was a smell he seemed to recognize but could not place. Now it came to him; it was the odor that had pervaded the room his wife had occupied. It was the smell of madness. But madness did not, could not, smell. He tried to shake it off, but recalled that after the Indian had left, he had found it necessary to open his windows to air out the room.

That smell, still with him, reminded him of those last days before Inger's suicide attempt, days that had left an indelible mark. And while it was true that the trauma of those events had irreparably damaged his personal life, he had come to believe that they had sharpened his instincts as a therapist. They had made him acutely aware of the depths to which a human being could sink. Unlike many of his colleagues, he no longer viewed the threat of murder or suicide as an abstraction. And although in his work he had not yet faced a life-and-death situation, he believed himself to be uniquely qualified to recognize one. Not that he would want to predict, at such an early stage, that the boy was capable of hurting himself or the girl, but clearly, violence was within the realm of possibility.

Moore wondered if the girl, Tanya, realized what she had let herself in for. There was a certain kind of woman who enjoyed living on the edge, courting danger, and Moore suspected that she might be one of them.

Moore knew that his only hope was that the girl was going to be in Brazil for three months. It might not be enough time to break the grip of his patient's obsession, but it would at least give him a head start. He could work with Prosenjit on a one-to-one basis for a number of weeks, without endangering his or the girl's life. The more he considered the challenge, the more he became determined to undertake it. For once, he felt that Stuart Gold, whom he considered to be an immature mama's boy, had made the right choice. He was convinced that if anyone could handle this case, it was he. With the girl out of town, the odds were at least even.

"Daddy," called Karin, "what's wrong?"

His daughter's voice startled him, and he looked down at her. She was eyeing him curiously.

"You look so scary," she said.

He realized that his hand was clenched over a rose. He released his grip, and the mangled flower fell to the ground.

"We're leaving right now, honey," he said, and he reached down, took her hand in his, and started off toward the car.

TANYA departed for Brazil on June 14. Although Dr. Moore did his best to persuade Prosenjit that it was a good thing that she had left town, Prosenjit remained disconsolate. He stayed in his dorm room playing *gazals*, sentimental Hindi love songs, late into the night, and fretting over the loneliness she must feel without him. Although Moore had called this delusionary, he didn't think it so. She had repeatedly refused to meet him for a farewell dinner and had become quite annoyed when he suggested that he accompany her to the airport, but he persistently denied the painful reality that she didn't want to see him anymore.

Instead, he recalled over and over the few euphoric moments they had had together, like the time she consented to play Ping-Pong with him in the I House game room. Ever since he was a boy, Ping-Pong had been his favorite sport and perhaps the only one he excelled in. One of his most prized possessions was his Ping-Pong paddle, and he was forever challenging people at the I House to a game. Whenever he had suggested playing a game to Tanya, she had rolled her eyes and told him it was a silly idea. But one evening she relented, and so it was with great joy that he found himself facing her. Immediately, it became apparent that she was not a good player. In order to keep the game going, he had to hit her soft high shots, down the middle of the table. But the physical contact with her—his hitting the ball and her hitting it back—was extremely gratifying. And while his being so much better than she frustrated Tanya, causing her to slam balls back, off the edge of the table, he had to admit that he liked this too. It was one of the few times in their relationship that he felt in control.

Replaying such happier memories only deepened his misery. It seemed that nothing could shake him out of his depression, until, only a few days after her departure, he received a most surprising phone call.

The call was from Alex Tarasoff, and it came at ten o'clock at night. Alex told Prosenjit that he had just gotten off work at the Union 76 station, and that he was calling from a phone booth. His rushed manner and the loud noise from the street made it difficult for Prosenjit to hear, but it seemed that for the last week, Alex had been having violent arguments with his father, the last of which had ended in Vitally's beating him up, and he was afraid to go home. He wanted to know if he could bring his sleeping bag and spend the night on Prosenjit's floor.

Prosenjit readily agreed. The fact that Alex had called in a time of need greatly pleased him. For while the two had spent a number of hours together over the last month, working on the Dodge and assembling stereo equipment, their friendship had been anything but intimate. Alex's crude sense of humor both offended Prosenjit and left him perplexed. They were not, as Jal would say, "birds of a feather." And yet when they were together, Prosenjit felt almost giddy with excitement. Strangely enough, his feelings were nearly as euphoric as when he was with Tanya herself. In his mind, the fact that Alex was willing to be his friend had great significance; not only did it mean that the Tarasoff family endorsed his plan to marry Tanya, but it was also indicative of Tanya's commitment to him, a commitment which she had been reluctant to voice.

In Prosenjit's mind, the phone call, coming just at this time, was a way for Tanya to keep her hold over him. It was as good as her saying, "While we are apart, we are connected through the family." This would be the manner in which such a separation would be handled in India, where frequently boys and girls who were betrothed were forced to spend years apart until the boy completed his university training. But if a commitment back home had been made, there was no problem. It was merely a matter of waiting, and in India, people had far more patience to wait for love.

Now the thought of having the brawny teenager camping on his dorm-room floor swelled his heart with happiness, and he dashed around, clearing a choice space for the sleeping bag.

* * *

An hour later, Prosenjit lay in his bed listening to the comforting sound of Alex swilling beer. The overhead light had been switched off, and a full moon illuminated the room.

"The guy owes me money and he doesn't want to pay," Alex was saying. He was sprawled inside his sleeping bag, a half-gone six-pack sitting next to his pillow. "I feel like punching him out."

"Your fists would do a good deal of damage, I think."

"The asshole went right through a stop sign," continued Alex. He was in an especially morose mood because one week earlier an accident in the Dodge had caved in the front fender and left his car immobilized. Although Alex said that it was the other driver's fault, the man was claiming that he had had the right of way. Alex's car had not been insured, and he didn't have the cash to pay for repairs. The mangled Dodge had been sitting for days just where he had left it, on a street corner in downtown Oakland.

"Will the repairs be that expensive, then?" inquired Prosenjit.

"Are you kidding? I don't even have the money to get it towed."

"Let me know if you are needing a loan."

"Oh, man, I don't want to take money from you."

"But I am offering it." Prosenjit lay in the darkness thinking that money, when it came right down to it, meant nothing. He was so certain that this friendship with Alex would seal his future with Tanya that he was willing to do anything to cultivate a closer bond with the teenager, including paying for his meals and giving him gas money. This inclination had already depleted the savings he had been putting aside for his younger brothers' education, and although he fretted about other unnecessary expenditures, where Alex was concerned, nothing was too much, including a sizable loan to repair the Dodge.

"If this joker doesn't come through by the end of the week, I'm going over to his house and beat his head in," vowed Alex.

"If someone was going to beat me up, I'd put my hands behind my back and take the beating."

"Yeah? Well, I'd knock the shit out of anyone who came near me."

"But if I really got mad," said Prosenjit, "I wouldn't try to hit him. I'd kill the person. Then that person wouldn't be around to get back at me."

Alex laughed and popped open another beer.

Prosenjit went on, "If I killed someone, I would turn myself in and take the punishment for it."

"Well, I'd like to get my hands on the guy who plowed into my car and wring his neck."

"Was Tanya with you when it happened?" ventured Prosenjit. He had learned to be careful about how he worked Tanya into the conversation, because Alex seemed to resent being questioned about her.

"Yeah, she was there. But she says she didn't see him sideswipe me."

"Were there many people at the airport, to see her off?"

"No," said Alex. "Who would want to see her off?" When Prosenjit didn't say anything, he added, "I don't see why you like my sister so much. She's not worth it."

"How can you say that?" said Prosenjit, pulling himself up on his elbow and moving closer to the edge of the bed.

"Try living with her sometime, then you'll see what I mean. I tell her not to fink on me about dropping out of school to work at the station, and she blows it. She says that Dad found one of my uniforms, but that's bullshit."

"I would make her a good husband."

There was the sound of metal hitting wood as Alex slammed the beer can down and rose up. "Jesus Christ."

"No, no. I want to marry your sister."

"Don't go telling her that. It'll turn her off."

"But I've already told her," cried Prosenjit, fearful that Alex, his future brother-in-law, would think less of him for acting in an ill-mannered way.

"She told you to kiss off, right?"

"No, no. Not in so many words."

"If she thinks you're all that serious about her, she won't like you. Just play it cool."

"Play it cool?"

"You should meet some other chicks."

Prosenjit knew that it was a mistake to ask the next question, but he couldn't help himself. "Does she have another boyfriend?"

"I don't know," said Alex. "She once told me about some guy she likes."

Prosenjit was trembling under the sheets. "Who?"

"Some guy. I don't know anything about him."

"Your sister plays a game with me."

"What else d'you expect from her?"

"She says she doesn't want to talk to me anymore."

"I told you, find yourself another girl."

"I only want one girl, and that's your sister. But she's like this description in a book I'm reading." Then Prosenjit began to tell Alex about the theories put forth in *Games People Play*. The part that seemed especially pertinent to his relationship with Tanya was a chapter entitled "Rapo."

"Rapo?" asked Alex, intrigued by the word.

"Yes. Let me read the part to you."

"That's okay," said Alex, who had little interest in being read to. "I already get the picture."

"It'll just take one second." Prosenjit switched on the light by his bed.

"Hey!" cried Alex.

"Listen to this." He started to read an excerpt from the book: "'First Degree "Rapo" or "Kiss Off" is popular at social gatherings and consists essentially of mild flirtation. White signals that she is available and gets her pleasure from the man's pursuit. As soon as he has committed himself, the game is over.'"

"That's called being a cock-tease," said Alex.

Prosenjit continued, "'In Second Degree Rapo, or "Indignation," White gets only secondary satisfaction from Black's advances. Her primary gratification comes from rejecting him—'"

"A major cock-tease."

"'Third Degree Rapo is a vicious game that sometimes ends in murder—'"

Alex cut him off. "Just turn off the light, will you?"

Prosenjit did as he was asked and settled down under the covers.

"This is just like your sister," he said, longing for sympathy for the way she had mistreated him, and at the same time, hoping that Alex would tell him that his suspicions were unfounded and that she really did love only him.

"Forget her."

"If I'm patient with her, I can win," insisted Prosenjit, on the verge of tears and grateful that the room was once again dark. "If I just keep on, trying more and more."

Alex rolled over on his side to face Prosenjit. "Did you really mean what you said—about lending me the money for the fender?"

"I always keep to my word."

"Far out."

A few minutes elapsed before Prosenjit said, "She knows that I love her because I showed her what I wrote in my diary."

Alex groaned. "Jesus Christ."

"If she still won't speak to me, I'm going to go and meet your father."

"Are you crazy?" Alex struggled up from the sleeping bag.

"I will. I told your sister that, too."

"Hey, if you go and talk to my father, you know what he's going to do? He'll beat the shit out of you."

"I won't tolerate her not speaking to me."

"Oh, shit!" Alex grabbed one of his shoes and heaved it at Prosenjit's bed. "Let me go to sleep."

DURING the week after Tanya's departure, after his second session with Larry Moore, Prosenjit was so distraught that he resisted the notion of returning to see the doctor. He informed Jal that he had decided not to go back. Upon hearing this news, Jal looked at him incredulously and said, "But I thought you found some relief in talking over the situation with a professional."

"Not so very much," said Prosenjit. "I liked the redheaded doctor with the pale face better. I will not go back to Dr. Moore."

"Then I wash my hands clean of you," said Jal and walked away.

Nevertheless, when the next day dawned, Prosenjit did not cancel the appointment. It remained set for Tuesday morning, June 24. He did his best to avoid Jal, ducking out of the way whenever he saw him approaching and averting his eyes when they passed in the dining hall.

In fact, he had begun spending more and more time with Alex. Alex so often stayed the night in his dorm room that the teenager fell into the habit of leaving his sleeping bag unfurled on the floor. The two were getting along so well that one night Alex suggested that they might find an apartment together. This pleased Prosenjit so much that he clapped his hands together and laughed like a little boy. It didn't matter that Alex couldn't really afford the expense, and that he, Prosenjit, would have to assume the lion's share of the rent. The important thing was that now Tanya might come and live with them. Then, on Sunday, Alex turned up with the classifieds under his arm and they went out in the newly repaired Dodge Charger, cruising the streets below San Pablo Avenue, looking for an inexpensive apartment. They managed to find a cheap place on Solano Avenue, only a few blocks from the Tarasoff home, that they liked enough for Prosenjit to put down a fifty-dollar deposit. It was the only real happiness he had known since she had left town.

Prosenjit sat in the waiting room, picking at a tear in the Naugahyde couch, managing to enlarge it to twice its former size. The problem was not that he didn't like Larry Moore, but that he was afraid of exposing himself in front of the man. How could he be sure that the doctor would not enjoy his disgrace? But when he heard his name called out and glanced up at the careworn face of Larry Moore, he felt an unexpected rush of relief. As he marched after Moore into his office, he arranged an artificial smile on his lips.

"What shall we talk about today?" asked the doctor, pulling out a chair and patting it. He looked at his patient, who was smiling enthusiastically. "Here, please sit down."

Prosenjit perched on the edge of the seat, gripping the armrests as if he were strapped in for takeoff. His hair and clothes were unkempt, and his eyes flitted around the room, avoiding Moore's gaze.

Moore gently prodded, "Have you nothing to tell me at all?"

"I stopped taking the medication, just as you told me."

"Good. Are you feeling better?"

Prosenjit tilted his head to the side to concede that he was.

"Is there something else bothering you?"

There was a long silence. Prosenjit shifted back and forth in his chair and cracked his finger joints. Then, in a small, self-pitying voice, he said, "The letter hasn't come. She lied to me again."

"Tanya?"

"Yes, Tanya," he muttered. "She promised to write to me. The last time I talked to her, two days before her departure, she said she'd post the letter straight away, and it's been nearly two weeks since she landed up in Brazil. I've waited every day, but there is nothing."

"What do you propose to do about this?"

"I plan to make her understand that she is a lying whore."

"But she is far away, in South America."

"I will write her a letter."

"But you've already done that, and apparently you haven't been able to get a response. I'm afraid, Mr. Poddar, that you have only yourself to wrestle with."

"She returns in ten weeks."

Moore frowned. "But it was our understanding, only last week, that you wanted to detach yourself from her. That you were going to try, at least, to stand back from yourself and take a long look at what's been happening."

He pouted. "I know what it is that's happening."

Moore's tone was firm. "Since being involved with Tanya is causing you pain, why continue to subject yourself to it? You have a choice. That's the most important thing I can teach you, that you do have a choice. You can continue to suffer, or you can say, 'Hey, I'm a dummy. I'm being set up by this girl and I'm just not going to take it anymore.'"

"Oh, what's the use," mumbled Prosenjit, looking down into his lap. "I'm going to be sacked from the program and I will no longer have my job at the towing tank. For so long the only thing that mattered was the girl. Now she's gone and there's nothing left."

"But you haven't been thrown out of the department," exclaimed Moore. "You told me yourself that your graduate adviser arranged for you to drop out before any bad marks went on your record, and I'm sure, if he's approached in the right manner, that the mechanic out at the towing tank will take you back."

Prosenjit swallowed hard and continued to stare into his lap. At that moment he almost wished that he had been sacked, and that he was on his way back to Calcutta, even if it was in disgrace.

"Listen," said Moore. "Last week you made a statement that was extremely encouraging. You told me that you were willing to end the relationship. To cut it off cold. It seems to me that you have the perfect opportunity to do that, now that she's gone."

"Only she will be back."

"Not for another ten weeks. A lot can happen in ten weeks." When Prosenjit didn't respond he said, "Don't you see that you only open yourself up to more pain by writing her another letter?"

"It is not Tanya so much that causes pain. It's the people at I House."

Moore sat up. "Now why do you say that?"

"They are having fun at my expense. They want to see me fail," he said, remembering the humiliation he had suffered when Jal and his chums had discovered him crying in the elevator on the night that Tanya had stood him up at the ice-cream parlor.

"Who, specifically?"

"Everyone."

"*Every* one of them?"

"Yes."

"That's a strong accusation."

"I have proof," said Prosenjit, his foot tapping the floor as if powered by its own motor. The "proof" that he referred to was a splotch of grease that he had discovered on one of his tapes. Just the other night he had been listening to the tape when suddenly the sound from the speakers had blipped and her voice had disappeared altogether. He had been stricken with apprehension. A whole vital section of the conversation was missing, a section that he might never hear again. When he had examined the tape under his magnifying glass, he had found a smudge of grease. It had taken him nearly ten minutes, working with alcohol and a Q-Tip, to remove the spot. By the time he had restored the tape to its original condition, he had come to the shocking conclusion that someone had broken into his room and listened to his tapes. He had immediately checked, but the lock on his door was intact and his diary untouched. "A person with dirty hands ransacked my room," he concluded. "I discovered the fingerprint."

"But I thought it was only a smudge."

He moved forward on his seat. "The smudge of grease caused by a fingerprint!"

"So, you've still been listening to the tapes, after all?"

Prosenjit flushed and glared resentfully. He had forgotten that in their first session, he had given Dr. Moore his word that he would no longer listen to the tapes.

Sensing his embarrassment, Moore said, "You don't have to feel ashamed. By listening to the tapes, the only one you hurt is yourself. The thing is, I don't see how you can blame the whole I House."

"Someone must have a key to my room and must have entered it without my permission. That same person secretly listened to the tapes. He had unclean hands and left the fingerprint behind."

"But even if it were true, that's one person—not everyone."

"They're all behind it. I can see it in their eyes."

Moore looked out the window, to the Campanile, the stilettolike tower that lanced the sky. "Are you sure that this fingerprint wasn't your own?"

"There is no possible way it could be my own!"

"But why would someone listen to your tapes?"

"To make an ass out of me. They all laugh at me behind my back!"

"Who could it be? Let's stick to just one."

"It could be many people, no doubt led by Jal Mehta."

"Did you ask Mehta if it was he who entered your room?"

"Yes, but he would not tell me the truth. He used to be my friend, but now he lies to me, too."

"If he was your friend, why would he have turned against you?"

Prosenjit pursed his lips. "All I know is I must move out of I House. I must get away from all of them."

Moore regarded him gingerly. "I can appreciate your feelings, but think this through. Where else could you go where you'd be looked after? At the I House at least you have three hot meals a day prepared for you."

Prosenjit gestured with his arms, as if pushing away the suggestion. "I can cook on my Sterno."

"I advise against moving. You're engaged in breaking off from Tanya. That will require all the concentration of energy you can muster. Leaving the I House now would be like abandoning your base camp before climbing Mount Everest."

"Only this. I can shift to an apartment on Solano Avenue with a friend."

"So everybody is not against you?"

"There is only just this one."

"And who is that?"

"Alex," said Prosenjit, with more than a little pride in his voice.

"Alex who?"

"Alex. Brother to Tanya." As he said this, he was surprised to see Moore rise up from his chair.

"Her brother?" The therapist ran his hand over his eyes. "I thought you said that you wanted to give the girl up? That's the reason you have come to me."

"Oh yes." Prosenjit nodded his head in assurance. "I have every intention."

"In that case," said Moore, "for God's sake, don't move in with *her brother*. That's precisely the wrong move!"

This advice, so contrary to what Prosenjit wanted to hear, turned him to ice. Clearing his throat, he insisted, "It will have no bearing on the matter."

"It's a mistake."

"It is a modern flat and even features an air conditioner."

Moore crossed around his desk. "Mr. Poddar. You don't seem to have gotten the point."

Prosenjit shifted uneasily.

"A break with Tanya means a break with her brother."

"But I have given a security deposit."

"Have you given notice yet, at the I House?"

"Not as yet."

Moore placed one hand on Prosenjit's shoulder. "Then I'm telling you, as your doctor. Ask for your deposit back. Wait for a few weeks before you make any move."

Resentment welled up in Prosenjit's eyes.

"Mr. Poddar? It's important, if we're going to continue. Did you hear me?"

"I don't know if Alex will agree to wait."

"It's not a question of what he will agree to. I will not repeat myself. You're going to have to tell this Alex that you've decided not to take the place with him. You are going to stay put at the I House. It's either that, or you can go elsewhere for help."

Moore's vehemence filtered through, and Prosenjit said, "You mean to say you will chuck me out?"

"Instantly, yes. You break all connections with the girl—including her brother—or we call it quits." They faced each other for a long moment. "Do you give me your word?"

A lump formed in his throat. He had no intention of giving Dr. Moore his word, but he also had an uncomfortable feeling that this man was like his father and must be listened to. He whispered, "Yes, sir."

"All right," said Moore. "I'm counting on you to behave like a gentleman, and a gentleman always keeps his word."

When the hour was up and Prosenjit had left the office, Larry Moore returned to his desk and leafed through Prosenjit's file, looking for the name of the other Indian that Stuart Gold had mentioned as having brought Prosenjit into the clinic. Here was a person who could keep him informed of any radical changes in his patient's behavior. He hesitated a moment. There was no doubt that eliciting the help of an outside party was an unorthodox move. If Prosenjit found out, he might quit therapy. On the other hand, it could prove to be a necessary precaution. Moore picked up the telephone and dialed the I House, asking for the room of Jal Mehta.

PROSENJIT really was giving it a try. He attended the therapy sessions, which continued with regularity through June and into July. Every Tuesday morning at ten, Prosenjit timidly entered Larry Moore's office and took his place in the chair across from the doctor's desk. He was making slow progress, finding it easier not to dwell on her. Once in a while a span of nearly twenty minutes would pass without her face filling his mind. But still, there were moments when she loomed up and possessed him like a great goddess. During these seizures he fought the impulse to bring her up in conversation, as though by not talking about her he denied her power. And indeed, the sharp and debilitating pain he had suffered was now turning into a dull ache. With every advance he made he congratulated himself on his strength of character. He was able to report to Moore that he had refrained from writing Tanya another letter; that he had given the tapes to Jal, to store in his closet; and, most difficult of all, that he had told Alex that he had made the decision not to move out of the I House. Saying this to Alex had required tremendous resolve, because he so much wanted Alex to think well of him, and he had been afraid that his pulling out of their agreement would anger his friend. But, seemingly, that had not happened. To his relief, Alex still dropped by his dorm room, bringing over stereo parts that needed repair and occasionally asking to borrow money.

It was in regard to this last connection with Tanya that Prosenjit was unwilling to surrender completely to Moore's program of recovery. Moore had admonished him to cut the ties completely and expunge Alex from his life. But Prosenjit rationalized that there was no reason to deprive himself of this last friendship when their encounters only brought him joy. So he concealed it from Moore. He continued to see Alex on the sly, knowing that his therapist did not approve, and experiencing a mixture of guilt and delight in pursuing the forbidden.

Moore knew that all of the actions that Prosenjit had taken to eliminate Tanya from his life had depended upon the strength of his will. Whenever the yearning for her seized him, he gave himself a stern rebuke and repeated to himself that he had finally and irrevocably broken with her. And it was for this very reason that Moore also knew it could not be considered a real recovery. Like an addict who has denied himself the pleasure of his drug, Prosenjit clung to his resolve with white knuckles, hoping against hope that he would not slip back into the arms of his obsession, but longing for it all the while.

It seemed to Larry Moore that this was as much as he could ask for. While it was obvious that his patient was as yet unable to find release from his obsession, there were moments when the girl seemed to recede from the foreground of his mind, and he would talk with great enthusiasm about his other activities, like the electronics hobby shop he had set up in his room. It was at times like these, when the Indian was lucid, that he became quite likable, and that Moore felt a surge of sympathy, almost affection, for him. He believed that Prosenjit's recovery depended on his ability to redirect the boy's attention to his work. He encouraged anything that did not have to do with the girl, asking him many questions about naval architecture and his work at the towing tank.

It did not take Moore long to realize that the towing tank was a sore point. Invariably, whenever the subject of the tank came up, Prosenjit's eyes would cloud over and a tremor would come into his voice. Prosenjit was sure that he had been a great disappointment to this man Stanfil, his friend and mentor, who had invested so much energy in teaching him to appreciate America and forget he was an Untouchable. According to Prosenjit, the chief mechanic had believed in him, entrusted him with jobs that he would never have assigned to the other students. But Prosenjit, because of his obsession with the girl, had lost the ability to respond to anything but her. He had neglected all of his responsibilities and destroyed Stanfil's faith in him. No matter how often Moore tried to assure him that the mistakes of the last few months could be corrected, Prosenjit would throw up his hands and cry that it was "useless."

Nevertheless, with the help of Dr. Moore, Prosenjit was beginning to realize that he needed something to fill the gaping hole that was his life. There were mornings when he awoke and was frightened by the sheer expanse of time, the interminable hours that stretched ahead of him. So it was a great triumph when, toward the middle of July and a few days after his fifth visit to Dr. Moore, he found himself tentatively entering the towing tank, where he had not been for two months. Hoping that he would be able to slip unnoticed into his old job, he had chosen the noon hour to return, a time when he knew Gunnar Stanfil would be on lunch break.

When he opened the door to the machine shop, he was relieved to find the room empty. He stood there a moment and ran his hand over the ribbed metal door, almost caressing it. A brisk wind blew in after him, catching up loose papers and plastic sheets and flapping them about. The air was full of dust from wood that had just been planed. He breathed in the pulpy smell, feeling fortified by it, choking a little. As he shuffled forward, he became aware that the floor was covered with a layer of sawdust, and he burrowed his toes under mounds of it, groping for a foundation. It was as though he had stumbled out of a sandstorm and was seeking solid ground again.

It was not until he was setting down his tool chest that he noticed that a sheaf of mechanical drawings was unfurled on the drafting table. He whirled around and saw that the drill press was covered with peelings of metal, and there were scraps of wood on the bandsaw. Then it all came to him in a rush: Stanfil and the others must have started building the model for Sea Lab. This was the event he had been awaiting for almost eight months.

It had been at least that long since Stanfil had first mentioned the manned underwater station, a government-sponsored contest designed to further oceanographic research. Every naval architecture department in the country would be competing for the contract. Under Stanfil's supervision, Prosenjit and the others had drafted the designs for Sea Lab, an underwater habitat that could be submerged to depths of five thousand feet and manned in oceans all over the world. It was back in December, without any real hope of winning the contest, that they had submitted their designs to Washington. Then, two months later, Stanfil had received word that their entry had been selected. It meant a substantial government grant for the tank, and prestige for all connected with it. The project was not scheduled to begin until the autumn, but Stanfil had taken them all out to celebrate at Alioto's, an expensive steak and lobster restaurant on Fisherman's Wharf.

The construction had obviously begun and was well under way. Prosenjit wrestled off his windbreaker and confronted the sheets of tracing paper on the drafting table. He pored over the calculations, losing himself in the symmetry of the designs. He could visualize the underwater habitat as if it were complete, submerged somewhere in the Pacific, gathering data off the ocean floor. Then—had it been thirty or forty minutes?—he pushed back his chair and checked his watch. It struck him that for the last blissful half hour, Tanya had been totally absent from his mind. As Dr. Moore had predicted, complete absorption in his work would exclude her from his life.

"Well, well," boomed a familiar, sarcastic voice. "Look who's decided to show up."

Prosenjit jerked his head around to see Gunnar Stanfil framed in the doorway. Scrambling to his feet, he called out, "Mr. Stanfil, sir, I am happy that Sea Lab is in full action!"

"Poddar, you're on my shit list." Stanfil marched over to where Prosenjit was standing at attention. "What makes you think you're working on Sea Lab?"

Prosenjit's face fell.

Stanfil snatched the plans Prosenjit had been working on off the table and rolled them up. "Scram."

"But I am so proud—"

"Like hell. You haven't shown up in months. Last time you busted five platinum gauges and I had to clean up the mess."

"I have recovered now, sir," he stammered. "I was having temporary nerves."

"I know all about your nerves," said Stanfil. "I'm fed up with hearing about you and your love life. I'm not going to have you screwing up Sea Lab."

"There will be no more problems with me, sir. I have seen two psychiatrists."

"Two?" sneered Stanfil. "You mean one wasn't enough?"

"No, I mean, there is only one that is treating me. He has succeeded in clearing up the confusion. I'm quite ready to come back to work, even to cleaning-up chores."

"Is that what your shrink tells you?" said Stanfil. "Shrinks don't know shit."

"This doctor expresses great confidence in me."

"What does some candy-ass know about real life?" Stanfil scoffed. "The only thing worse than a shrink is a prison shrink. Someone who pokes his nose through the bars telling the guys they don't have any problems, when they're four in a cell and won't get laid for years."

Prosenjit twisted his hands. "Sea Lab needs an expert arc welder. One that is precise." He looked beseechingly at Stanfil.

"Arc welder, my ass. I made my mind up weeks ago you couldn't come back, and that stands today. Now clear out."

"Very well, sir." Prosenjit closed his tool chest and started across the room, stopping for a last look at the model ships arranged in the display case. The *Sita*, the tanker he had assembled a few months earlier, was the centerpiece of the case.

"Take it with you," said Stanfil.

"I'd prefer that you keep it," he said, his eyes on the cement floor. "I made it for you."

He started toward the door, his shoulders stooped and his head down. Suddenly it flashed on Stanfil that perhaps tools and hard work could accomplish more than any shrink could ever do. "Wait," he called. "What do you think I'm going to do with that goddam tanker?"

Prosenjit turned, daring to let his eyes meet Stanfil's.

"I'm putting you on probation."

"Probation?"

"One more screw-up and you're out."

"Yes, sir," cried Prosenjit. He bowed his head in thanks. Somehow he felt that life was about to begin again. He took a deep breath and said, "I won't give you any cause for regret."

BY mid-August, a few weeks after he had returned to his job at the towing tank, Prosenjit was feeling remarkably better. He was genuinely absorbed in the Sea Lab project and had even gone back to work on one or two of his own inventions. When he had demonstrated to Gunnar Stanfil how one of these gadgets worked—a cigarette dispenser that popped up a cigarette, fully lit—Stanfil had been so enthusiastic that he had suggested marketing it in Japan. The chief mechanic's praise had swelled Prosenjit's heart.

"I am feeling so much better, doctor, since I am done with her," he said, at the start of his sixth session with Moore.

Larry Moore nodded and leaned back in his chair.

Prosenjit had almost come to look forward to this hour, every Tuesday morning, that he spent with the young doctor with the careworn face. Just as it had always been so important to him to be the perfect student, it was now important to be the perfect patient. He wanted to win the doctor's approval, and he knew that by proving that he was cured, he would do so.

"I do not even think of her as a bad person. It's as if she doesn't exist."

"Yes, I see that you have a lot more energy for yourself these days."

"Oh, very much so. It used to be that I would wake up in the morning and think about her straight away, but now I hardly bother."

"I can see the change in you."

Prosenjit beamed. In fact, there had been only one really noteworthy incident in the last few weeks. He had written a letter home, to India, complaining about the pain that the American girl had inflicted on him and begging his parents to arrange a marriage. His father had sent back a formal note saying that he was not prepared to do so until Prosenjit had returned and proved himself recovered. He had referred to his son's passion as a "disease," much like a brain tumor, that had to be excised, and had used the Bengali expression *haather putul banano*, meaning that the American girl had turned him into her glove puppet. This letter, so scathing in its content, had only increased Prosenjit's determination to be done with Tanya.

"Do you think it will be soon, doctor, that I can graduate?"

"Graduate?"

"That you will give me a clean bill of health?"

"We're just starting to make progress. Let's wait awhile, at least until after she returns."

Prosenjit was crestfallen. He had expected Moore to share his feeling of triumph. It seemed to him that he had made more progress than the doctor was giving him credit for. "But I am full steam ahead with Sea Lab," he exclaimed. "I will never go back to what it was!"

"That's probably true, but I want to be there with a net, just in case you have a momentary slip."

"According to Alex, she is to return in some four weeks' time."

"Alex?" Moore frowned. "Have you been seeing Alex again?"

"By accident only," Prosenjit lied, regretting that he had let the name slip out. "I bumped into him on the street."

"When? What street?"

"Oh, close to Telegraph, the other day," he rushed on. "He waved from across the street."

"Did you stop to talk to him?"

"No, we barely spoke."

"But you see, don't you, how getting involved with that family will put you right back on square one."

"Oh, I see that. Quite clearly."

"You're sure of that?"

"I washed my hands clean of them."

Moore looked at him suspiciously.

"It is the girl who doesn't want to let me go. I tried to break with her once, but she called me again, and at I House she sent her emissaries after me, and wouldn't leave me alone."

"That's why I think we should be prepared for what might happen when she returns."

"I already know. I will have nothing to do with her."

"But she may call you."

A little smile appeared on Prosenjit's face.

"What will you do then?"

"I will tell her flat out not to bother me."

Larry Moore said, "You might be prepared with a simple but firm phrase, letting her know that you don't want to see her and you would appreciate it if she didn't call you anymore. I'll help you write it, if you like. You can tape it on your telephone, so when she calls, you can read it to her."

"She thinks if she can fix it so I am with Alex, she will end up with me."

Moore darkened. "Explain what you mean."

"I know she's behind the plan that Alex and I get a flat together. She's put him up to it."

"How has this communication taken place?"

"I just know how her mind works. She wants me to live with her brother so she can come live with us, in the same flat."

"Is this something Alex told you?" Moore asked guardedly.

"No, no. I have not talked to Alex. Only that I keep thinking, if it's so important to her that I live with her brother, then maybe she does love me."

Moore, exasperation mounting, said, "Mr. Poddar, you've got me thoroughly confused. I thought we were making progress—"

"We are making progress!" cried Prosenjit. "Just tell me what to do!"

Moore thought for a moment. "I think we should add another hour a week, for the time being. Especially in light of the fact she will be home soon."

"It's useless."

"It's not useless. You've been doing so well. You've got to expect setbacks now and then."

"Only I thought I was cured!"

Moore shook his head solemnly. "Give it some time. Matters of the heart take a long time to heal."

THE Dodge Charger cruised slowly down San Pablo Avenue. "You watch your side of the road," said Alex, "and I'll watch mine." He hummed along to the Beatles' song "With a Little Help from Your Friends," while Prosenjit sat rigidly alert, staring out at the storefronts that passed. They were looking for the gun shop that was in the neighborhood. Alex had recently been assigned to work the graveyard shift at the Union 76 station, and thought it would be a good idea if he bought some pellets for his air gun.

"There it is there," said Alex, pointing toward a row of one-story buildings that included an Army-Navy surplus outlet and Brothers Collateral Loans. He pulled over and parked. Three attractive girls dressed in faded workshirts were coming toward them, passing a joint back and forth. Whistling under his breath, Alex nudged Prosenjit and said, "Come on, let's go," and jumped out of the car.

Alex grinned at one of the girls, who had feathers jutting out of her hair, but she ignored him and, taking a hit off the joint, exhaled smoke in his direction as she passed. "Bunch of freaks," he said with a laugh, turning around and flipping her the bird. "Did you see that?" He glanced over at Prosenjit, but his attention seemed to be elsewhere.

"No, what?"

"What's with you today?" muttered Alex. "You ought to lighten up." He strode ahead and turned into a building that was paneled with rough-hewn planks of wood and looked much like a Wild West trading post. The shingle over the door read, "Frontier Gun Shop." Prosenjit followed him inside.

Ever since Prosenjit had heard that Alex had received a letter from Tanya, telling him that she might come home early, his behavior had been unnaturally tense and distorted. Whatever spontaneity he had once enjoyed was gone; he rigidly steered every gesture, controlled every emotion, as though he were living in a police state. He was determined she was not going to catch hold of him again, try as she might. But deep down he knew he was weak, and he was ashamed of this weakness, almost as one would be ashamed of a foul body odor.

The Frontier Gun Shop was a windowless room that was as cool and dark as a cave. The interior walls were paneled with knotty pine, polished to a high gloss and adorned with antlers and stuffed quail. Rows of rifles, standing on end, lined the shelves, and handguns of every shape and size rested on a bedding of fern-green felt under a six-foot-long glass counter.

Alex walked over and leaned against the counter.

A salesman was cleaning a glass display case that held antique rifles and war paraphernalia. When he looked up and saw Alex, he said, "Is that Alex Tarasoff? How're you doing, brother?"

His tone of familiarity flattered Alex, and he grinned. "Hey, Rudy," he said, "Do you mind if I show my friend the .38 caliber Smith and Wesson? The one with blued steel and the Airweight frame?"

"Model 37?"

"That's it."

Rudy took the gun out of its case. Alex turned to Prosenjit and said, "This gun handles better than any handgun in the world. This is what I'm going to get when I turn twenty-one." He raised it in the air and pretended to fire. "There're so many crazies out there," he went on, "you got to be on your toes all the time. Late at night they're not content just to rob you. They want to do bodily harm."

"The world is full of bullies," agreed Prosenjit.

"You got to learn how to control it, just like you learn how to drive a car," said Alex, clicking off a few make-believe rounds. "Here," and he handed the gun to Prosenjit, who turned it over in his hands, a spark of interest showing in his eyes.

"It's a beaut," said Alex.

"It's better than a prayer," said Rudy.

"How much does this baby run, Rudy? About two hundred bucks?"

"Two-fifty."

"Does the bullet explode in pieces when it hits the body?" asked Prosenjit.

"You can buy the kind that flatten out. They do the most body damage," said Rudy.

"I would like to own this gun," said Prosenjit.

"Well, forget it," said Alex. "They don't sell guns to foreigners. Only American citizens can buy guns."

"That's right," said Rudy. "You have to be over twenty-one, be a citizen of the U.S., and have a clean record."

"Could I buy a special permit to own one?"

"No, man, the laws are strict," said Alex. "Why do you think I use an air gun? Don't you think I'd rather have one of those?" He pointed at the handgun cabinet. " 'Course, if you get lucky, you can buy one on the street. I got a friend who found a sawed-off shotgun in the trunk of a car in Oakland."

"Who sells them on the streets?"

"Muggers, junkies. Hey, Rudy. You got any CO_2 pellets, box of five hundred?"

Rudy put a round tin full of pellets on the counter and slid it to Alex.

"Can your pellet gun kill a person?" asked Prosenjit.

"Shit yes, if you aim right. 'Course, you got to be real close."

Rudy scoffed, "A pellet gun's not going to kill a squirrel."

"If you aim at the face and hit 'em in the eye it will. The pellet goes straight into the brain."

"How far does the pellet travel into the body?" asked Prosenjit.

"About an inch and a half, two inches," said Alex.

"Am I permitted to buy one of those?"

"Sure," said Rudy. "Come around anytime."

Prosenjit stared wide-eyed at him.

"It's a good thing to have," said Alex. "I mean shit, if I'm getting robbed, I can at least defend myself."

Later, when they were driving back to the I House, Prosenjit couldn't help wondering why Tanya was coming back early. Perhaps something unpleasant had occurred in Brazil. Telling himself that it wouldn't hurt to inquire, he found himself asking, "How has your sister been enjoying her holiday?"

"I don't know. I guess she's having a real good time."

The thought that she had been having fun filled him with anger, and he said, "I think all she went down there for was to whore around."

"What's wrong with you? You know she doesn't do it for money."

"But she does do it."

"Well, maybe she's not a virgin, if that's what you mean."

"I feel sorry for her."

"What are you talking about?"

The old anger rose.

"Why don't you forget my sister?"

"It is very bad. Somebody should tell her not to be cheap with herself. Make her come to her senses."

"Well, if anybody tells her anything, it's not going to be me or you."

Prosenjit gripped the sides of the car seat and averted his face so Alex could not see his distorted features. He felt the fury surging through him, taking hold of his being once again. Silently, he prayed to Kali to remove his terrible obsession, but it was too late. His heart beat violently, and there was a strange noise in his brain, like wind through a tunnel. He was barely conscious of the ride home, and when they pulled up in front of the I House, he stumbled out of the car and went directly to his room.

WHEN the knock sounded at his door, Larry Moore lost no time in opening it. He had been pacing nervously ever since the telephone call, an hour earlier, that shook him up. He found himself confronting a strong-featured, smooth face. A face that matched the well-spoken voice he had heard over the phone.

"Doctor?" Jal Mehta reached out and gave him a firm handshake. "Perhaps I'm overreacting, but I don't think so."

"Overreacting?" said Moore. "When you tell me he's trying to buy a gun?"

"It's so unfortunate, really." Jal grimaced. "I've known him half my life. He's always been touchy, but he's the most generous and decent chap you'd ever want to meet. He'd never hurt a fly. I mean that literally."

"Buying a gun is no idle gesture," said Moore, indicating a chair. "It means he intends to act out his fantasies."

Jal sat down. "At first, after you called me, I thought no, I don't want to do anything more on this matter. You see, I had hoped that the burden had been taken off my shoulders after I turned Prosenjit over to Dr. Gold."

"Yes, I gathered that much from the file."

"You see, before she left town, I had been finding it increasingly difficult to communicate with him. Sometimes he would ask for my help, which I was quite willing to give, and then he would accuse me and my friends of wrong intentions. The whole atmosphere was contrary. I thought my interference was only making matters worse."

"You were wise to pull back. But tell me, what happened last night?"

"I hadn't seen him in the dining hall, so I went to his room. It was obvious he hadn't been out all day. He was lying on a soiled sheet and the blinds were drawn. There was such a stench in the place you wouldn't believe it."

"What the hell happened? I was under the impression that conditions had been improving."

"Yes, yes, that's true, up until the point, a few days back, when he went off with the girl's brother."

Moore paled. "He told me over and over that he wasn't seeing Alex."

"Oh, no, they have been very close, with Alex coming frequently to I House."

"He's been keeping that from me." Moore paced the room. "He's probably been lying about other things, too." He whirled on Jal. "Tell me the rest."

"He was looking very strange, and he said, 'Jal, please do not see me anymore. This is the end between us.' I asked him, 'Why, what has happened?' And that's when he muttered something about going to San Francisco to buy a gun."

After Jal left his office, Moore remained seated in his chair, staring out at the Campanile, from where, just a few weeks earlier, a student had jumped to his death.

He was ruminating over what would happen if he went ahead and blew the whistle on Prosenjit. His dilemma was one that went to the very heart of his profession. Should he break with the time-honored principle of confidentiality and disclose to the police that Prosenjit was threatening the life of Tanya Tarasoff, thus rupturing his relationship with Prosenjit, and causing him to be placed in a treatment and evaluation facility, like Herrick Hospital? Or should he keep silent and continue to build on the positive relationship he had managed to form with the boy, and avert danger in that way? It was a dilemma that had as many hues as a prism.

On the one hand, the principle of confidentiality that had been drilled into his head throughout his years of study held that as a precondition of psychotherapy, there must be a compact between therapist and patient that statements made by the patient would be held in the strictest confidence and never disclosed. This principle had its roots in the Hippocratic Oath, and although the code was not so absolute as the one that existed between priest and penitent or lawyer and client, it was still binding. According to the guidelines of the American Medical Association, a physician could not violate the principle of confidentiality "unless he is required to do so by law or unless it becomes necessary in order to protect the welfare of the individual or of the community."

As far as Moore was concerned, in no branch of medicine was the bond between doctor and patient more intimate than in psychiatry. The only exception to the all-inclusive principle of confidentiality was if there was a clear potential for harm done by the patient.

On the other hand, Moore always questioned his ability to predict future behavior. Just because he had a Ph.D. in psychology didn't mean he had a crystal ball. Even the fact that Prosenjit had been making threats to get even with the girl was not necessarily significant. It had been Moore's experience that most patients who came in for help were struggling with destructive impulses, and often made threats, even expressed the wish to see someone dead. The venting of anger was not only routine to the therapeutic process, it was also promising. If a patient had an outlet for his rage, the chances were greater that he wouldn't have to act it out.

Moore had been taught that the best predictor of future violence was a history of past violence, and in Prosenjit's case, there was none. Absolutely none. Still, Prosenjit—being the innocent that he was—had never been involved with a girl like Tanya Tarasoff. If one was to believe him, Tanya was the tormentor and he was her hapless victim. She was repeatedly enticing him to come closer, and then when he yielded, spurning him. No matter how he had tried, Moore had failed to make Prosenjit see that he was participating, too; she couldn't humiliate him unless he showed up on schedule to be humiliated.

But what to do with the girl? From the stories Prosenjit had told him, and from what Jal Mehta had been able to corroborate, Moore had formed a picture of a flighty, capricious teenager. For all Moore knew, she might return from her vacation and not even make an attempt to see Prosenjit. Or with Moore's help, Prosenjit might muster the strength to keep away from her. But in his gut, Moore tended to think that neither Tanya nor Prosenjit could keep themselves from being drawn into their flirtation with death.

Such as Prosenjit's talk of buying a gun.

Moore rose from his chair and walked to the bookshelf. He took down the *Welfare and Institutions Code and Laws Relating to Social Welfare*. He opened it to the index and looked up commitment procedures.

Twenty minutes later, Larry Moore entered the Cowell Hospital cafeteria. He stood at the door and scanned the tables. He spotted the curly red top of Stuart Gold's head, across the room. He was sitting opposite Barbara Lena, a middle-aged therapist.

As Larry approached their table, Lena gave him an easy smile. "Here comes our Young Dr. Moore," she said with a drawl of intimacy, pushing aside her sandwich and bag of corn chips and making room for him.

Moore slid in next to her. "Stuart," he said, "I'm glad I found you."

"What's up?" said Gold, prying his attention away from a plate of brisket.

"We've got a problem on our hands with Prosenjit Poddar."

"Poddar?" said Gold, trying to jog his memory.

"Stu's up to almost sixty patients a week," cracked Lena, "so he tends to lose sight of a few of them."

"The Indian student you diagnosed as a paranoid schizophrenic. The thin little fellow who's totally obsessed with the American girl."

"Oh, right," said Gold. "Another case of unrequited love."

"I think he's dangerous."

Gold frowned. "I remember him now. Passive, blunted in affect. A timid little thing."

"Maybe not that timid. I've just had a visit from a friend of his who says he's buying a gun."

"Is that right?" said Gold, his equanimity seemingly undisturbed.

"That's right. He's been threatening all along to get even with her."

"I hear that sort of thing all the time," said Lena, through a bite of her sandwich. "It's hard to know who to take seriously."

"Most of the time patients are seeking a way to vent their rage," said Gold. "That doesn't mean they're going to do anything about it."

"Somehow this feels different."

"You're especially in the dark with these fellows from the Far East," said Gold. "They're hard to read."

"That's just it. Back in India, he might be able to handle the stress, but he's struggling to cope in a culture he's utterly unprepared for. It's driving him crazy."

"Listen," said Gold. "If I had thought he was really crazy, I would have checked him into the hospital right away. Obviously I didn't."

"You diagnosed him as psychotic, for Christ's sake. And you prescribed Thorazine."

"I wanted to give him time to calm down," said Gold, shifting uneasily. "He was looking for a way to save face. With those people, saving face is everything."

"All I know is, the girl was supposed to be away for another month but now, I'm told, she could be coming home anytime."

Gold shook his head. "And here I assumed you had this under control."

"I thought I had, too. But he's gone behind my back and bought a gun. I'm going to have to confront him about it, tomorrow morning. I'm going to take that gun away."

"You'll lose him for sure," snapped Gold. "I guarantee you. He'll be out the door faster than you can blink an eye."

"The number-one rule," said Lena, "is to keep the patient coming back for treatment. As long as you have him in tow, you have some control over his acting-out problems."

In a sense, Moore thought they were right. Keeping Prosenjit in therapy might be the best protection Tanya had. By confronting the boy and rupturing the therapeutic relationship, he might be increasing the danger to her rather than reducing it.

"I just wish you had come to me sooner," put in Gold. "I'd hate for this to get back to Powelson."

"It may have to."

Barbara Lena rolled her eyes. "Powelson? You must be mad." She and Gold exchanged a quick glance.

"Just don't do anything rash." And then Gold added, "Just remember, you're under no obligation to act," making an allusion to the common-law rule that as a therapist treating a voluntary outpatient, Moore was not legally required to warn those who might suffer danger.

"Jesus. We're talking about a human life," said Moore, his voice rising in volume and causing several others sitting nearby to turn and look at them.

Gold leaned in closer. "All I'm saying," he hissed, "is that you may not have enough experience to handle this case."

"You assigned it to me."

"Maybe it's time to turn it over to someone with a little more experience."

Moore edged forward, only inches from Gold's florid face. "You're forgetting one thing. The girl. Even the most experienced therapist is going to have absolutely no control over what she does. I think she's doing her best to provoke my patient to extreme behavior."

Lena and Gold stared at him.

Moore went on, "She's been out of the country for eight weeks. That gave me some room to work with him. When she gets back, there's no telling what may happen. She may push him into killing her. I don't think she realizes what she's doing, but she may be setting up her own execution. How're you going to control *that*? Huh, Stuart? By transferring the case?"

ON the morning of August 18, Prosenjit furtively approached Larry Moore's office. He formed his lips in a stiff smile and knocked on the door. A moment later, Moore opened the door and Prosenjit moved in with the mechanical evenness of a robot.

Already in a state of hyperalertness, he was thrown off balance by Moore's opening line. "I understand that you have been seeing Alex all along."

"Alex is the only friend I have left," he replied stubbornly. He was not going to allow himself to be stripped of the last relationship that was important in his life.

"Not only that, but I've heard you've bought a gun."

The muscles in his face twitched. "Only not for hurting her but to save her."

"What do you mean?"

"The girl is prostituting herself. But I believe that she can learn how to become good again. I merely want to teach her a lesson."

"How will you do that?"

"I will pay someone at I House one hundred dollars to secure her sexual favors. Maybe I will ask Gorian Newaz. After he brings her back to his room and before they start having sex, I will burst in and rescue her. Then I will take her off to my room and say, 'Do you see what you have gotten yourself into? Don't you see that I have really saved you from a terrible fate?'"

"Mr. Poddar," said Moore, rising from his chair, "do you realize that what you just said doesn't make sense?"

Prosenjit smiled mysteriously.

"You do not realize that fact?"

"Only you said I was getting better!"

"Is it because Tanya is due to return?"

"It is no matter that she is returning."

"I'm going to ask you to give me the gun."

Prosenjit waved his arms, as if to push away his words. "There is no gun."

"If you don't give it to me, I'm going to go to the police."

"But I've already told you, I'm not going to hurt her with it."

"Then I'm going to have to take the necessary steps to have you detained in the mental ward at Herrick Hospital for observation."

"It's just as I thought," cried Prosenjit, now rising from his chair and walking hurriedly toward the door. "You're against me too," and he stalked out of the office.

Larry Moore immediately telephoned the campus police. He was informed that two officers would be dispatched shortly, to interview him in his office.

The knock on his door came at three-fifteen in the afternoon. When Moore opened the door, he found himself facing Johnny Teel, a pudgy man just over five feet tall, with twinkling blue eyes and a boxer's flattened nose; and Everette Atkinson, a taciturn man who stood nearly a foot taller than his partner and hid behind glasses as thick as Coke bottles. In his hand Atkinson held a note pad.

Moore informed them that he had been treating an Indian student, Prosenjit Poddar, who resided in room 607 of the International House, and that he believed that this patient was capable of doing bodily harm to a girl named Tanya Tarasoff. He explained how Prosenjit, when confronted about a gun he had bought, had refused to turn it over to him. "In my opinion," he concluded, "unless Poddar is committed for observation, the girl is in danger of losing her life."

Both Teel and Atkinson, having never before been requested to incarcerate a person without a court order, insisted on examining the regulations in Moore's *Welfare and Institutions Code and Laws Relating to Social Welfare*. Although worded uncertainly, the regulation seemed to call for detainment for observation only after the attending medical authority had written a letter requesting it. Moore agreed to comply.

"Here, Stuart, I've got something for you to sign," said Larry Moore, taking a letter out of its envelope and sliding it across Gold's desk.

Gold scanned the page. "What're you coming to *me* for?"

"Powelson's out of town. I need you to cosign it."

"Can't this wait until he gets back?"

Moore shook his head. "Tanya will be back before Powelson is."

"It seems to me that the first step is to ask Poddar to voluntarily commit himself."

"I've done that. This morning. He refused. I confronted him about the gun and asked him to give it to me. He refused that, too."

Gold shifted uneasily. He looked at the letter as if it were a scorpion. "This really is the kind of thing Powelson should authorize."

"Are you going to tell me that I shouldn't breach confidentiality?"

"For Christ's sake, confidentiality doesn't even enter into it. I just think this has been going on for a long time now—what is it, two or three months? Why can't you wait another week or ten days until Powelson gets back?"

"I have to act *now*. If you sign the letter, the police will pick him up and take him into Herrick for seventy-two hours of observation. Once they get a load of him there, he'll have a hard time getting out. In any case, we'll both be off the hook."

Gold squirmed in his seat. "I don't see how that gets us off the hook."

"Look, Yandell's already signed it," said Moore, pointing to the signature of the acting director of the psychiatry department. "Now I need an M.D.'s signature."

"But his record gives no indication he's had any history of violence."

"Stuart, we can't just close our eyes and hope that this will go away."

Gold let out a sigh.

"He's an Untouchable," said Moore. "Doesn't that say anything to you?"

"Not particularly. There are a hundred million of them."

"Not in this country there aren't. He's *one* in a hundred million. Do you realize what kind of odds he had to overcome just to get here?"

Gold shook his head.

"His grandparents had to clean shit out of latrines. When he was growing up, the other kids in the village wouldn't play with him because he was stigmatized as unclean. They thought he might contaminate them."

"Are you telling me that just because he's had an underprivileged background he's dangerous?"

"You don't seem to realize that we're talking about a brilliant boy. Top of his class before he met her. Now he's flunking out. He's letting everything he's worked for his entire life go down the drain. If he gets sent back to India it will be a disgrace he'll never live down. In his mind the only way he can hold on to his career and his self-respect is to kill her."

"What gives you such a crystal ball?"

"Is that it, Stuart? Is that what you're going to be asking when you're confronting her body in the morgue?"

Gold looked up with doleful eyes. He picked up his pen and signed the letter.

A late-afternoon sun fell on the barricaded shopfronts along Telegraph Avenue. The Bank of America, The Mediterranean Café, and Cody's Bookstore, all once shining plate glass, were now, after the last spell of rioting, boarded up with raw sheets of plywood. Disheveled street vendors squatted next to Navajo blankets on which were displayed leather crafts and turquoise jewelry. In the air hung the moist odor of body excretions and patchouli oil, defying the sudden gusts of wind that sent leaflets fluttering into the gutters.

It was four in the afternoon on a windy August 20. Even though classes were not in session, a steady stream of students and street people flowed down Telegraph, heading toward the vortex of action, Sproul Plaza.

Larry Moore elbowed his way through the crowd, heading in the same direction but attempting to move at a faster pace. His face was set in grim determination, and he seemed oblivious to the bodies that jostled him.

He couldn't get his mind off of Tanya, the girl he had never seen or talked to. She had been described to him in such detail that he thought he could recognize her if they met by chance. Beguiling green eyes that slanted upward like a Mongolian princess's. A little girl's body that was slender as a reed. Long dark hair that swung with every step she danced. He knew secrets about her that would make her cringe. He had heard her voice on a tape recording, teasing and taunting, saying things she should never have said to the Indian boy. She had become so real that last night she had appeared in his dream.

Moore wondered whether he had become too identified with his patient, if his much-vaunted objectivity had deserted him. He felt obliged to ask himself an onerous question: Had Tanya Tarasoff succeeded in seducing him, too?

He had to admit that when he had listened to Prosenjit's recounting of the girl's inconsistencies, they had triggered off angry memories of his own not-so-distant past. He couldn't help but wonder whether any of his silent rage toward his wife, Inger, had transferred itself to Tanya. It occurred to him that perhaps by tacitly siding with Prosenjit against the girl he had even incited him. This monstrous thought drove him forward.

As he neared Sather Gate, he saw the usual crowd of demonstrators milling about in the Plaza. Approximately a hundred of them, chanting slogans and carrying pickets. They were contained on two sides by a cordon of police, wearing flak jackets and holding bayonets, their unsheathed points tilting toward the sky. Undaunted, Moore threaded his way through the demonstration and ran up the steps of Sproul Hall. He swung through the heavy glass doors. Inside, the corridor was cool and silent. His footsteps echoed on the marble slabs. He stopped in front of the registrar's window and asked, "Where do I find the police?"

"In the basement at the rear of the building," said a voice from behind the glass partition.

Moore found his way to a door on which was tacked a cardboard sign marked "Police." He went in. The fluorescent lights gave off a harsh yellow sheen. There were about a half-dozen uniformed cops strapping on armored vests and shin guards. He recognized the white helmet with the red cross of a paramedic, who was loading medical equipment into a satchel. No one paid any attention to him. "I'm here to see Chief Beall," he said to a lieutenant who was counting canisters of tear gas and entering numbers into a log.

The lieutenant glanced up. "The chief's not here."

"I phoned earlier and he told me to come in."

The lieutenant eyed Moore, saw a youngish man in a tattered cashmere sweater and faded jeans, with shoulder-length hair. "Who are you?"

"I'm from Cowell Hospital. This is an emergency—"

"An emergency?" He snorted.

Moore reddened. "I'm Dr. Moore." He thrust the envelope at him. "Chief Beall told me to hand-deliver this."

The lieutenant took the envelope. "I'll make sure he gets it."

Moore left the office.

Hours later, when the demonstrators had gone home to watch themselves on the six-o'clock news, and the Blue Meanies had checked in their flak jackets and gas masks for the day, William Beall, chief of the campus police, returned to his office to plan the next day's defensive. Ever since the People's Park uprising in May, he had been requisitioning sophisticated riot gear, and tonight his mind was on the new gas grenades that could be ejected through the exhaust system of a police vehicle, which his men fondly referred to as Puff, the Magic Dragon. It was only after he sat down at his desk with a cup of coffee that he noticed the letter. When he unfolded it he saw that it was from Cowell Hospital, and then he recalled the brief phone conversation he had had with the psychologist that morning. It seemed ages ago. He wearily flattened the page out on his desk and read:

August 20, 1969

William Beall, Chief of Police
Room 2, Sproul Hall
Campus

Dear Chief Beall:

Mr. Poddar was first seen at Cowell Hospital by Dr. Stuart Gold, June 5, 1969, on an emergency basis. After receiving medication he was referred to the outpatient psychiatry clinic for psychotherapy. Since then I have seen him here seven times.

His mental status varies considerably. At times he appears to be quite rational, at other times he appears quite psychotic. It is my impression that currently the appropriate diagnosis for him is paranoid schizophrenic reaction, acute and severe. He is at this point a danger to the welfare of other people and himself. That is, he has been threatening to kill an unnamed girl who he feels has betrayed him and has violated his honor. He has told a friend of his (Jal Mehta, also of International House) that he intends to go to San Francisco to buy a gun and that he plans to kill the girl. He has been somewhat more cryptic with me, but has alluded strongly to the compulsion to "get even with," and "hurt" the girl.

I have discussed this matter with Dr. Gold and we concur in the opinion that Mr. Poddar should be committed for observation in a mental hospital. I request the assistance of your department in this matter.

Sincerely,

Lawrence Moore, Ph.D.
Clinical Psychologist
Department of Psychiatry

ON the afternoon of August 22, Prosenjit was working on Sea Lab when he heard the crunch of tires over the gravel drive and the sound of car doors slamming. Through the window he saw two uniformed police officers approaching. There was no doubt in his mind now; Dr. Moore had betrayed him. He sank lower into his chair and, like a spider from a dark corner, watched as they entered Gunnar Stanfil's office.

A few minutes later Gunnar Stanfil tapped him on the shoulder and whispered that apparently one of his "shrinks" had lodged a complaint against him, and that the police were there to question him. However, Stanfil, contemptuous of shrinks, said he had already assured them that "everything could be straightened out."

Careful to show only casual interest in this information, Prosenjit shrugged and said, "I'm happy to talk to the officers." By the time that Stanfil returned with the police in tow, he was hunched over a steel casing, apparently oblivious to their arrival. Stanfil cleared his throat, and Prosenjit glanced up.

"Oh, officers," he exclaimed, jumping up and approaching them. "I would shake your hands, only mine has so much dirt," he said, indicating his own grease-covered hand and grabbing a rag.

After introductions were made, Stanfil nudged Prosenjit and said, "I thought I'd hang around. You might want me here." Prosenjit nodded, and Stanfil remained standing a few feet to one side, twisting the corner of his mustache.

As always in the presence of authority figures, Prosenjit became meek and deferential. It was important to him that he win the police officers' respect. Besides, he liked the pudgy fellow, with the seamed face and the crinkly blue eyes. The man had a jolly manner about him, and Prosenjit imagined that, unlike everyone else, he was actually sympathetic to his situation.

Prosenjit answered their questions in a solicitous manner, explaining that the young lady in question was a language major at Merritt Junior College in Oakland and that when she was in the area she came to the I House to practice her different languages with the residents. He told them that on a number of occasions, he had eaten lunch and dinner at the Tarasoff home and that her brother, Alex Tarasoff, frequently drove him to work.

Then Officer Teel, the pudgy one, said, "What do you think it was that alarmed your therapist so much?"

"Dr. Moore? Oh, those things I said to the psychiatrist were just play-acting."

"If you have a problem," said Teel, "maybe we can help. We probably take more time with students than any other police department in the world. If a student has a problem, we make it our own."

"No, there is no problem."

Teel and Atkinson exchanged a look.

"Maybe it would be a good idea if you came on down to the department, after you get off work," said Teel.

"Please," said Prosenjit, "would it be better for you if you brought me there now?"

"That would be most obliging, if you wouldn't mind."

Prosenjit scurried off to collect his tiffin carrier and tool chest. While he was gone, Gunnar Stanfil said to the officers, "From now on, I'm going to keep an eye on him. Don't worry about a thing. He'll be working five to six days a week, eight to ten hours a day, and he won't have time for any more foolishness."

They drove to the campus in silence. What Johnny Teel and his partner, Everette Atkinson, had elected not to tell Prosenjit was that the day before they had questioned Jal Mehta, who had confirmed that Prosenjit had made numerous statements that he would get even and kill Tanya Tarasoff. Jal had told them that he thought "Mr. Poddar should either be committed to a mental hospital or should go back to India." However, when asked if he would mind making a written statement in regard to Mr. Poddar's behavior, Jal had declined.

During the drive to the police department, Prosenjit told the officers that his father, who was the court inspector for the district magistrate's office of Dinajpur, would be quite interested in the police procedures of this country.

"Oh yeah?" Teel turned around. The boy was smiling and seemingly unconcerned. "What's the punishment for a crime, back in India?"

"They are cutting off your hands, if you are a thief. And the head, if you are a murderer."

"Sounds pretty strict."

"Oh, very much so." Prosenjit laughed.

To Johnny Teel, the boy looked like a timid little runt that the wind could blow away. The only indication that he might be feeling nervous was that he kept buttoning and unbuttoning the cuffs of his shirt.

Atkinson turned the squad car into the driveway behind Sproul Hall and parked. The officers led Prosenjit down a ramp into the basement of Sproul, where the headquarters was housed. There they were joined by a Lieutenant Halleran, who ushered them into an empty office and closed the door behind him.

Teel began by asking Prosenjit how he liked school and his job at the towing tank. When he was satisfied that Prosenjit was feeling more at ease, he leaned closer and said, "Now tell us, why do you keep bothering the girl?"

Prosenjit stiffened. "Actually it is she who is interfering with me." He proceeded to tell them how she had taunted him at the I House dances and had stood him up on several occasions.

"Was she your girlfriend?"

"Yes."

"Did you ever have sex with her?"

"I am not interested in sex with her. But she was having it with someone else and threw it up to me."

Embarrassed for the boy, Teel averted his eyes. "We've heard from several people that you've threatened her."

"If they say this, I certainly don't want anything else to do with her."

"Are you saying that you didn't threaten her?"

"It bothered me that she was so free with herself. But not anymore. I'm done with her."

"You'll leave her alone?"

"I might have some trouble avoiding her, socially, but I will go out of my way to do so whenever possible so as not to cause trouble."

The three officers asked Prosenjit to wait while they left the room to confer. They were gone less than ten minutes. When they returned, Prosenjit rose from his chair and stood before them, his head bowed.

"Well." Teel cleared his throat. "There's no one who says that the girl herself is afraid of you. I see no reason to be concerned."

Prosenjit lifted his eyes.

"We've decided to take your word that you'll stay away from her," said Atkinson.

Teel added, "You seem as normal as any one of us. Like a rational young man." Atkinson and Halleran voiced their agreement, and then, one by one, they complimented Prosenjit on his short hair and clean-cut appearance, saying that he had been a pleasure to deal with compared to the hippies who were overrunning the Berkeley campus. "Those people have no respect for law and order," muttered Teel, as much to himself as to anyone else.

Prosenjit smiled broadly. He wished with all his might that his father was there to make the acquaintance of this good-natured policeman. It seemed almost too good to be true, but then Teel was giving him a congratulatory slap on the back and was asking if he wanted a lift back to his dorm.

When they pulled up in front of the I House, Prosenjit invited the officers up to his room, saying, "Maybe you would be keen to see the workshop I've fixed up?" The policemen spent a few minutes admiring the ship models and electronic gadgets that were displayed on his shelves. Much to Prosenjit's delight, Officer Teel seemed particularly impressed. He told Prosenjit that his inventions were so ingenious he ought to get them patented. As Teel was leaving, he handed Prosenjit a business card and added a heartfelt, "If you ever need to talk, give me a holler."

THE following Thursday, August 28, Larry Moore entered the gray fortress of Cowell Hospital. It was his first appearance at the clinic since he had delivered the letter to Chief Beall and since the return of Harvey Powelson. Moore's face showed signs of sleeplessness, and his lean body looked almost gaunt under his flannel shirt.

As he climbed the stairs to his office, he passed Neal Ross, his regular tennis partner, who gave him a sheepish greeting and hurried off. Moore paused on the landing and watched Ross's back recede down the hall. What did this brush-off mean? Was it possible that rumors of his breaking confidentiality and going to the police had already spread through the clinic? His telephone had been conspicuously silent over the last few days. It was starting to dawn on him that his colleagues—even the ones he counted as friends—were reluctant to get involved.

Later that morning as Moore was making his way down the hall, Dr. Harvey Powelson stepped out of his office and collared him. "I need a word with you," said Powelson. Detecting a slight tremor in the chief of psychiatry's voice, Moore braced himself and entered his office.

Dr. Harvey Powelson had taken over as chief of psychiatry in 1964. The charismatic doctor had about him the look of a high school quarterback, not big enough to be a pro, but endowed with a spry, athletic stance. Sporting a full beard and tweedy jackets, Powelson had quickly gained a reputation as a maverick, prominent in the Free Speech Movement and outspoken in his support of hallucinogenic drugs and experimental therapies. He was the kind of man who embraced new philosophies with the exuberance of youth, and it was not long before the clinic became known as a model psychiatric center, attracting some of the best young minds from around the country.

But within the last year, to the amazement of all, Dr. Harvey Powelson's politics had inexplicably taken a sharp turn to the right, so much so that he took on all the characteristics of a law-and-order zealot. As an administrator, he had become authoritarian and inflexible. He turned with a vengeance against the hippies on campus, calling them "spoiled brats" and "self-pitying assholes." In a recent address to a psychoanalytic association, he had stated, "All long-haired freaks should be thrown into a concentration camp and force-fed." And in a move that his colleagues at the hospital particularly decried, he aligned himself with Dr. Hardin Jones, professor of medical physics and physiology, who had been barnstorming around the country on the platform that smoking marijuana produces severe neurological damage.

Powelson even went so far as to inform several therapists that he wanted them to work closely with the campus police, who he referred to as the clinic's "sister agency." He gave the therapists direct orders that if any patient reported drug usage, like smoking a joint or dropping acid, the individual's name should be passed on to the police. Although this dictate was in violation of the university's policy on confidentiality, Powelson made every attempt to enforce it.

The change in Powelson's personality was so disconcerting that members of his staff had begun to jokingly predict mass purgings of the ranks. Old-timers at the clinic, once considered close confidants of Powelson, now found themselves cast off like unwelcome relatives, and younger therapists were regularly called into his office for interrogation and disciplinary action. With the rules forever shifting, gossip was rife and paranoia ran high. The final straw came in January of 1969, when Powelson created a stir by appearing at a staff meeting with his beard shaved off. No one had ever seen the chief of psychiatry without his beard. Standing behind the podium, he had surveyed the shocked faces of his staff before he spoke. "Do you see this mouth?" he had asked, pointing at his tight, thin lips. "This is the mouth of a Presbyterian minister. This is the mouth of my grandfather." The event was further confirmation that his personality was undergoing a radical change. Some of his colleagues speculated that the transformation was the result of his divorce from Dorothy, his wife of twenty years, and his recent marriage to a former patient. Others close to him thought that it was a reaction against his own children's apparent involvement with drugs. Whatever the cause, nearly everyone agreed that his effect on the clinic had been highly detrimental, and that the atmosphere at Cowell was beginning to smack of totalitarianism.

As soon as he had closed the door, Powelson snatched up a sheet of paper and whirled on Moore. "You owe me an explanation," he said, struggling to control himself.

Recognizing the paper as a copy of his letter to Chief Beall, Moore took a deep breath. "You were on vacation," he said. "I had to act quickly."

"Go on."

"I conferred with Drs. Gold and Yandell and they agreed that I should have the patient put into Herrick for both his protection and the girl's."

"You're aware, of course, that you've breached the ethics of your profession?"

"In what way?" asked Moore, his lips tightening.

"By breaking confidentiality with your patient and going to the police."

"I had no choice. I asked him point-blank what his intentions were toward the girl. It was clear from his answer that he was contemplating homicide."

"You realize, don't you, that by betraying his trust, you destroyed whatever chance you had of helping him?"

"It was past that point. And besides, I think he *wanted* me to break confidentiality. His telling me of his intentions was his way of saying, 'Look, I'm out of control. I'm going to kill this girl unless you stop me. Won't you please stop me.'"

"But you're bound to silence by the rule of confidentiality."

"There is no such rule. There are only guidelines. When someone's life is in danger it's my right and duty to inform the authorities.

"That decision rests with *me*, not you."

"All right, if you have any doubts about my diagnosis, why don't you see the patient for yourself?"

"I don't need to see him," said Powelson. "And I'll tell you why." He went behind his desk, yanked open a drawer, and picked up a sheaf of papers. He fanned them out on his desk. "The police file."

Moore went white. "Police file?"

Powelson was livid. "Last Thursday, Detectives John Teel and Everette Atkinson brought your patient down to the station for questioning. They also talked to other people familiar with the patient." He fingered out a sheet, scanned it, and said, "Jal Mehta, his best friend from India, reports that Poddar has made threats against the girl, but when the police asked him to make a written statement, he refused."

Moore tried to interrupt, but Powelson held up his hand. Gunnar Stanfil, chief mechanic at the Richmond Field Station, calls the Indian a 'love-sick puppy.' Said his relationship with the girl interfered with his work for a while, but for the last few weeks he's been 'shipshape.' "

"But you yourself know that paranoid schizophrenics often function very well at their jobs—"

"Oh really?" said Powelson. "The police did their own appraisal and decided that your patient appears quite rational."

"They aren't psychologists. I am. And I'm telling you he's fixated on taking revenge against this girl."

"He told the police that he had an excellent relationship with her and her family, too. Apparently he eats meals at their house, and the girl's brother drives him to work. He assured them that he didn't realize he was bothering her, and if she felt that way, he'd leave her alone."

"He's lying," cried Moore. "You know yourself that a paranoid schizophrenic can be quite cunning. And the more brilliant he is, as in the case of this boy, the greater is his capacity to dissemble, to cloak his psychotic drive. The police have fallen for it."

"They gave him a warning to stay away from the girl, and they feel that's enough. They've concluded that commitment is not necessary."

"I wouldn't try to give out traffic tickets. They shouldn't try making psychiatric evaluations!"

"One day you just may be giving out traffic tickets."

"Did the police find the gun?"

Powelson stepped around his desk and directly confronted him. "Look, Moore, I've had enough. The 'gun' in question is a child's BB gun, and he hasn't even bought it yet. The police say he's harmless, and I stand behind their judgment. So you do exactly what I say. Call Chief Beall and tell him you've made a mistake. Tell him that I said that the police are our sister agency, that we work together, and that I wouldn't want any action taken by someone on my staff to embarrass them."

Moore was stunned.

Powelson went on, "Pick up the letter you sent him. Get all the copies of it and destroy them."

"I don't see why it's necessary to go that far," said Moore, thinking that it was a felony for a doctor to destroy legal documents and determining that he would quietly take the Poddar file home, safely away from the clinic.

"You're on probation, Moore. I don't trust your judgment. I'm putting a supervisor on all your cases. One false move—and I don't just mean with your Indian—and you're finished. Now get out."

Utterly shaken, Moore turned and walked out of the office. Powelson had left him with the impression that the whole episode with Prosenjit had been his fault and that he had really caused people a lot of trouble and inconvenience. It was as though he were in the middle of a nightmare. To top it off, he still had to face the embarrassment of calling Chief Beall, James Yandell, and Stuart Gold and asking them to return their copies of his letter.

Over the course of the next week, matters only got worse. When Moore tried to talk to his colleagues at the clinic, it was obvious that they didn't want to get involved. Some refused to take him seriously, acting as though he were just a beginner in the complex field of mental health. Others, like James Yandell, who had had enough confidence in Moore's feeling about Prosenjit's homicidal potential to have signed the letter of commitment, now seemed to equivocate. Yandell told Moore that he had a great deal of respect for the campus police's ability to deal with psychotic and disturbed students. He hinted that because Powelson and the police had jointly concluded that the situation was not desperate, it was possible that measures short of commitment, such as an interview at police headquarters to administer "a sharp reminder of reality," might still be appropriate.

Much was said by staff members about the need to maintain the tradition of strict confidentiality at Cowell, a tradition that Moore knew to have been violated by Powelson numerous times, particularly in marijuana-related cases. He was reminded that while many patients talk of suicidal or homicidal impulses, few ever take action, and if therapists were to heed these threats and "break the container of the therapeutic relationship," psychotherapy wouldn't stand a chance. One vociferous colleague even went so far as to tell him that such a breach of confidentiality "destroys our capacity to assure all of our other patients, without reservation, that their communications will be kept forever in confidence."

There was not a single person, not even from among his staunch female admirers, who was willing to go to bat for him against Powelson. The case had been taken out of his hands, and he felt as though he had been shoved aside and abandoned. He had even begun to doubt his own judgment. Certainly the girl must be home by now, and he wondered what, if anything, had happened between her and Prosenjit. The silence from Jal Mehta's corner only reinforced his doubts. As the days passed into weeks, he began to ask himself, what if he had been wrong about Prosenjit, after all of this? What if a sharp reminder of reality *had been* sufficient to stop the boy from acting? It wasn't that he accepted his colleagues judgments, really, but he considered them to the point of being paralyzed. After all, he told himself, he was only thirty-four years old, with not all that much experience in the field. He wanted to say "The hell with all of you" and push ahead, but at the same time, it seemed to him that he had exhausted every recourse.

TANYA flew back from Brazil on the afternoon of September 10, laden with packages her aunt was sending home to her mother. After managing to stuff them under her seat, she settled back and thought longingly about the young man she had met on a street corner in Rio de Janeiro. Naturally, it had happened during the last week of her vacation, when she was on her way home. She had seen him sipping mango juice in front of one of those little juice stands that were all over the city. He was dressed like a hippy and looked like he might be American, so she had wandered over and stood near him. He had the pale freckles and blue eyes of an Irish schoolboy. It didn't take him long to notice her and start up a conversation. He told her that his name was Patrick and that he was a "bootlegger" from Milwaukee, an image which immediately fired her imagination. When she pressed him to explain what a bootlegger did, he laughed and said, "Monkey business." He told her all about his plans to travel through the Andes and visit Machu Picchu. They ended up spending a romantic weekend together at the Sheraton Hotel, smoking grass from the huge stash he had concealed in his knapsack, and looking out at the white sands of Copacabana beach. When they parted, she had cried, and he had promised to try to visit her at Christmastime. She counted out the months on the fingers of her hand. Christmas seemed such a long way off.

But the main thing on her mind was whether or not she had been accepted as a student at UC Berkeley. Surely the letter from the registrar must have arrived. By the time the plane landed, she had worked herself into a fitful state. Hoping that her mother had had the sense to bring the letter along, she pushed her way through the customs line, impatiently craning her neck to see if anyone was waiting for her behind the glass partition. When finally she emerged, dragging a suitcase and two straw packages, she spotted her mother, Alex, and Helen, slumped on chairs. Dropping her belongings, she ran toward them. "Mama," she cried, hugging her, "did the letter come?" Her mother looked at her blankly and shook her head. The disappointment was almost too much to bear. "Are you sure?" she demanded, fighting back the tears.

Lidia shrugged. "Not unless your father has it."

And then, if this wasn't bad enough, as they were loading her cases into the car, she learned another bit of news. As of the first of the month, Alex told her, he had moved out of the house and into an apartment with Prosenjit Poddar. "You're kidding," she groaned. "How could you do that to me?" Up until that moment she had had every expectation that after their three-month separation, she would never again have to deal with that Indian.

After she had had a bite to eat and had distributed gifts to the rest of the family, she withdrew to the quiet of her room. The fifteen-hour flight had left her exhausted, but now she found she was too disturbed to sleep. Her worst fear was that somehow her father had managed to intercept the letter. The annoyance of Prosenjit seemed insignificant compared to the larger issue of how she was going to handle her father. He could be very cunning at times, and she didn't know what to expect. She lay awake in the darkened room, listening for the sound of his car in the driveway, wondering whether or not she had been accepted to Berkeley, and thinking with irritation about Prosenjit, who had managed to insinuate himself into her brother's life.

She remembered that last week before she escaped for Brazil. In the end, Prosenjit's jealous accusations, his talk about hiding bombs in her purse, and his disclosure of that crazy diary had actually prompted her to leave town. Even though she had stood him up and consistently refused all of his invitations, he never seemed to get the message that their relationship, or whatever you wanted to call it, was over. The incredible thing was that even after all of that, he still expected her to write him a letter.

* * *

Ten blocks away, Vitally Tarasoff stumbled out of the cool din of Pete's Tavern on San Pablo Avenue and looked around for his car. The blaze of afternoon sun made him dizzy. For a moment he forgot where he had left it and, steadying himself against a parked car, glowered at the rush-hour traffic. He was still rankled because as he had left work his boss had given him an order in the wrong tone of voice, making him feel like a lackey.

By the time he pulled into his driveway he had fallen into a self-pitying mood. The sight of his six-year-old Helen, holding back the drapes, peeking out of the bay window, lifted his spirits but little. As he walked in the door, he swung her into the air and crooned in a thick, sodden voice, "How's my baby girl? How's my doll face?" The thought of fleeting childhood and his own advancing years made him lachrymose. Holding her against his chest and rocking her back and forth, he moaned, "You're the only one left." Still holding her and repeating those words, he walked into the kitchen.

Tanya lay inert under the covers, listening to the sound of his steps receding into the kitchen. Then she heard her mother's timid voice. "Vit, have you forgotten—"

He cut her off. "Mother," he slurred, "the whole family's gone, except our baby. They grow up so fast. Once they go, they have no appreciation for everything we've done. They don't give a good goddam."

"Vit, she's home."

"Hunh?"

"She's in her room sleeping."

"What do you mean? She isn't supposed to be back until to-morrow."

"No, the flight was today."

"Does she know I want to talk to her?"

"Shush, don't wake her up, Vit. It was fifteen hours on the plane."

"I don't give a goddam." Tanya could hear him yank open and slam the refrigerator door. She knew he was grabbing a bottle of beer. His voice rose in volume. "Who does she think she is? A princess?"

As though rising to a challenge, Tanya swung her feet out of bed and reached for her robe. Tying it around her waist, she walked toward the kitchen. When she reached the door, she took a deep breath. "Hi, Dad," she said, and entered the room.

He swung around. His eyes were glassy, the brown irises like balls of lead floating in oil. "My baby's back," he said, opening his arms.

She couldn't help but feel that gush of love. "I missed you," she said, and ran to him, planting a wet kiss on his cheek.

When he released her, Vitally said, "What's the matter? I heard you couldn't take your aunt?"

"No, she was real nice, but there was nothing to do there."

"What do you mean? You go all that way and there's nothing to do?"

"It was pretty quiet."

"That sister of yours is a dead-ass," he said, turning on his wife. "I told you that before she went."

"Well, now our little girl is home," said Lidia, happily carrying plates and place mats to the table, "and I've made her favorite dinner."

Tanya began to set the table, feeling encouraged that he seemed in a good temper, and yet reminding herself that his mood could shift at any minute. "Olga sent presents for everyone. Isn't Mama's dress pretty?"

Vitally glanced at the flowered print sticking out from under his wife's apron and grunted. "What about the money that good-for-nothing husband of hers owes me? I'll bet she didn't send that."

"Oh, Vit," said Lidia. "Fifteen years ago."

"Lousy freeloader." He plopped himself down in the chair at the head of the table and set down his beer. He was in his undershirt, and Tanya noticed his powerful shoulders. Helen scrambled onto the seat next to him. "I want a swivel straw," she said to her mother, as Lidia poured out her glass of milk.

Tanya put a platter of meat loaf and cabbage on the table and sat down. Vitally reached over and whacked off a section, sludging it onto his plate.

"Hey, Mama," said Tanya, frowning at the four place settings, "aren't we waiting for Alex?"

"Alex," boomed Vitally, "is never setting foot in this house again! If he does, he's going to get his ass whipped." He spooned a mound of mashed potatoes out of the serving dish and slapped it on his plate. "Couldn't hack school, so he drops out to work at some lousy gas station."

Lidia sighed. "He only had one semester to go."

"I told him to get the hell out. He was killing your mother."

Lidia sighed again and stopped eating her meat loaf. Tanya looked down at her plate, thinking that nothing had changed.

"If it wasn't your first night home," he said, shaking his fork at her, "I'd really give you something to be unhappy about."

"What do you mean?"

"You knew he quit school all along, and you never told me."

Tanya bit her lip, trying not to let him provoke her.

"Vit, please," said Lidia, shaking her head. "Have some peas," and she pushed the bowl toward him.

"So, where's his apartment?" asked Tanya.

"He's living in some dump down on Solano," said Vitally.

"What I don't understand is how he could move in with that Indian," said Tanya.

"Because he's a nothing, that's why. A big zero."

"I helped them move," said Lidia. "Just like men," and she gave Tanya a look. "They didn't have one thing for the kitchen, not even a kettle. I gave them some of our old pots and pans and silverware, and then we went shopping. You should have seen all the special teas that Indian bought—"

"Mama," erupted Vitally, "I don't want to hear it. And I don't want Alex sneaking around here. Do you understand me?"

"It's so weird." Tanya frowned. "I had no idea Alex even knew him all that well."

"I'll tell you another thing that's weird," said Vitally. "Helen," and he touched the child's bare knee, "go get me that letter."

Tanya's heart started to beat violently.

Helen skipped out of the room and returned a moment later holding an envelope. She handed it to her father.

"This came for you," and he threw it in front of Tanya, "while you were gallivanting around São Paulo."

Tanya picked it up with trembling hands. The Seal of the Regents of the University of California was embossed on the upper left corner. "How come it's been opened?" she said, feigning innocence. Her father didn't respond. She took out the letter and scanned it. It was her notice of admission to Berkeley, beginning that fall. A dream come true.

"I told you not to apply there," he said.

She remained silent, staring back at him.

Lidia began to scrape food from the plates and stack them on top of each other.

"You did it behind my back!"

"I wanted to see if I'd get in. It's a great university."

"Big deal! You got in. It's not going to do you any good."

"Yes it is," she said softly. "I'm going."

"Over my dead body!"

"Mama said I could." She looked to her mother, who was busy rinsing plates at the sink, her back to the room.

"Your mother agrees with me," he shouted. "We don't want you anywhere near that freak show. Isn't that so, Mama?"

Lidia nodded weakly.

"If you think we're going to allow you to end up on drugs, you're crazy!"

"Dad, that's ridiculous."

"Ridiculous, is it?" His face darkened a shade. "I forbid you to go. End of discussion."

"It's not the end of it," said Tanya, rising from the table. "I'm going to Berkeley."

He jumped up, trembling with anger. "Don't you dare talk to me like that!"

She ran from the kitchen and into her bedroom, locked the door, and hurled herself face down on the bed. In her hand she clutched her letter of acceptance. It didn't matter anymore that her father had forbidden it. The incontrovertible fact was that she had been admitted to Berkeley. With an animal ferocity she kept repeating that to herself, over and over. She was going to Berkeley. To Berkeley! That's where life would begin! She visualized herself passing under the row of plane trees that lined Sproul Plaza, and breezing into her first class. She had fought for and won her ticket to freedom, and she was taking it, no matter what. If she had to get a job and move out of the house, she'd do that, too.

A few nights later, Prosenjit lay on a mattress on the floor of his new apartment at 1737 Solano Avenue, just around the corner from the Tarasoff home. For quite some time, he stared up at the cottage-cheese ceiling, mesmerized by the glimmer of tiny sparkles embedded in the plaster. With a groan, he rolled over on his side. All of his belongings were piled against the wall. Although he and Alex had moved into the apartment nearly two weeks ago, they still had not put the furniture in. The problem was not that they didn't own any—because last Sunday Prosenjit had purchased a sofa and a dresser at a garage sale—but that Alex had not gotten around to borrowing a truck to haul it over.

Prosenjit rose from the mattress and paced the room. The shag carpet was badly stained, and the room was empty except for a bridge table and two stools, arranged in the kitchen nook. He peered out the small window that fronted on Solano Avenue, thinking how hard it had become to endure the hours after dark, and longing for the arrival of Alex. It occurred to him again that perhaps he should have listened when Dr. Moore counseled him not to move from the I House. There, at the I House, he never had occasion to be alone. There were always lively conversations to be had in the dining hall, and fierce chess games taking place in the smoking lounge, at any time, day or night. He hated to admit it, but he even missed Jal Mehta. For a moment he considered calling Jal up and suggesting an outing to the cinema, but then he remembered their last encounter. Jal would expect him to apologize for the things he had said. He wondered why he had to always be the one to apologize, when it was the others who were taunting him, having fun at his expense. He twisted his hands in anguish. At that moment he felt more isolated and helpless than ever before in his life. No one was looking after him; no one cared. He was like an infant put in his crib and left alone, who drops his pacifier and wails to the four walls because no one is there to pick it up.

He wandered into the kitchen nook and switched on the overhead light. The only cookware in evidence was one crock pot, sitting on the stove, and two blackened frying pans. In the cupboard were a stack of plates and the three mugs that Mrs. Tarasoff had given them on the day they moved in. When Prosenjit had complained that they needed more cooking utensils, Alex had suggested that they throw a house-warming party so they wouldn't have to purchase any. The party was planned for the following Saturday night, and in the meantime, Prosenjit had been cooking all of their meals in the one pot.

When he examined the vegetable curry he had prepared for dinner he saw that a rubbery jell had hardened over the surface. As he turned on the burner, he picked up a spoon and punched through the film, stirring the sodden mush as it heated. He glanced at the clock and calculated that Alex had left work at least two hours ago. Then the fear hit him that maybe Alex wouldn't come home at all. He reached for two of the plates from the cupboard and set them out on the table.

Midway through his meal, Prosenjit heard the front door slam. "What smells in here?" hollered Alex as he marched into the kitchen. When he saw Prosenjit, he grinned. Under one arm he carried a large brown bag, and under the other was tucked a wad of greasy overalls, which he casually dumped on the table. He bent over the pot and sniffed it. "What is this shit?" he grimaced, rearing back. He reached into the bag, took out a beer, then loaded the remainder of the six-pack into the refrigerator.

"I thought you would come from work straight away," said Prosenjit in a reproachful voice.

"I stopped by my mother's house," said Alex, straddling the stool across from Prosenjit.

"You mean you have already eaten, then?"

"Yep," said Alex, oblivious to Prosenjit's disappointment. "It makes my mother happy to cook me dinner. I just have to eat fast and get the hell out before my old man gets home."

Prosenjit went on chewing without looking up. No doubt Tanya had been there. He could imagine the brother and sister, so alike in the simian cut of their faces, sitting across the table from each other, laughing and talking. He said in a sullen voice, "I waited until the curry got cold."

"Hey, don't get all bent out of shape. I never said I'd be home."

"We agreed that unless you said otherwise, I would have supper ready. Now, unless you become more responsible, I will never cook another meal."

"Are you giving me some kind of ultimatum? 'Cause in that case, you can forget about my ever eating here again."

There was a long silence. Prosenjit blinked, then pushed the curry around on his plate. He yearned to ask Alex all about Tanya, but he knew from experience that that subject only brought him grief. He hoped that if he just kept quiet, Alex would bring her up of his own accord. He was determined not to mention her, no matter how much he yearned to.

"Look," Alex was saying, "the minute you start laying some trip on me, I'm gone," and he made a gesture with his hand to imitate a jet plane zooming down the runway and taking off. He put the beer bottle to his lips and took a long swig.

Prosenjit's voice was barely audible. "I didn't mean it as an ultimatum."

"Hey," Alex said, "forget it. Look what I brought you," and he reached into the bag and pulled out a pint jar of what appeared to be homemade preserves. "Check this stuff out," he said, sliding it across the table. "Mango jam."

"Yes, mangos are very fine," mumbled Prosenjit, not even looking at the jar. "The best mangos in the world come from Dinajpur, near my family's home."

"Yeah, well, I guarantee you this shit's better. My aunt in Brazil canned this herself. She sent it to me because she knows how much I dig it," said Alex. "A couple big jars so I wouldn't run out."

Prosenjit jerked his head up. The mango jam had obviously been carried back by Tanya. Suddenly it took on a new interest. "I will give it the taste test," he said, grabbing the jar and twisting off the lid. "There is not a time in the world more happy than when the mangos come out on the trees, before the monsoon."

Alex watched while Prosenjit spooned a dollop of the yellow-orange preserve onto his plate.

"Sweet chutney." Prosenjit sighed. "It makes me feel at home." He fully expected that now Alex would bring her name up. He dipped a forkful of curry into the mixture and put it in his mouth, savoring the tang. When Alex didn't say anything, he asked, "Where did it come from?"

"I told you. My aunt."

"Yes, yes, I know. But how did it come to you?"

"In six-pint jars."

The pungent sweet-and-sour taste rather sickened him, and Prosenjit was unable to swallow. He reached for a napkin and quietly spat the food into it.

"Jesus Christ," said Alex. "Don't waste it." He got up, put the jar in the refrigerator, took out another beer, and headed for the door.

Prosenjit rose, pushing back the stool. "Wait," he said, unable to contain himself. "What does your sister say about our sharing a flat?"

Alex turned around. "What d'you mean?"

"Only that I wanted to know—is she keen on it?"

"It doesn't matter to her, one way or the other."

Except for an imperceptible tremor that caused his eyelids to flutter, Prosenjit showed no reaction. "Did she ask about me?"

"When?"

"Tonight, at dinner."

"No. Why should she ask about you?"

Prosenjit's expression was stony.

"She's all excited about going to Berkeley," said Alex, sitting back down on the stool. "You know, she got accepted for the fall."

That thought only increased his worry that now he would lose her for certain.

"Of course, my old man said she can't go. I think she's going to have to move out of the house."

"Does she want to come live with us?" He could scarcely conceal his excitement.

"I doubt it." Alex laughed, "Not with the way she feels about me. Not to mention you."

"What do you mean, *me*?"

"You're not exactly her favorite person."

Prosenjit's voice remained impassive. "Don't worry. You can tell her she'll never have the discomfort of seeing me again. I'm out of her life."

"I didn't mean that she hates you or anything. She just thinks you're a pest."

"Okay! I said it's finished."

"Well, it's been over for a while, hasn't it?"

"Is that what she said about it?"

"Oh. She did say one thing. She told me to tell you not to bother her anymore."

"I'm not bothering her!"

"Hey, I'm just passing on the message."

"I don't care about her anymore! I'm different now!" His face was dark and contorted. "You had better make her understand that, the next time you see her."

"Tell her yourself. She's coming on Saturday night," said Alex, referring to the house-warming party they had planned.

"If she comes to the party, I won't be here."

"Great," said Alex, heaving his beer bottles into the trash bag. "Don't come. No one will miss you." Grinning, he got up from the stool and moved toward Prosenjit. "But if you don't set up the stereo first, I'm going to beat your head in."

"I will attend to everything that needs preparation," said Prosenjit in a sullen voice, "and then be gone."

"Everything?" Alex laughed. Reaching behind Prosenjit, he grabbed his arm and twisted it behind his back in an armlock. Leaning into his ear, he said in a mock-threatening voice, "That means cleaning all this shit up in the kitchen and mopping the floor, right?" He tightened his grip, and Prosenjit stifled a cry. "That means making the guacamole-and-onion dip, too."

"I know."

"Promise?" He wrenched his arm higher. "Say yes."

A whimpering "yes" escaped Prosenjit's lips.

"Do you give?" said Alex, nearly bending Prosenjit's shoulder joint out of its socket.

"Yes."

Laughing, Alex released his arm and danced out of the kitchen. Prosenjit massaged his aching shoulder and fought back the tears. For a long while he sat in front of his plate, staring down at the lumps of congealed curry. He carried his dish to the sink, turned on the faucet, and waited for the water to get hot. All the while he assured himself that he wouldn't attend the party on Saturday night, no matter what. But he was as edgy as a jumping bean. There was no use going to bed, he thought, because he'd never fall asleep. Looking around, he decided to set to work on his first task, and surprise Alex with a clean kitchen.

AT seven o'clock on Saturday night, Tanya was still debating whether or not to go to her brother's party. It wasn't that she expected anyone good to be there. She knew just about all of his friends, and there wasn't one that was worth looking at. Not only that, but she was sure to see Prosenjit, and that would be awkward. According to Alex, he was still pining away for her. But it *was* a party, and parties were hard to pass up. Especially when one had been out of town for nearly three months and was feeling cut off from the world. Besides, why should she let Prosenjit dictate where she could or couldn't go? Going out of her way to avoid him gave him much too much importance.

As soon as she walked in the door, she could tell that the crowd was just what she'd expected, only crummier. It was a strange mixture of I House losers and Alex's friends—the kind of guys who hung around at stock-car races, pretending to be Hell's Angels. The stereo was blasting, making conversation impossible. Then her eye caught Prosenjit Poddar, standing like a cadaver behind the breakfast nook. He had that same skinny little body, as wiry as a bird. The expression on his face was so intense that his skin was covered with a thin sheen of oil. She found the beseeching look on his face especially sickening. She knew that with one smile she could transform that look into one of doglike devotion. A feeling of revulsion welled up inside her. She hoped he was listening to the refrain of the song, "Every time you make love to me, I want to run."

By the time twenty minutes had passed, she was bored. She glanced around to make sure that Prosenjit hadn't snuck up behind her. Somehow she sensed his eyes were on her. When finally she picked him out of the crowd, she was surprised to see that he was talking to another girl. The girl was someone she didn't recognize. She had curly red hair and a heart-shaped face, and Tanya had to admit that she wasn't unattractive. She watched them for a moment, laughing and joking with each other. The amazing thing was that the redhead actually seemed to be enjoying herself with Prosenjit. Annoyed, Tanya turned away and poured herself a glass of white wine. With glass in hand, she walked over to Alex.

"Who's that girl with the red hair?"

Alex squinted at the girl. "Don't know."

"How can she be here if you don't know her?"

Alex shrugged.

"Just make sure you keep your creepy roommate away from me."

"Lay off of him," warned Alex, "and he won't bother you."

She threw him a look and moved away.

Sometime later, as she was making her way through the room, she noticed that Prosenjit was leaning against a doorway, some six feet off, still engaged in conversation with the girl. She almost wished that he would come over and try to talk to her so she would have a reason to tell him off. Just then a casual acquaintance, a girl named Cathy Taylor, touched her arm and inquired about her trip to Brazil. Tanya whirled around and said, "It was fabulous. I had a great time." She glanced in Prosenjit's direction to see if he was within earshot, then added loudly, "I met a guy."

"Oh yeah?" said Cathy. "A long-distance romance?"

"Yeah, I think I'm in love." She sighed.

"Where's he from?"

"Milwaukee. His name's Patrick."

"What was he doing in Brazil?"

"Just cruising around." Tanya raised her voice. "He's in the import-export business. He calls himself a bootlegger." She laughed. "The thing is, he's so cute. I was amazed that a guy like him would pay attention to me."

"How long were you together?"

"Oh, just for the weekend. But it was real intense." She glanced toward Prosenjit, who was pretending not to be listening. "It was just like being married. We stayed in this great hotel, right on the water."

"How romantic."

"It was unbelievable. I've never experienced such freedom." She glanced at Prosenjit again and noted that a stricken look had come over his face. She touched Cathy's arm and said in a confidential tone, "There's a big difference when you're with someone who knows what he's doing."

"What d'you mean?" asked Cathy.

"The thing was, he was so uninhibited. It gives me chills just to remember it." She turned again toward Prosenjit, who was staring at her as if transfixed.

"So is he coming here to see you?"

"At Christmas, I hope. I don't know if I can stand the wait."

"Find out if he has any friends who want to come with him," Cathy said, laughing.

"Don't worry, I will." When she walked away to refill her glass, she made a point of passing close to Prosenjit. Although she did not acknowledge him, she could feel his eyes all over her, adoring her. It gave her some satisfaction to know that the red-haired girl meant nothing, and that she still owned his heart. And while she felt a slight degree of guilt for sucking him back in again, that old feeling of revulsion welled up inside, making her want to punish him. A moment later, by the refreshment table, he came up behind her and cleared his throat, as if he had something to say. Pretending not to see him, she tossed her head and walked off. As she passed, she couldn't help but sneak a glance in his direction, and at sight of his hurt, imploring eyes, she suppressed a laugh.

TANYA and her mother each held one of Helen's hands as they approached the cluster of colorful tents and booths that had been set up on the playground of the Thousand Oaks elementary school. Children's voices, like a tinkle on the wind, reached them, and then a rustling through the trees, and the delicious smell of burning leaves and caramel apples. Tanya put her face into the wind and closed her eyes. The sounds of far-off laughter brushed her like a feather, and then suddenly an ominous presence reached out and touched her. She was certain that eyes were watching her from the trees. She picked up her pace and glanced around, seeing nothing. Then the tug of Helen's hand, pulling her through the gate and into the crowd, made the feeling of uneasiness vanish.

The Thousand Oaks Carnival was an annual event that kicked off the beginning of the school year. Tanya had been coming here ever since she had moved to Berkeley at the age of thirteen, and for the last few years she had brought Helen along. It always reminded her of how glad she had been to get back to school after the idle days of summer had grown monotonous. She had been one of those children who counted down the hours until the first day of class, wondering who her new teachers would be and if perhaps this year she'd end up popular. There was even an excitement attached to going to the stationery store to stock up on school supplies. She loved to outfit her notebook meticulously, neatly printing the tabs that went inside the colored dividers, and smelling the lead shavings when she sharpened her pencils. Now that she was about to start Berkeley, she felt the same sense of expectation. But this year there was a hurt, too, that she couldn't escape.

Thus far, her father had remained violently opposed to her attending the university. Every time she brought up the subject he derided Berkeley as a "freak show." She knew that reasoning with him did no good and, remaining every bit as determined, went about her way, making quiet plans to circumvent his authority.

There was little doubt in Tanya's mind that his refusal to let her go would result in her having to move from the house. At first, she had been afraid she wouldn't be able to afford it. When she had confessed her fear to Cindy, Cindy had thrown her hands up in exasperation, telling her that this was just another one of her excuses to hide from life. Then Cindy had sat her down and actually worked it out on paper. Tuition for a California resident was relatively inexpensive, running about two hundred dollars a quarter. If she could manage to find someone to share an apartment with, living expenses would not be unreasonable. There was even a remote possibility that Tanya could move in with her, as Janice had been dropping hints that she was thinking of sharing a place with her new boyfriend.

In preparation for the inevitable, Tanya had begun looking for a job. Through the student union, she had applied for a position as a research assistant to a Portuguese language professor in the comparative literature department, and because of her natural fluency with the language, she had been encouraged to think that she stood a good chance of getting it.

Everything was working smoothly, except for one gnawing concern. She didn't know how she could find the nerve to tell her mother she was leaving. The truth was, it wasn't the telling, it was the leaving. What frightened her was that with both herself and Alex out of the house, Vitally would have no one left to take his frustrations out on but her mother. Tanya felt responsible for her mother's well-being, both physical and emotional. In the past she had found herself in numerous situations in which she had been able to deflect her father's anger and save her mother from a beating. She was racked with guilt at the thought of what might happen when she was gone.

"I wonder if they put my cake out," her mother was saying, as they neared a table where slices of homemade cakes and pies were being sold.

Tanya glanced at her mother's anxious face and remembered the poppy-seed cake she had baked. She saw Lidia's eyes darting from one cellophane-wrapped piece to another, searching for it.

"Maybe they no like," said Lidia.

"Look, Mama," said Helen, unaware of her mother's preoccupation, "the grab bag," and she strained toward a line of children who were waiting to stick their arms into a barrel full of presents.

"You just hold on," said Tanya, tightening her grip on her sister's arm. "Let's go get a brownie," and she steered Helen toward the cakes, her eyes scanning the table. "There it is, Mama." She pointed to her mother's cake, still intact and sitting behind the counter.

Tanya and Helen waited while their mother chatted with the woman who was selling the baked goods. Finally Lidia turned to them and confided, "She says she's saving the nicest until last."

"I could have told you that," said Tanya, relieved. Oh, how she wanted to see her mother happy. Anything to make her happy, since she herself was about to cause so much pain. It was only last week that she had broken the news to her that she was going to Berkeley, no matter what. Immediately Lidia's face had scrunched up in worry. "Your father," she had moaned, "he will kill you."

"The only way he'll ever find out is if you tell him," said Tanya, knowing that while her mother could never be counted on to take her side in an argument, she would never betray a confidence.

"But when you start school, he'll know for sure."

"How can he? He's at work all day."

Lidia shook her head. "It's much too dangerous."

Even though Tanya knew that her mother was right, she had used every argument she could think of to assuage her fears, short of telling her that she was leaving home. At first Lidia had fretted, but gradually her anxiety had given way to resignation. Then, the day before, she had offered to take Tanya on a clothes-buying expedition to Macy's bargain basement. The two set out by bus, first thing in the morning. Lidia spent hours rummaging through the racks of clothes and waiting in the try-on room, while Tanya modeled various outfits that were appropriate for the university. When they were done, she treated Tanya to a chocolate soda at Blum's coffee shop in Union Square. They arrived home just before dinnertime, exhausted and laden with packages. The noise of the TV was coming from the front room, and with a conspiratorial smile, Tanya and her mother had slipped in the back way and hidden the purchases from Vitally.

Her mother loved her so much, thought Tanya, as she looked over at Lidia, who was twisting the strap of her handbag while she stood talking with the cake lady. Now she was about to leave home and abandon her.

"I want a bird," said Helen at her side. "Can you win me a bird?"

"I'll try," said Tanya. She bought two brownies and gave one to Helen, who stuffed it in the pocket of her jumper and ran off toward a booth that was full of parakeets, tweeting in their cages. Tanya followed, slowly unwrapping her brownie. As she raised it to her lips, a shiver of uneasiness passed through her. She again had the sensation that someone was watching her. She glanced around but saw no one. It must be the nightmare, she thought. She had felt weird ever since that morning, when she had awakened with a start from a terrifying dream. In the dream she had gone to a party given inside a house with many rooms. Something had been chasing her, an unknown entity that she never saw. She hid inside a bedroom that had no furniture, only faded flowered wallpaper. There were other people in the room, but she knew that she was the target, that the entity was after her. If she could only get out of the house, she would be safe. She snuck down a long flight of stairs toward the front door, and then she felt it come after her. She jumped, flying through the air at first and then falling, spiraling down and down. She woke up before she hit bottom, her heart pounding and her back and neck covered with a thin sheath of sweat. It had been a bad omen for the rest of the day.

Now, as Tanya stepped up to the counter of the parakeet stand, she tried to shake off her fear. Inside the booth, about ten feet from where she was standing, were two dozen cages of birds, stacked one on top of another in a wobbly pyramid. Three flat glass plates were set on stands directly in front of the cages. Tanya could see there were a few dimes on the plates, and heaps more on the ground beneath them. She took some coins out of her wallet and began to flip them, one after the other, at the glass plates.

Again she felt a pair of eyes on her back, and she glanced around. This time she thought she saw a shadow pass behind a nearby booth. She turned to Helen and said, "This game is impossible."

Lidia came up beside them. "We'll buy you a bird at the pet shop."

"No." Helen pouted. "I want one of these."

Tanya asked for more change and tried again. Amazingly, a dime landed on one of the plates and didn't bounce off. Helen pointed at a powder-blue bird and the cage was handed down.

"What're you going to name him?" asked Tanya as they were walking home, carrying the cage. Out of the corner of her eye she thought she saw a figure flitting by, between the trees.

"Tweetie."

"That's a good name."

"Oh, for heaven's sake," said Lidia. "There's that nice Indian boy who lives with Alex."

Tanya's heart stopped, and she whirled around. She saw him, standing at the corner, partially hidden behind a lamppost. He was watching her, his eyes boring into her. It hadn't been her imagination after all. "Mama," she snapped, "don't ask him home with us."

"I had no such idea," stammered Lidia.

"I can't get rid of him."

"Shush. Don't let him hear," hissed Lidia.

"I don't care what he hears. He's following me, Mama. I know it." She wrapped her sweater more tightly around her to take away the chill.

"Why would he do that?"

"I don't know. He's crazy."

"He's scary," said Helen, at her side.

She couldn't help but glance at him again, and as she did so, he caught her eye. His pleading expression reached out and clutched for her. She knew then that she was powerless to keep him out of her life.

"He and Alex live right around the block," said her mother.

"I know that."

As they arrived at the corner, Tanya averted her face and stared straight ahead, as though he weren't there. Lidia gave him a weak smile and tightened her grip on Helen's hand. They passed him without incident.

TANYA went to her first class at the university on Monday morning, October 6. It was Physical Anthropology 1, taught by Professor Washburn, who had received such high marks in the Slate Supplement, an unofficial rating system compiled by students, that the cavernous auditorium of Wheeler Hall was filled to capacity. She heard that she would learn about *Australopithecus* and the ascent of man. Then the lights were dimmed and she watched a slide show of the monkeys and apes of the primate family. Among these were slides of nocturnal creatures called lemurs, which crawled around in the darkness and had gleaming yellow eyes. When the lights came up and Tanya had risen from her seat and was making her way down the steps of Wheeler Hall, she couldn't help but think of Prosenjit.

A few days later she received a phone call from Cindy, informing her that Janice was definitely moving out of the apartment. The girls agreed to meet for lunch at Merritt Junior College, where Cindy and Janice still attended class.

"Move in as soon as you want," said Cindy, after they had set their trays down and begun to eat.

"I need about a week," said Tanya, as she took a bite out of her cheeseburger. She had committed herself to taking the room, and now there was no turning back. "If you want, I'm sure I can raid my mom's kitchen for some old pots and pans."

"We've got all of that stuff," said Cindy, shooting a glance in the direction of Janice, who sat across the table. "That is, unless Janice ruins another pan."

"Listen, dear," said Janice, laughing, "I've got news for you. You're the one who burned the shit out of my good Teflon pan."

As usual Janice was a stand-out, in full makeup and a set of false eyelashes. She wore a hat that drooped over one eye, partially hiding her face. "Unlike *you*," she said as she examined her manicured nails, picking at a fleck of deep red polish, "I'm sure *Tanya* will keep the kitchen clean."

"Oh yeah?" said Cindy. "Do you know how many times I've filled the ice-cube trays or put up a new roll of toilet paper?"

Janice took a sip of Tab and let her eyes meet Cindy's for a long, icy moment. "Anyway," she said, turning to address Tanya, "just shove all of my things to one side of the closet. I'm leaving most of my stuff because it won't fit in his little fleabag of a closet. You know the kind that's really a wardrobe with an old sheet hanging over the front?"

Cindy rolled her eyes. "Just your style."

"You can use my sheets too," said Janice, ignoring the crack. "They're not the right size for his bed."

The girls agreed that Tanya would pay Janice's share of the rent while Janice tried out a live-in relationship with Gary, her new boyfriend. If, within four to six weeks, the experiment seemed to be working, she would permanently give up her room to Tanya. If not, they would deal with the problem when it came up.

When Janice got up to go, Cindy said, "Why don't you see if Gary has any cute friends?"

"I thought you didn't like Gary," countered Janice.

"I don't, but that doesn't mean I wouldn't like his friends."

"See you."

"At least keep your eyes open," called Cindy, as they watched Janice sail through the cafeteria as if she owned the place.

It was some minutes later that Tanya noticed Prosenjit Poddar standing in the doorway, watching her. The instant her eyes met his, he smiled and moved in her direction, as if in a trance. "Oh no," she said, feeling a surge of physical revulsion. She kicked Cindy under the table. "Save me."

Cindy whirled around to look at Prosenjit. He moved stiffly, with the mincing steps of an automaton. When he reached the table, he bowed slightly in Tanya's direction. Not for one second did his eyes leave her.

Tanya and Cindy exchanged looks. Tanya tapped her nails on the table. Finally she could stand it no longer and said in a frozen voice, "Would you mind telling me what you're doing here?"

"I am here to talk to you," he said, a twisted smile on his face.

"There's nothing to talk about," said Tanya, looking off into space.

Cindy whispered in her ear, loud enough for him to hear, "Tell him to fuck off."

"If you think I'm bothering you," he began, "I won't interfere anymore."

"You *are* bothering me. So why don't you just leave?" She couldn't bear to look at him.

He sat down at the far end of the table, on Tanya's side. "Just tell me why you won't talk to me anymore."

Cindy could stand it no longer and blurted out, "Why are you always following her around? You know she doesn't like you. She despises you as a person." When Cindy saw that he wasn't paying attention to what she was saying, she yelled, "She doesn't want anything to do with you, so leave her alone!"

He didn't respond. He seemed neither angry nor hurt, simply resigned to sit at Tanya's side like a dog.

"Just ignore him," whispered Tanya.

"That's pretty hard to do," said Cindy, now really rankled. "Let's split."

As they were getting up, Prosenjit said, "I'm here to find out once and for all how you feel about me."

"I told you. I'm not interested," said Tanya, moving away from the table.

"Fuck off, you creep!" yelled Cindy, following after her.

On the bus home, Tanya told Cindy that she suspected Prosenjit was stalking her. After Cindy had heard the details of how Tanya had caught him lurking behind a tree at the carnival, she urged her to go to the police. But Tanya dismissed that idea, saying that he was a harmless pest, and that all the police could do was cause trouble.

Later that night, Cindy telephoned Tanya. "Tanya," she said, "I'm getting really bad vibes from that guy. I think you should leave town."

"Oh, sure. I've just spent the last six months of my life trying to get into Berkeley and you tell me to leave town."

"I'm serious. The guy could do something dangerous."

"I can't believe you."

"Listen, I just took out a loan and I can give you five hundred dollars. Take it. I don't even care if you pay me back."

"Cindy," said Tanya, "I'm not going to blow my entire future by freaking out over some jerky guy."

"I'm worried, that's all."

"Well, forget it." It was then that Tanya informed Cindy that she had her own plan. "I'm going to burn that sari he gave me," she said.

"What?"

"I'm going to burn the sari. I'm going to put it in a trash can, set it on fire, and tell him about it."

"What sari?"

Tanya explained how it was the custom in India, when a boy and girl were engaged, for the boy to give the girl a sari. And that some months ago, Prosenjit had given her a sari.

"You accepted it? How could you do that?"

"Oh, I don't know. I didn't want to hurt his feelings."

"Well, for God's sake, don't burn the damn thing!" cried Cindy.

"That's what I'm going to do. And the next time he comes sneaking around, I'm going to throw the ashes in his face."

"You do that and you're asking for it."

"Yeah, but that'll really make him leave me alone."

"Or just the opposite. If you burn that sari, he'll kill you. I'm not kidding."

Cindy begged Tanya to seek some help from a school counselor, preferably one at the I House who knew the Indian. Her last words to Tanya were "Do you promise you'll call someone tomorrow?" Tanya agreed, saying, "All right already. Now, can we talk about something else?" But this promise, extracted after so much arm-twisting, didn't quell Cindy's fears. An hour later, as she was lying in bed unable to sleep, the notion of telephoning her own mother popped into her mind. Lately there had been so much friction between the two of them that they had not spoken in months. She hesitated, remembering the last unpleasant encounter, but then the fear that something bad was going to happen prompted her to dial the number. It was only when she heard her mother's voice, warm and familiar, that she felt some relief from her premonition.

L ATE in the afternoon of October 8, around closing time, Gunnar Stanfil was sitting in his office at the Richmond Field Station when Jacob Buehler, a student from Africa, poked his head in the door and asked to have a word with him.

"What is it?" asked Stanfil. His feet were propped up on his desk and he was sipping a cup of coffee.

"It's Poddar, sir," said Buehler. "I think you should come look. Something's very wrong."

"Where is he?"

"In the model."

"Oh, Christ." Stanfil heaved himself out of his chair and strode down the hall.

From behind him Buehler called, "He hasn't come out all afternoon."

Stanfil groaned. For the last few weeks there had been something pent-up and edgy about Prosenjit, and then just yesterday something had happened that, in Stanfil's mind, really upset the applecart.

Stanfil had been sitting in his office shooting the breeze with Ed Spies when the telephone rang. It did not take much for him to recognize the low, throaty voice of Tanya, who had called the tank several times, back in April and May, asking for Prosenjit.

"How long've you been back?" Stanfil asked, in response to her cheerful hello.

"Just about a week," she said, and then with a laugh, "Why? Has he missed me?"

Stanfil was so taken aback that he waved at Ed Spies to get his attention, covered the mouthpiece, and whispered, "Tanya just asked me if Poddar missed her!"

Spies shook his head in disbelief and replied, "That's sick."

When Tanya asked to speak to Prosenjit, Stanfil was so reluctant he considered saying that Poddar no longer worked there. He hesitated and then, realizing that it would do no good to interfere, gruffly told her to hold on while he called him to the phone.

Stanfil did not know what Tanya had said to Prosenjit, but whatever it was, the boy had walked away from the telephone trembling with anger. When Stanfil casually inquired about the call, Prosenjit turned away, muttering something incomprehensible about a sari.

"What's that you said?" asked Stanfil.

"She said she's going to burn it," he cried. "She's going to throw it in my face!"

Stanfil was stumped.

Now, as Stanfil was locking up, Ed Spies caught up to him and said, "I just tried to talk to Poddar. He's in there sobbing."

"The best thing is to just leave him alone," said Stanfil. "Nobody wants an audience."

Stanfil entered the hangar. The clang of heavy machinery blotted out all other sound. He stood in the doorway of the cavernous room, squinting into the darkness. In the melancholy greenish light all he could see was a dim jungle of churning machines. He moved forward toward the model. It was a large steel structure, built as a replica of the hull of a ship, approximately fifteen feet long and four feet wide. On most days the interior was lit by fluorescent lights. Now the lights were switched off, and it looked like a gloomy cave.

"What the devil is he doing with the lights off?" Stanfil muttered. He bent down and peered in. He could see nothing. The hole was dank and airless. He backed away and fumbled for something on a shelf, grabbed up a flashlight, turned back. "What can you expect when they go to shrinks," he grumbled to himself. He clicked on the light and threw the beam into the darkness. The sight he encountered shocked him. Prosenjit was at the other end of the hull, huddled up on his knees, his head buried in his hands, sobbing. Stanfil recoiled in embarrassment.

Why did I take him back in the first place? he thought. Maybe he should have been thrown into that loony bin, after all.

Drawing in a deep breath, Stanfil called out, "Hey, Prosenjit, come on outside." When there was no answer he called again, "Hey, come on out of there!"

There was a long silence. If there was one thing Gunnar Stanfil couldn't stand, it was to see a man crying. "Prosenjit," he called, "come on out. We'll go for a walk or something."

There was another silence. Then Prosenjit's voice came, weak and tremulous. "No, man, just go away. Leave me alone."

Stanfil wondered if he should crawl in, grab him by the leg, and yank him out. He leaned into the hull, but somehow, the notion of reasoning with the boy while he was in such a state was abhorrent, and he drew back. He turned and stalked out of the hangar, and said to himself, Fuck it. If he wants help, he'll ask for it.

OCTOBER 8 was the last day that Prosenjit showed up for work at the towing tank.

On Thursday morning, October 9, he called Gorian Newaz, an acquaintance who lived on the fourth floor at the I House, and told him he had something important to discuss with him. They arranged to meet in the lounge in the student union, at three o'clock, the next afternoon.

At the appointed time, Prosenjit made his way through the lounge. Sitting down on one of the Naugahyde couches, he pulled his wallet out of his pants and, as he waited, methodically counted out one hundred dollars in ten-dollar bills, then replaced the money in his wallet. He reflected that if he had accepted a job with the Garden Reach Shipbuilders back in Calcutta, as his parents had wanted, this never would have happened. His family would have come to his rescue and would have gone out and loudly vilified the girl in public places. Then his father would have fixed up a marriage. It was not until he began mulling over the qualities that were important in choosing the ideal wife, deciding that she should be trustworthy, frank, well educated, and good-looking, that he saw Gorian Newaz appear in the doorway. "Here I am," he said, jumping up and waving his arms. Newaz walked over and sat down next to him.

"What's new?" asked Newaz.

Prosenjit said, "I have this American girlfriend. I think you know her. Tanya Tarasoff?"

"Oh, yes. I remember her from the dances."

"She's my girl, but not to sleep with, of course."

Newaz smiled, embarrassed by the unexpected confession.

"I am having some difficulties with her, and I want to teach her a lesson." Then, sliding his wallet out of his pocket, he said, "I will pay you one hundred dollars to buy the sexual favors of Tanya."

Newaz stared at him, speechless.

The way Prosenjit outlined the plan, he wanted Newaz to bring Tanya back to his room at the I House in order to have sex. Prosenjit would be waiting in another room, on the same floor. On his way up to the fourth floor, Newaz would stop at the house phone, which was by the elevator, and alert Prosenjit that they were on their way. Right before they started to have sex, Prosenjit would burst into the room with his gun and "save" her.

"Well, I don't know," said Newaz, waving away the money that Prosenjit was trying to put in his hand and rising from the couch. "This is a lot to think about." Actually, he thought the proposal was insane, but he had always had a soft spot in his heart for the Indian and could see that he was going through some sort of an emotional crisis. "Why don't I let you know in a couple of days?" he said, as he backed out of the room.

The next day, Prosenjit returned to the Frontier Gun Shop on San Pablo Avenue and purchased two pellet guns, one a Crossman CO_2 pellet pistol, and the other a Daisy BB-type pistol, and a box of CO_2 cartridges. He intended to use the guns in the raid on Newaz's room.

After a few days, Prosenjit became irritated that he had not heard from Newaz and called his dorm room. He demanded that Newaz proceed with the plan. When Newaz politely refused, saying that he had always thought Tanya Tarasoff was a nice girl and did not want to do anything to insult her, Prosenjit slammed down the phone.

One week later, when Tanya was visiting friends up at the I House, she heard a rumor that Prosenjit had tried to give Gorian Newaz one hundred dollars to proposition her. Fuming, she sought Newaz out in his room, and he confirmed the story. "Well, you can tell him for me that I hate him," she said and stalked out of the room.

The following morning, at Cindy's urging, Tanya telephoned the

I House and explained that she was having some trouble with a former resident named Prosenjit Poddar and needed to talk to a counselor who was acquainted with him. She was put through to Dr. Donna Dickenson, the foreign student adviser, who said that she was extremely busy, but that Tanya could come see her the following week.

"Next week?" said Tanya. "Is that the soonest you can meet with me?"

"Well yes, unless you feel it's a matter of life or death."

Tanya hesitated a moment. "Next week will be fine," she said, and they made an appointment for Tuesday, October 28, at ten in the morning.

On Sunday morning, October 26, at five o'clock, Alex Tarasoff finished working the graveyard shift at the Union 76 station. He drove over to the all-night liquor store near the corner of Solano and Alameda and bought a six-pack of Coors. Standing in the parking lot, he downed one beer, then hurled the empty can into the bushes. The sun had not yet come up, and the only sounds to be heard were the hum and suction of street cleaners. On the drive home he looked forward to eating the last half of the Sarah Lee Black Forest cake that he had left in the refrigerator, and going straight to sleep. When he pulled up to the curb, he was surprised to see a light shining from the front window.

Alex walked into the living room. All the lights were on, but the apartment was quiet. Seeing that Prosenjit's door was slightly ajar, he peeked in. It was dark inside, but he could see Prosenjit, lying on his mattress with a blanket thrown over him. His eyes were wide open and he was staring into space. Without looking in Alex's direction, Prosenjit said, "I keep thinking about your sister."

"What about my sister?"

Prosenjit huddled deeper, under the blanket. "I love your sister."

"Oh, Christ!" Alex walked out of the room and into the kitchen.

A few minutes later, as Alex was sitting at the table eating the Sarah Lee cake, Prosenjit padded into the room on bare feet. He was fully dressed, and it was apparent to Alex he had not changed his clothes in days.

Prosenjit sat down on the stool across from him and didn't utter a word.

Finally, annoyed by the silence and the pair of pitiful eyes that searched his face, Alex said, "You better start going in to work at the tank or else we won't be able to pay the rent." Prosenjit didn't respond. "I've got my share," said Alex, who was paying a third of the rent. "You better have yours. If you weren't laying around like a cry-baby all the time, we'd be okay."

"Maybe you can invite her to come over here," Prosenjit persisted.

"Even if I did, she wouldn't come."

"I'll be all done with your sister after I talk to her, one more time."

"It won't do any good." Alex wiped his hands on a paper towel and pushed back from the table.

"I can't do anything until I talk to her."

Alex jumped up. "What the fuck are you talking about?" He grabbed Prosenjit by the shoulders. "You know, now you're starting to upset my mother, too!"

Prosenjit put his hands behind his back and said, "I can't help it."

Alex shoved him in the chest, knocking him back against the wall, and shouted, "We're going to get thrown out of here, goddammit!" Prosenjit was crying softly and did not raise his hands to defend himself. Alex grabbed him by the collar of his shirt and threw him down on the floor. Prosenjit cowered away from him, dragging himself along the rug toward the bathroom. Alex yanked him up and pinned him against the bathroom sink, yelling, "I don't like to see my mother upset!"

"No, please!"

Alex slugged him in the stomach. Prosenjit clutched his midsection and fell whimpering on the bathroom tiles. Sobs wracked his body. Alex kicked him in the side and said, "From now on, just leave my sister alone," and stomped down the hall.

Prosenjit heard the jangle of Alex's keys and the front door being flung open. He cried, "Please don't go!" The cry was so weak it could barely be heard.

The front door slammed shut and the house was silent.

When Prosenjit awoke, a soft light was coming through the blinds. He became aware of the faint ticking of the clock, and he paced his breathing to it. He could go on like this for hours, he thought. Then it seemed as if the clock had stopped, and he held his breath. His skin was damp, and he shivered. Soon his body was shaking so violently that he rose from the mattress and put on a sweater. He was dimly aware that his body hurt in many places.

He looked in Alex's room, but the bed was empty. He wanted to rush over to Tanya's house, but he was afraid that he would do her harm. Then he thought, Oh what's the use, and he sat back down on his mattress and burrowed under the covers. He didn't want to hurt her, really. He put his head back down on the pillow and called out to the goddess Kali to give him courage to stop. He again became aware of the ticking clock. His ears received each increment of sound as an unpleasant jolt. He lay contemplating the water stain which was smeared like blood over the beige walls of his bedroom.

An hour later, he found himself standing on the cement walkway leading to Tanya's door. He rang the bell.

There was a shuffling noise and Mrs. Tarasoff opened the door. Her solid body was massed under a terry-cloth robe. "What you want, bothering us all the time?"

"I have come to talk to Tanya."

"Tanya doesn't want to talk. Tanya's not here."

"I am her friend."

"What kind of a friend are you? Tanya doesn't have friends like you."

He stepped forward and leaned through the doorway, trying to see if Tanya was in the house.

Lidia Tarasoff stood her ground. She bleated, "Go out. Tanya's not here."

He pressed up closer, his hands jammed in his pockets. He saw Mrs. Tarasoff glance over her shoulder. Then he noticed the child Helen, staring at him with round, frightened eyes.

Mrs. Tarasoff gestured with her arms to shoo him away. "You go now. Tanya already left for school."

After he was halfway down the path he heard Mrs. Tarasoff yell, "Why don't you go back to India? When my husband comes home, he'll beat you up."

On his way back to the apartment he felt hungry, and he realized that he had not eaten for two days. He stopped at the Coop market to buy some fish. He stood in front of the meat section staring at the packages of frozen halibut and sole, the whitish flesh frosty under plastic wrap. He didn't know whether he was going to harm her, or whether he was going to ask her to straighten up. Why he should kill her, or why he shouldn't kill her. It disturbed him that he had upset her mother. The mother would plan a marriage for her, but probably not with him. While he was waiting in line at the checkout counter he remembered all the things he had told the therapist at Cowell Hospital, and he was ashamed of himself. All those things were foolish, really. They were just play-acting.

Then, very distinctly, he heard Tanya's voice. She was laughing. He pictured her sitting on a couch with another man. He tried to see who the man was. At first he looked like Gorian Newaz and then he seemed to resemble Jal Mehta. Tanya and the man were sitting close to each other, fully dressed. The image aroused Prosenjit, and he was impatient to return to his apartment. Putting down the package of fish, he hurried out of the store.

A T four that afternoon, Tanya was awaiting the arrival of Alex. He was coming over to pick up her and Helen and drive them over to Helen's ballet class. He was late, as usual, and as the minutes passed, Tanya was becoming more and more reluctant to leave the house.

For the last few days she had been feeling exhausted. She supposed it was anxiety. Her period was over two weeks late. The ramifications of this were really too horrible to contemplate. Even though she had said that she "loved" Patrick and had even told Cindy that she would like to "marry" him, she was not ready to have his or anyone else's baby. Particularly now, just as she was starting her first semester at Berkeley, and a whole new life. But there she was, left to deal with the situation all alone, while the man in question was traipsing around God knew where, without a care in the world.

As she was helping Helen get into her ballet costume, a pale pink tutu and matching tights, the telephone rang, and she reached over to answer it. There was silence on the other end. A long, heavy silence. She held the receiver to her ear and said hello again. The sound of breathing, a man's breathing, became audible. "Who is this?" she demanded, then slammed down the receiver and sank onto the bed, gripping one of Helen's satin toe shoes in her hands. A moment later, when she put the slipper on her sister's foot and tried to lace the strings, she was surprised to find that her hands were trembling. When Helen asked what was wrong, she smiled and told her it was nothing.

Her pulse quickened when, five minutes later, she heard the sound of the front door opening and the tromping of boots. "Hey, Mama," Alex hollered from the living room, "you got anything to eat?" With a squeal of glee, Helen jumped off the bed and ran down the hall toward the kitchen. Tanya stood up and followed slowly. By the time she reached the kitchen, Alex was taking off his jacket and her mother was bustling around the stove.

"What's wrong with you?" her mother was saying to Alex. "Don't you have any food at your apartment?"

Alex pulled out a chair and sat down. "Man, I'm not going there. Poddar's acting real freaky."

Tanya shuddered and pulled out a chair.

"Oh, don't start talking about that Indian again," said Helen, pushing up on the tips of toes and trying to balance. "He's so creepy."

Lidia turned to face Tanya. "Did you talk to that counselor at school?"

"Mama, you're making too big a deal out of this," said Tanya.

"He was here this morning," her mother said, turning back to Alex, "and I said to him, 'Why are you bothering us so much lately? Why do you insist on coming here?'"

"What'd he say?" asked Alex, between spoonfuls.

"The same old stuff," said Tanya. "He's a broken record."

"I don't know why it should take you so long to talk to someone," persisted Lidia.

"Mama," Tanya spun around. "I don't know what you think talking to some counselor at school is going to accomplish. They aren't going to be able to keep him away from me."

Her mother shook her head in frustration. "Tanya, you'd better get your coat," she said, indicating Helen, who was waiting impatiently by the door.

"Mama," said Tanya, "would you mind taking her? I don't feel well."

"What's wrong?"

"Nothing. I think I'm getting a cold." After her mother had left the room, Tanya leaned closer to Alex and hissed, "Alex, I can't take it anymore, with him following me around."

"What can I do?"

"Something. Anything. I don't know. He's your roommate."

Her mother appeared in the doorway, buttoning up her lamb's-wool coat. "What's that you said?" There was a worried look on her face.

"Nothing, Mama," said Tanya.

Helen clutched her mother's hand and began pulling her toward the front door.

"We'll be back around six-thirty," said Lidia, "and I'll make you some good hot soup."

Alex stood up, grabbed his jacket, and started down the steps, into the chill twilight.

Tanya watched the three of them through the window. The setting sun cast shadows on the lawn. Helen danced across the grass, balancing on her toes, leaping up against the cloudy sky. Alex's dragster sat by the curb, waxed and shining. He crossed around to the driver's side, while Helen and her mother huddled together waiting for him to unlock the passenger door.

Tanya reached for the book she had been reading and sat down in her father's big chair. When she heard the car engine rev, a chill went through her, and she shivered. She glanced up and saw them pull away. She thought about how in just a few days she would be gone from the house and living on her own. The unknown frightened her, dulled her excitement, so that all she was left feeling was a numbness. At this point she was going on blind faith that once she got over the first hurdle of being on her own, she'd be fine. Of course, now there was this problem of a late period, but she guessed that she'd be able to deal with that, too. She turned back and began to read her book, *I Never Promised You a Rose Garden*.

As soon as the dragster pulled away from the curb, Prosenjit's palms started to sweat. From his hiding spot behind the oleander bush, he could see a light coming from the front room. He shivered under his windbreaker.

Straightening up, he stepped out from behind the bush. Her father's car was not parked in the driveway, so he assumed that only Tanya was at home. As he was crossing the street, he watched her, sitting behind the window. She appeared to be reading a book. Her face, smooth and childlike, was illuminated by a spot of light.

Her head was tilted to one side and her eyes were cast downward, hooded under moon-shaped lids. The therapist had told him that he could control himself if he wanted. But this notion only angered him. Why wasn't Dr. Moore there to stop him? Why wasn't anybody watching out for him? He had posted a letter to his father pleading that a marriage be arranged, and all he had gotten in response was a scolding. Balling his hands into tight fists, he promised himself that under no circumstances would he send any more letters home.

Suddenly a man in white overalls, carrying a tool chest, emerged from behind the Tarasoffs' house. The sight so startled Prosenjit that he reared back, nearly losing his balance. Turning on his heels, he trotted halfway down the block. When he spun around he saw that the man was loading his gear into the back of a van marked Pacific Gas and Electric. With dismay, he watched the man walk back into the Tarasoffs' yard. He crouched down behind some shrubbery, squinting into the deepening sunset, waiting for the man to reemerge. It seemed like ages before he did, carrying a stepladder. Prosenjit watched while he angled the ladder into the van and slammed the double doors. Prosenjit bent low and soundlessly tiptoed up the block. By the time he reached the Tarasoffs' house, the van had pulled away.

As he crept along the sidewalk in front of her house, the headlights of a car approached. It must be her father, returning from work. His heart beat violently, and he gripped the knife he had brought along to protect himself. The car was almost up to where he was standing, the headlights blinding him. Suddenly it swerved sharply and pulled into the driveway next door. With relief, he watched a middle-aged woman struggle out from behind the wheel, clutching a sack of groceries to her chest. Suddenly the impulse seized him to call out to her. She could stop him from going up to Tanya's door. But, as if paralyzed, he remained rooted to the spot, while she started up her front steps. Then he shook himself and began to move across Tanya's lawn, crying, "Lady, lady!" But she didn't hear him. Her door closed behind her.

Tanya didn't look up when he tiptoed up the steps. He turned the knob, but the door was locked. He rang the bell. A moment later he heard the sound of a bolt being clicked back. The door opened a crack and one eye looked out.

He was willing to forgive her even now if she would just talk to him. It was strange how just being close to her made him feel whole. He took a deep breath and said, "I want to talk to you."

"Well, I don't want to talk to you." Her voice sounded contemptuous.

He didn't budge.

She said, "My father will be home any minute." When he remained standing by the door, she said, "If my father comes home, he'll kill you." She tried to slam the door on him, but he threw the weight of his body against it and jammed his foot in the crack.

"I must talk to you," he insisted.

"I said no!"

He gave a violent shove, and the door flew open, hurling him into the room. He fell headlong, thrusting out his arms to break the fall and landing on his knees. When he rose to his feet, she was standing squarely in front of him. It was then, when he looked into her eyes, that he saw an expression he had never seen before, an animal fear.

All thought left Tanya's mind. If she had been laboring under the misconception that this man was not a danger, that belief was now gone. A scream rose in her throat.

Fifteen blocks away, on the corner of Arch and Grove, Helen and a dozen other little girls were practicing *pliés* in front of a long mirror. An old woman was playing "Claire de Lune" on a baby grand. Every so often, Helen glanced over at her mother, who was sitting on a folding chair in the corner, but her mother seemed distracted, and Helen couldn't catch her eye. From the distance came the faint sound of sirens, whining through the streets. The noise mingled with the tinkle of the piano and made it hard for Helen to concentrate.

Later, when Helen and her mother were waiting for the bus, Helen said, "I'm scared for Tanya."

"Don't say such things," scolded Lidia.

A few minutes later the bus arrived. The bus driver, who had known them for years, gave Lidia a second look and said, "Why are you looking so strange?"

Lidia shrugged and dropped some coins into the slot. As the bus lurched forward, she clutched Helen's hand and pulled her down onto the seat across from the driver.

Prosenjit and Tanya stood facing each other.

He grabbed at her hand and felt the touch of flesh. She backed away shrieking. All he could see was her open mouth and wide, staring eyes. Cat eyes.

It was a high piercing scream.

"Don't screech!" The shriek jumped out of her throat like a cat, clawing at his face.

The whole room was filled with the scream, coming at him, ripping and slicing at his face. He didn't want to hurt her, but the scream terrified him. He pulled the pellet gun out of his pocket and aimed at the sound. He fired in the air to stop the screech. He was firing wildly, one round after another.

He watched while a welter of pellets struck her body and embedded themselves in her skin. His vision was foggy, but he could see her put her hands up around her face, trying to ward off the shots.

He heard the gun click empty.

Then the screech came toward him and he didn't know what it was going to do to him.

He pulled out the knife. It was a thirteen-inch butcher's knife with a jagged point and the serrated edge of a saw.

He held the knife above his head and plunged down on the screech. He felt the knife go into something smooth. There was no resistance. The knife went in and came out softly. She was screaming and he just wanted to stop the noise. He plunged down again and felt something warm spurt onto his face. Again and again. Then they were in the kitchen and he saw something splatter across the white refrigerator door. She was running and he was following. He watched the blood trickle down her legs. He could even hear the squish of the blood in her rubber thongs as she ran. She was crying, "Help, help, help." He chased her out the front door. Her thongs left bloody footprints on the cement steps. Then he looked down and her leg was on the knife, and they were both lying on the front lawn. The struggle was over. She was stretched out next to him. The expression on her face was peaceful, like a young bride's. He let his eyes wander down her body, so slender and childlike. The dark slits in her knit dress looked like tiny mouths filling with blood.

He became aware that a dog was barking wildly, from next door, and that his entire body was shaking spasmodically. Slowly and with some surprise, he realized that blood was gushing out of a deep slash in his left hand. He looked around at his surroundings. A young boy was standing behind the oleander bush, where he himself had hidden. Then he noticed that the woman who had come home with her groceries was standing on her front porch. He struggled to get to his feet, and when he did, he was dizzy. In a stiff and jerking motion he walked across Tanya's lawn and up her front steps.

He followed the bloody footprints back to the kitchen and dialed the operator, asking for the police. It seemed an interminably long time before he was put through. When he heard the officer's voice, he said, "I just stabbed my girlfriend." He did not understand why the officer kept asking him to repeat his name, and then requested that he spell it out for him. "My girlfriend needs the immediate attention of a physician," he said, and then he realized that he was crying. He reassured the officer that he would remain at the location until the ambulance and the squad car arrived.

He sat down at the kitchen table. The room was perfectly still. The smell in the air reminded him of Tanya. He felt very lonely in the house now that she was not there. He wondered how he could get through the night without her. Repeatedly, he counted the number of checks on the vinyl tablecloth. Then the sound of sirens became louder and louder. The knowledge that someone was coming to get him filled him with tremendous relief. As if in a trance, he rose and walked toward the front door. There were footsteps on the porch and a loud knock. A strong-looking man in a police uniform came through the door.

Prosenjit put his hands above his head and cried, "I did it. I stabbed her."

The police officer quickly patted him down for weapons and, finding none, told him to lower his hands.

Lidia and Helen Tarasoff rode in silence. When they reached the intersection of Tacoma and Solano, the bus stopped and the automatic doors opened. Turning toward them, the driver said, "You have to get off here because the street's closed."

When they stepped down onto the sidewalk, they saw, halfway up the block, police cars with red lights flashing. A crowd of people were standing in front of their house.

Helen said, "That's our house, Mama."

Lidia made the sign of the cross over her breast. Firmly gripping Helen's hand, she started to run.

Many of their neighbors were standing on the lawn. Grace Quigley, who lived next door, was crying. Thirteen-year-old Michael Ostrowski, who had witnessed the stabbing, was sitting on the steps. Alma O'Hara, who had come out of the house when she heard Tanya's cries for help, was being questioned by the police. Others, too, were milling around, whispering among themselves.

Still clutching Helen's hand, Lidia Tarasoff stepped forward. Many of the neighbors, noticing them for the first time, fell silent and stepped back. When Alma O'Hara saw them, she started to wail.

Then they saw Tanya. She was lying face down on the lawn. Her neck, shoulders, and legs were covered with blood. She looked very pale.

Lidia Tarasoff pulled her youngest daughter to her, lifting her from the ground and fiercely pressing her face into her breast so she couldn't see.

But out of the corner of her eye, Helen caught a glimpse of Prosenjit. She couldn't see his face because it was turned away, but she could see that his clothes were splattered with blood. He held his hands above his head. There were police officers all around him, but he wasn't struggling. He was moving slowly. Then he turned and his eyes met hers and held for an instant. The expression on his face was different than she had ever seen it. The misery had gone out of it. It was as though he was relieved. She watched while he let his hands fall to his sides. Then he placed them behind his back and she heard him say, "Handcuff me. I killed her."

Epilogue

TANYA Tarasoff was pronounced dead on arrival at Herrick Memorial Hospital. The coroner's report determined that the cause of death was shock and hemorrhaging resulting from eight major stab wounds to the chest, abdomen, and back. The report also confirmed that she was six weeks' pregnant at the time of death.

Prosenjit Poddar was arraigned and charged with first degree murder. He pleaded innocent by reason of insanity. During his trial, extensive testimony was introduced in support of the contention that he had been tormented to the point of becoming so mentally ill that he suffered diminished capacity and could not have harbored malice aforethought at the time of the killing. On August 26, 1970, he was found guilty of second degree murder, that is, murder without premeditation, and was sentenced to five years to life in the California Medical Facility in Vacaville.

Poddar appealed and, four years later, the California Supreme Court overturned his conviction on the ground that the trial judge had not given adequate instructions to the jury on the meaning of diminished capacity. A new trial was ordered. The trial judge agreed to a compromise: Poddar's release in return for his deportation to India. In September of 1974, Prosenjit Poddar returned to Calcutta, where his father arranged a marriage for him. Two years later, he received a scholarship to resume his study of naval architecture at a prestigious institute in Hannover, Germany, where, according to his old friend Jal Mehta, "He is leading a normal life with his wife and daughter."

However, the untimely death of Tanya Tarasoff was not to fade into obscurity. It was to have ramifications that would go far beyond the murder of one girl.

As a result of that murder, the long-festering tension at Cowell Hospital erupted in angry dispute. Staff members accused Dr. Harvey Powelson of authoritarianism, harassment, and illegally attempting to destroy evidence in a murder case. Powelson responded by firing nine therapists, including Larry Moore and Barbara Lena. Between 1970 and 1972, various committees investigated Powelson's conduct. Most of them recommended that he be replaced. In September of 1972, Powelson resigned, although denying that his decision had anything to do with these recommendations.

Feeling vindicated by evidence that came to light during the trial of Prosenjit Poddar and the subsequent resignation of Harvey Powelson, Larry Moore went into private practice in Oakland, California.

In September of 1970, Lidia and Vitally Tarasoff filed a $200,000 wrongful death suit against the Regents of the University of California and the City of Berkeley for failing to warn them that Prosenjit Poddar had threatened the life of their daughter.

In 1974, the suit reached the California Supreme Court and *Tarasoff* v. *Regents of the University of California* fulminated into one of the most controversial landmark decisions in state history. The court's decision, now referred to simply as *Tarasoff*, altered the time-honored rule of doctor-patient confidentiality and laid down the imperative that if a psychotherapist has reason to believe that his patient may harm someone, the therapist has a legal duty to warn the potential victim, his friends, relatives, or the authorities. In 1976, the Tarasoff family was awarded an undisclosed sum of money and the court altered its decision, saying that a psychotherapist treating a mentally ill patient is required to use "reasonable care" to protect threatened persons. Although the Tarasoff duty-to-warn rule applies only in California, it is cited as precedent in every state in the union. In any doctor-patient relationship, "Protective privilege ends where public peril begins."

DEBORAH BLUM was born in Los Angeles and is the daughter of a Hollywood screenwriter. She was a sophomore at Berkeley when the murder of Tanya Tarasoff occurred. After returning to Los Angeles to work as a documentary writer/producer, she became fascinated by the Tarasoff case and began an investigation that was to last seven years and take her twice to India. She is currently working as a film producer. *Bad Karma* is her first book.